POWER, POVERTY, AND PRAYER

POWER, POVERTY, AND PRAYER

The Challenges of Poverty and Pluralism
in African Christianity: 1960-1996

Ogbu U. Kalu

Africa World Press, Inc.

P.O. Box 1892
Trenton, NJ 08607

P.O. Box 48
Asmara, ERITREA

Africa World Press, Inc.

P.O. Box 1892
Trenton, NJ 08607

P.O. Box 48
Asmara, ERITREA

Copyright © 2006 Ogbu U. Kalu
First Africa World Press Edition 2006

Book design: Sam Saverance
Cover design: Dapo Ojo-Ade
Cover art (wood carving) by El Anatsui entitled "Ancestral Fence Crumbling" (1986) provided from the art collection of Professor Ogbu U. Kalu, Isiugwu-Ohafia, Southeastern Nigeria

Library of Congress Cataloging-in-Publication Data

Kalu, Ogbu.
  Power, poverty, and prayer : the challenges of poverty and pluralism in African Christianity : 1960-1996 / Ogbu U. Kalu.-- 1st American ed.
     p. cm.
  Includes bibliographical references and index.
  ISBN 1-59221-393-6 (hardcover) -- ISBN 1-59221-394-4 (pbk.)
  1. Africa--Church history--20th century. 2. Christianity and politics--Africa--History--20th century. 3. Poverty--Africa--History--20th century. 4. Poverty--Religious aspects--Christianity--History--20th century. I. Title.

  BR1360.K25 2005
  276'.082--dc22
                              2005023667

Dedicated with gratitude to the memory of my father, Shadrack Uke Kalu, 1904-2002. A faith-full elder of the Presbyterian Church of Nigeria. He was like a sheath of corn fully ripe.

Table of Contents

MAPS

DIAGRAMS

TABLES

Acknowledgements

This reflection began with an invitation from Dr Kwame Bediako of Akroffi-Christaller Memorial Center in Ghana to examine the patterns of church-state relationships in Africa from a historical perspective. The fruit of that endeavor was shared in the pages of the Toronto Journal of Theology in the fall of 1999. I elaborated on the ideas for courses offered at the Faculty of Religious Studies, McGill University, Montreal, in 1997. The interest of the students inspired more work which was shared at Emmanuel College, University of Toronto, in 1998, and finally at the Divinity School, Harvard University in 1999. The chapter on Daughters of Ethiopia was first shared at Princeton Theological Seminary under the aegis of my mentor Professor Andrew F. Walls and the Project on Currents in World Christianity. He has encouraged me at every stage of this enterprise.

I owe a debt of gratitude to many such as Professor William Klempa and Dr Geoffrey Johnston in Montreal; Professor Roger Hutchinson and Dr Phyllis Airhart in Toronto; and Professor Larry Sullivan at Harvard. Professor Sullivan's robust intellect and friendship won my deepest affections. The final part of this manuscript's journey ended in the Bavarian city of Bayreuth, Germany, where my friend Professor Ulrich Berner sacrificially combed through the manuscript, copyedited it, and vigorously dialogued about its many assertions. His secretary, Frau Menchen, a woman with an incredible spirit of charity, provided all the logistic support during my sojourn at the University of Bayreuth in 2000. The manuscript also benefited from a full reading by the doyen, Professor Theo Sundemeier of the University of Heidelberg. He recommended it to the German Missiological Society, which funded the publication with Peter Lang of Frankfurt am Main. I am very grateful to all. A special debt of grati-

tude goes to John Kamalwa of Bamasaba, Uganda. He was a doctoral
student at the time but, as a brother, spent many hours sorting out
my computer problems. Happily, he has completed his doctoral dis-
sertation which is now published as a book. I enjoyed the unalloyed
assistance from the staff of Iwalewa-Haus (Afrikazentrum), University of Bayreuth. Finally, I thank Kassahun Checole, the publisher
of Africa World Press, and his assistant, Damola Ifaturoti, for this
opportunity to produce a corrected version with fewer "howlers". I
crave pardon for any obstinate errors as I negotiate between German
and American proof-readers.

Ogbu U.Kalu,
Chicago,Illinois.
Summer 2005.

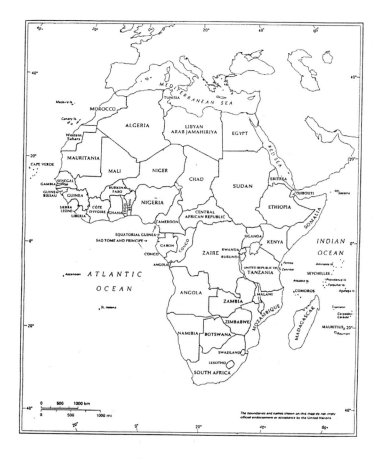

African States, 1993

Preface

THE PROBLEM

In the early 1990s a certain tone emerged in African church historiography that sought to bring it back into the mainstream of world Christianity. Historians recognised its tremendous growth. Adrian Hastings, the consummate historian, theologian, and social activist, intoned that:

> Black Africa is today totally inconcievable apart from the presence of Christianity, a presence which a couple of generations ago could still be unreasonably dismissed as fundamentally marginal and a mere subsidiary aspect of colonialism.[1]

Kwame Bediako who built an ashram in the lushy hills of Akropong in Ghana endeavoured to reconstruct the roots of the revitalization of African Christainity as a non-western religion. He recalled the absence of African participants in the famous Edinburgh Conference of 1910 and traced the contours of this surprise element in the transformation of African Christianity to the development of the vernacular translation of the message, a theme that Lamin Sanneh, the Gambian scholar raised prominently in 1989. Bediako compared the vitality of contemporary African Christianity with its heritage in the second century and declared that African Christianity has now acquired a greater consciousness of its African identity and character. The greater challenge for the future is how to be of service to Africa as she voyages into the political realm of the twenty-first century.[2] Not only have "new dimensions" emerged in African Christian spirituality, as Paul Gifford has posited, but the roles of Christian leaders in the contemporary political crises have enlarged tremendously.

Both Bediako and Gifford list the cases of Togo, Benin, Ghana, and
Liberia in West Africa; Kenya, Uganda, Tanzania and Madagascar in
East Africa; Zaire, Malawi and Zambia in Central Africa; and South
Africa as examples.[3]

Indeed, the March 1996 election in the Republic of Benin is a
good case in point. Without resorting to monocausal analysis, there
is little doubt that the religious factor was the crucial element. Ironically, Soglo, a former World Bank economist, came to power with
the support of the church. The Catholic archbishop of Cotonou brokered the constitutional crises in the effort to overthrow the Marxist
military dictator, Kerekou. Once in power, Soglo shifted allegiance
to vodoo priests. It should be noted that the majority of the Beninois
bow to traditional gods and the python is the controlling spirit. Benin
was formerly known as Dahomey, a name that means 'in the belly of
the python'. In the Republic of Benin, the Roman Catholics are next
in numerical strength followed respectively by United Methodists,
African Independent Churches and Pentecostal/Evangelicals.

Soglo declared vodoo the national religion and installed a
vodoo national holiday. He decorated the streets of the capital city,
Cotonou, with vodoo symbols. Meanwhile, vodoo priests practiced
their sacrificial rites in the glare of national television and blared
their confident support for Soglo in the proposed national election.
During the first balloting, that confidence appeared prophetic as
Soglo led the pack. Ultimately,however, there was no clear majority
and two of the candidates dropped out. Soglo and Kerekou were the
remaining contestants in a run-off.

The Christians became alarmed. Meanwhile, it was alleged that
Kerekou had become "born-again" under the ministry of an Assemblies of God pastor, and that he demonstrated his new-fangled allegiance in statements and actions even in his northern native home.
All over the nation, Christian groups of all hues undertook long
periods of fasting and praying in support of Kerekou. They turned
out in large numbers to vote. Tensions mounted to such an extent
that while the results were awaited, pandemonium enveloped the
capital city, Cotonou. On 23rd March ,1996, as two thieves were
pursued through the Dantokpa market, the largest market in West
Africa, people fled fearing that the army was about to take over and
save Soglo from an imminent defeat. The chaos spread into the
suburbs as garbled versions reached the hinterlands. In addition, it
was rumoured that the Catholic archbishop of Cotonou had fled the
country. Churches were filled through the night begging for God's

intervention. Early in the Sunday morning, on March 25th, the announcement came that Kerekou had won. Sunday services turned into thanksgiving victory dances in the churches. The atmosphere was electric as people imagined the victory of the Christian God over the vodoo python.

This example in the Republic of Benin draws attention to certain salient factors: there has been pulsating criticism that the church in Africa has, for the most part, failed to produce an adequate theology and an institutional force to oppose the encroaching power of the state or to deal with the problem of pauperization at its source. While the church has danced around the tail of the python, repairing the havoc caused by the tail, it has gamely avoided the head. Contemporary literature not only privileged the collusion of the mainline churches, but abandoned the notion that the African indigenous churches that emerged in the interwar years were sublimated anti-colonialist forms, arguing that they were not politically-conscientized and that the matter has grown worse with the implosion of Pentecostal religiosity in the post independent period.

These conclusions require re-examination in the face of the paradigm shifts that have brought ethnicity and religion onto the centre stage of African socio-political realities. However, the reassessment of the enlarged religious space should neither focus on elitist power nor measure the tensile strength of political engagement through the pronouncements of church leaders and institutional organizations. A re-understanding of political theology as people's God-talk about the meaning of Christ in the midst of their conditions would open the vista more creatively. As Ruth Marshall has urged, more attention should be given to the huge body of believers and to popular forms of Christian beliefs and practices.[4] The concern here is that the implication of the rapid growth of Pentecostalism since the 1970s has received inadequate scholarly study. The pre-eminence of functionalist sociology in the study of world Christianity ignores the social and political theology of the movement. Indeed, it is the religious belief that informed and guaranteed its success. Moreover, the influence is seeping rapidly into the mainline churches through the charismatic movement.

Much of the literature focuses on the global, especially the American influence, ignoring the creative local processes. Consequently, a web of conspiratorial scenarios is woven that alleges that the American Moral Majority has conspired with the Central Intelligenece Agency to nurture a conservative political ideology in Africa.

This outsider perspective is built on an ideology best articulated by Eric Hobsbawm's The Age of Extremes: the redundancy of African history. He argues that everything that has happened in Africa is an empty mimicry of what has really significantly happened elsewhere. His historiography is built on the grand narrative assumption that Europe is the end point of all grand narratives. It ignores local vitality; that the dialectics of the local and global is about how the one flows in and out of the other in a continuous process of reciprocal influence. The outside perspective is not only a poor reading of the context, it misses the new politics of engagement in African Christianity that may explain the rising crescendo of religious violence in many African countries. Lamin Sanneh has, in both Turban and Crown and Piety and Power, drawn attention to the deeper level of Islamic understanding of the political uses of power.[5] At the core of the concern in this text, however, is the problem of Christian understanding of power and her engagement with contrasting perceptions by the state and by other competing religious groups. This fact has created the dilemma of pluralism.

This discourse is telescoped around three concepts:(i) the power available for developing communitiesnotwithstanding (ii) the poverty which dogs our heels, and (iii) the presence and the prayer of the church. Poverty surely means different things to different people and is manifested at different levels; however, even the most ardent theorist would be astonished by the increasing pauperization of African communities. Political scientists have dubbed it Afropessimism. The problem lies at that interface of history and theology. The perception here is that reeds do not grow where there is no marsh, and that behind all the malaise is a spiritual dimension needing a spiritual discernment that does not ignore the avalanche of social-science data.

The goals here are twofold. The first is to explore the internal history of the goodspell in Africa after the bugles of the political independence. As one bard sang, when the whites left us, it is now "we on us". What did the various faces of Christianity in Africa accomplish with the gospel? Did they develop a new political ideology to ensure that the goodspell would bring joy in the midst of legitimacy crises? Why did the political field enlarge so tremendously after 1990 for religious operators? The second goal of this text is to examine the significance of new forces in the religious landscape such as the rise of Pentecostalism which is at the cutting edge of African contemporary experience. What is its response to the scourge of poverty in the African ecosystem? Moreover, the voice of Christian women has become significant in addressing the feminization of poverty and the adverse effects of patriarchy for church and society.

The choice of poverty as the overarching conceptual scheme arises from many factors: poverty was of primary concern to Jesus. It also occupied the attention of theorists during the 1960's. At the root of African underdevelopment is what Dennis Goulet, in *The Cruel Choice*, calls "vulnerability." This term succinctly characterizes the failure of many low-income countries to maximally tap their resources, meet their development goals and consequently left Africans to suffer elitist domination and increased pauperization.[6] Even the shift of the discourse to liberation instead of development signaled the elitism and jaundiced perception of social revolution as an alternative recourse in the concept. Development buttressed modernization theory and autocracy. Democratization, in this context, perceived in constitutional arrangements is vitiated by a corrupt political culture. As one pundit observed, democracy does not work with empty stomachs. All constitutional arrangements fall at the beck of "money bags."

At the root of underdevelopment is an ethical factor, namely, the emphasis on the modern market and the modern state. People in the third world had great hopes that once freed from the colonial yoke, they would have a great future with better human conditions. However, international economies colluded with unwholesome internal factors to create a dependency syndrome. This politics of economic stagnation has internal explanations but is for the most part externally induced. It could best be explored through the pages of World Bank Reports. The reason is simply that the World Bank and the International Monetary Fund are the vanguards of the Western liberal economics devised the modernization theory for newly-independent African countries designed to move them into mass-consumption societies, following W.W. Rostow's five-stages. Colonial governments, which themselves were manifestly undemocratic, created equally non-democratic societies in the process of decolonization and expected these to succeed with no governmental experience and with nation-states made up of tribes and tongues that were brought together, each in a daze and each without any patriotic allegiance. The new capitalist economy paid little attention to the base resources because cold war ideology was supreme. Poor leadership and corruption took their tolls. Meanwhile, western advisors convinced the new African rulers that their problem was the multiplicity of tribes that served as centrifugal power nodes. A reconciliation system that permitted "tribalism" would lead to failure. The solution was the mobilization theory that wiped out countervailing, indigenous power nodes. Soon, one party states sprouted under a stream of dictators who called themselves "father of the nation." Within a few years, the military sacked the dictators and replaced them with praetorian and prebendary state structures. All practised the politics of the belly.[7]

The World Bank Report (1994), *Adjustment in Africa: Reforms, Results and the Road Ahead,* has chronicled the matter, even though it was greeted with hostile reviews, as a misguided ideological effort to claim a small modicum of success in the midst of abject failure. The reports' methodology and analysis have been attacked and the recommendations characterized as impracticable. Indeed, social scientists perceive the World Bank and the IMF as the problem, because the social cost and economic decline of countries that implemented the Structural Adjustment Program (SAP) have been staggering. The SAP, as devised by the bank and IMF, rejects "country ownership," the idea that recipient countries should decide their own development goals. It meant undertaking certain measures, such as cutting public expenditures, debt and deficits; freeing up trade; and opening and deregulating the economy in exchange for substantial periodic payments of aid money. The program would be monitored by the IMF and the continued flow of aid would be contigent on the country's macoeconomic performance. It is designed to take over the economies of debtor nations and to run them in such a way that the IMF could collect for the Club of Rome.

Perhaps we should compare this with two earlier reports; *Accelerated Development in Sub-Sahara (1981)* and *Sub-Saharan Africa: From Crisis to Sustainable Growth* (1989). Both reports give the impression that the crisis in Africa has been intractable. For instance, the 1981 report identified two problems, namely, the implosion of the state and the centrality of political factors in the rapidly declining conditions in Africa. The wisdom here was to pare down the role of the state and to encourage responsible policies and practices. By 1989 the catalogue had worsened: predatory, static policies stifled entrepreneurship and investment, led to instability as incompetent and unpredictable management of the public sector and failed legal systems; meanwhile, environmental degradation and human rights abuses proliferated. Therefore, the 1994 report recommended a number of ideological shifts. It prescribed the need to redirect and to rebuild the potential for African states to attain good governance. This is measured by the degree of accountability, transparency, and openness in decision-making, efficient public management, and the rule of law. Political and economic liberation should dovetail and be undertaken simultaneously in order to be perceived as mutually supportive.[7] This is in tune with the ideology of the second liberation, a consequence of the fall of communism, and the triumph of liberal capitalism, and the divinity of the market. Is this a dramatic shift from the modernization theories of the 1950s which held that democracy would be the outcome of economic and social modernization? Such theories had argued that only fairly literate, affluent industrialized and urbanized societies could maintain democratic politics. No, it was a change, for the World Bank tended to blame its agents – the African states – rather than its own core policies and the undergirding ideology. Many of the myths in Word Bank prescriptions have so far gone unchallenged.

A tendency by World Bank to monopolize all policy options led to the model advocated in its 1993 report, *East Asian Miracles* which failed to consider the differences in sociocultural and value systems between East Asia and Africa. Besides, East Asia model was built on the state as the key agent, an interventionist state that literally selected the sectors for control.[8] To deal with disastrous micro-economic fall out, non-governmental organizations (NGOs) proliferated as agents of poverty alleviation programs, designed to sedate the impoverished masses while the IMF recovers the debt. The model is to bypass the corrupt state and carry the global market message to the grassroots. Besides, many of the socioeconomic discourses ignore the moral bedrock of the society on which the true future of the communities may rest. Modernization theories tend to assume that religion and ethnicity are atavistic forces that will disappear. Much to the contrary; these forces are crucial in the new politics. Ethnic rivalry, the resurgence of Islam with its emphasis on territoriality, the enlargement of political space for Christianity complete the background context.

Equally crucial is the fact that Africa is on the receiving end of the dark sides of globalization: the debilitating impact of economic globalization on the poor nations, the policies of the international financial institutions, the unequal distribution of new communication and production technologies, and the foreign capital investment for greater profit without concern for human and environmental consequences. As institutionally weak partners in a global economy and in cultural interaction, the poor nations inevitably experience economic decline and cultural uncertainty, and thus slide even more deeply into debt.

THE STATE AND SOCIETY IN AFRICA

Commentators note the complexity in a typology of states in Africa. For instance, in 1960, nearly all African countries modeled their constitutions on the example of former colonial powers; either on Westminster (English) or the Republican (French). This excludes the Arab and Islamic countries of the North Africa such as Egypt, Libya, Tunisia, Algeria, and Morocco, whose orientations are towards the Near and Middle Eastern Arab countries. Soon after independence many structures changed beyond recognition towards an authoritarian presidential system. In some countries, a one- party system emerged directed either towards African socialism or geared towards Marxist-Leninist ideologies but with a tightly "democratic centralist" structure. In others, that is, in a large number of countries, military groups swept away the constitutions or intervened frequently enough to create praetorian conditions. Only in a few cases did the original constitutional framework remain as semicompetitive or polyarchic systems. Of twenty- six polyarchies at the beginning of the 1960s only six turned out to be reasonably functioning and stable in 1980 (Botswana, Gambia, Kenya, Lesotho, Mauritius, and Senegal). Of the socialist states, four turned out relatively stable (Guinea, Congo/Brazzaville, Tanzania, and Zambia). The relatively stable authoritarian states included Ivory Coast, Gabon, Malawi and Swaziland. By contrast, twenty-two countries had a military government in 1980, which, following several changes in government, also included praetorian states such as Nigeria and Uganda.

In the wake of the collapse of the Soviet Union in the 1980s, the second liberation (after the liberation from colonialism) began. As could be expected, the World Bank and the IMF turned Africa's liberation from home dictators into a political conditionality for funds. When French President Francois Mitterand declared his support at La Baule in 1990, "conferences" began in Africa to oust dictators. Some lost, others manipulated the votes (in Cameroon and Togo), Mobutu held tight to power, the military used subterfuge to survive in Nigeria, democratization produced war in Somalia and Rwanda, while others, as in Ghana, changed their stripes. With the new wind, old political theories were blown off the ramparts. The modernization theory by Lipset and Apter which considered mobilization and the one- party structure as the most viable option, became discredited. The dependency theory advanced by Lowenthal that ignored the force of internal political conditions, became flawed especially in states composed of major regional, cultural, and ethnic divisions.[9]

Meanwhile, new ideologies jostled: the secularist against the non-secularist, the theocratic, and otherwise, and yet there is no African state that ignores the religious factor or is antireligious in principle. One core characteristic in the evolution of African states is that the rise of the monopolistic state (which Lamin Sanneh dubs a "theological state") has gone pari passu with both the diminution of civil or human rights as well as economic decline. Musa I.M. Abutudu explains this with the model of class formation. He argues that the state, through development plans, patronage, expenditure, employment, illegitimate accumulation of public wealth and alliance with multinationals or metropolitan bourgeoisie creates and furthers the long-term interest of a dominating class. Thereafter, the apparatus of state is deployed to consolidate the class, the regime, and the personal survival of the ruling group. They privatize the state and turn it into a prebendal state. Andreas Thimm has, therefore urged a clear restatement of the relationship between human rights and economic development.[10] In conclusion, the fundamental problem in Africa is not lack of resources, but the failure of political leadership. The modern African state is a colonial creation, extractive in its design. Its mission was not to serve the people but to dominate and exploit them. Despite independence, and despite improvements brought by numerous democratic elections, the nature of that state remains intact. The primary solution is to change the nature of the state.

PRAYER AND POVERTY

In reflecting on the pattern of the churches' responses to the challenges of the implosion of state power and the empty bowls of the poor, we must first examine the character of the presence of the church in Africa. There are enormous regional differences ranging from the predominantly Muslim northern zone through the heavily Christianized southern and central sectors and the divided western region. In West Africa, a combination of Islam and traditional religion has affected the Christian presence. In a 1990 survey of West Africa, Muslims had the majority in Niger, Guinea, Mali, Guinea-Bissau, Gambia, and Senegal. They make up a large force in Nigeria. Traditional religion held major sway in Benin, Togo, Cote d'Ivoire and Guinea-Bissau, and also held second place to Islam in Guinea, Mali, and Senegal.

Generally, missiometric surveys show that Christianity in Africa has grown exponenetially in the last decade. Even in areas of alternative challenge, the percentage of growth has been phenomenal. Guinea is perhaps a good example of what has happened to Africa's fallow grounds. Between 1919 and 1952 only the Christian and Missionary Alliance, the Roman Catholic Church, and a small Anglican group in Conakry were allowed to operate. Gradually, other groups came in. But in 1967 the Guinean Catholic archbishop was implicated in a coup and the anvil fell on Christianity, only lifting after the death of Sekou Toure in 1984. The new government opened the door to missions, declaring complete freedom to all religions and open society as in Cote d'Ivoire. They saw that the restrictions, repressions, and Marxist socialism produced economic disasters. Guinea in 1984 was in ruins, its spirit broken. Since then, the missions have poured in to fill the gaps. The implication of this example is that the second liberation wind has a tendency to favor Christianity because the moral bankruptcy of its enemies has been betrayed in broad daylight. There is a connection between the wind of God (the activity of the Holy Spirit) and the liberation of nations or exposure of the bankruptcy of their leaders.

As Adrian Hastings has argued, the relationship between church and state in Africa is complicated by the fact of overlap as each claims some form of absolute loyalty over the same people and pressed to various degrees.[11] Christians belong to two cities, and have woven various theologies in response to the challenge. Some of these theologies arose from conflicts in European societies, through time, and were merely reproduced in Africa. In others, the circumstances in the pattern of European presence in Africa further bedevilled matters. Thus, churches in preapartheid South Africa produced self-serving theological emphases. It has become necessary therefore, to restate the theological foundations for the Christian participation in the politics of poverty alleviation. As Karl Barth intoned, democratic conception of the state is the justifiable expansion of the thought of the New Testament (I:145) and Boenhoefer concurred. We shall not, however, pursue this lineas de Gruchy has ably done so recently.[12]

Rather, the take-off here is Paul Gifford's assertion that "the most significant development within African Christianity during the decade, 1980-1990, was the mushrooming of new churches." The new churches refer to the born –again Christians who have left the mainline churches. But it recognizes the born-again Christians who operate within the mainline churches. These are referred to as "charismatic." Thus, there is a charismatic wind blowing in Africa that deserves scholarly attention because it has forced changes on the society, mainline churches and the African indigenous churches. Gifford measures its growth by its numbers, the strength of missionary personnel, and finances. He concludes that while Roman Catholics have grown and remain a formidable force, Pentecostalism and charismatism have grown more rapidly and at the expense of both the mainline churches and the African indigenous churches. He adduces five reasons for the weakness of mainline churches: (i) governments' efforts to co-opt mainline churches,(ii) the elitist "Big Man" model of leadership, (iii)NGO-ization of churches by funding agents in a bid to avoid corrupt regimes, (iv) weak theology and (v)problem of identity as faith churches thrive on faith gospel of health and wealth and a certain understanding of spirits in the African environment. The barriers between Pentecostals and Evangelicals have collapsed and many AICs are joining the Pentecosta' bandwagon as their nondenominational ecclesiology creates a new form of polity.[19] The question is, what is the impact of the rise of charismatism on a) the state and b) the African societies characterized by high population growth, most of whom are in the rural areas, illiterate and increasingly impoverished? In many parts of Africa the largest sector of the population comprise of children, youths, and females. It is necessary to state that the mainline churches are currently responding to the Pentecostal challenge, to the implosion of state power, and to the pauperization of the society in a robust manner.

But as Adrian Hastings argues in his African Christianity (1979), there are certain factors that determine the impact of the church on the state, namely, the size or number of adherents, ecclesiastical organization, the spread of and quality of adherents, and the pattern of colonial church-state relations precisely because post-independence relations tend to be part of a continuation or in part, a reversal of what went before. He includes the theological emphasis, for example, other worldliness, the attitude towards other churches and religions, and the overall character of worldwide relationships. Various patterns exist in different states in Africa based on varied local conditions. In all situations, the voice of the church could only be listened to based on the level of democratic culture in which the government could admit public opposition.

In the polyarchies and praetorian states of Africa, the churches have tended to express their views. One example is a booklet entitled Christian Council_Response to Ghana's Search for a New Democratic System (1990). The chairman of the council, Rt. Rev. D.A. Koranteng, observed that there are three reasons for the publication. Among them, it was to thank God that "we in Ghana now enjoy a climate in which we are able to discuss freely the political future of this country and share the official contribution made to the National Defence Council Government." This was innocuous and did not involve a challenge over human rights or social policies. Indeed, it concentrated on political structure. A proactive image of church-state relations in Ghana is painted in J.S. Pobee's Religion and Politics in Ghana.[13] But even in a praetorian state such as Nigeria, the voice of the church is strong. Indeed, the Christian Association of Nigeria (CAN) operates as a civil society, harnessing the energies of those discriminated against because of tribe and religion.

The current situation in South Africa is a different model of the Christian presence in a distraught society. There is a unique quality in which a cardinal theological concept is placed in the center of the political road to recovery. I have dubbed it Simunye Theology, that is, an effort to achieve unity through repentance. This is what the Truth and Reconciliation Commission, a seventeen -member group led by Bishop Desmond Tutu and Dr. Alex Boraine, stands for. One may argue that the initiation of such an organiszation was facilitated by the fact that approximately 70% of South Africans attend church. Nonetheless,the matter is more complex.

In the background there are certain facts: the antiapartheid battle was borne by a host of conscientized youths,even younger than Steve Biko. Their future then is now, and their present is laden with such expectations. Young whites, on the other hand, wonder why their teeth should be set on edge because the fathers ate sour grapes. They are disquieted. The ranks of the white fathers were broken between diehards and liberals. The blacks are not united as the Inkatha. Representing an old society feels awkward in a young state. As affirmative action creates a black middle class, resentment ripens in the homelands. And yet a certain haunting tune punctuates television programs: "Si-mu-ny-e-e, we are one"! It is a Zulu word breathing the hope for the future, anxious for the return of love for one nation. But can people sweep the past under the carpet? The South African government has therefore set up the Truth and Reconciliation Commission composed of eminent churchmen, theologians, and laypeople, to provide a forum where aggrieved people can speak openly about the brutality they suffered under apartheid from white and black alike. This catharsis or self-purging process should lead people to truth,forgiveness, and compassion,if not reconciliation. The theological underpinning is immense. Criticism abound questioning whether it will re-open old wounds, provide possibilities for prosecution and justice, or mainly serve as a sanctuary for those who brutalized others? Is it an African way of achieving reconciliation?

Finally, if the cutting edge in contemporary African Christianity is the implosion of Pentecostal/charismatic religiosity, the implications for the future are immense; therefore, Pentecostal/charismatic political theology should be seriously examined. The salience of the movement may create a dilemma for the practice of pluralism. The case of Nigeriacan serve as an illustration. The size of the country, the balance between Islamic and Christain populations, with a regional divide, the international interest in the mineral and human resources, the conflation of oil politics with Arab nationalism, all have immense economic import. These attributes have combined to produce a series of violent religious conflicts. Scholars have proffered many analyses: some focus on violence, others on dysfunctional religious politics; some on theological pathways to harmony, others on the impact of economic policies on religious crises. All agree that the declaration of secularity as a state ideology has not sufficed.

Ironically, charismatic power may enhance the power of women in African churches. This is an important aspect because of the rising voices of the daughters of Ethiopia in African churches. In the early 1990s some women in the continent formed a circle to produce literature and to engage in the theological discourse . They have achieved much through the years with over fifteen titles. But there is a plurality of voices in the female camp. We must listen to these voices and examine the exits that each segment of that constituency proffers. Obviously, academic women do not speak for all.

The Pentecostal view of history is that societies live in the midst of the whirlwind of the Holy Spirit that is the driving force of human favor; Jesus declared that he was indwelt by the Spirit of the Lord. The mind of Christ was, therefore, pneumatic reasoning, perceiving the compassion and the mercy of the vulnerable. This is set against the instrumental reasoning of the secular state and its exploitation of others as instruments to achieve ends. As Paul Felton would argue, the charismatic emphasis is an attitudinal and lifestyle change directly opposed to the pervasive egoism of secular society.[14] Does Pentecostalism or any church in Africa offer beauty for the ashes on the faces of impoverished Africans? Does any church offer an alternative religious space for creating a new community characterized by a combination of emphasis on personal salvation and social justice? The burden of the following chapters is the concern questioning whether any meaningful church history can be done in this generation, in Africa, that ignores the responses of African churches to the three forces of the implosion of the state, the impoverishment of communities, and the crescendo of religious conflicts that threaten sociopolitical stability; life, property, and the ideal of pluralism.

Notes

1. Adrian Hastings, "Christianity in Africa", in *Turning Points in Religious Studies*. ed Ursula King (Edinburgh: T&T Clark, 1990), 208.

2. Kwame Bediako, *Theology and Identity* (Oxford: Regnum Press, 1992); *Christianity in Africa*. (Maryknoll, NY: Orbis, 1995), 235. Lamin Sanneh, *Translating the Message* (Maryknoll, Orbis, 1989).

3. Paul Gifford, *New Dimensions in African Christianity*. (Nairobi: AACC, 1992); *African Christianity: Its Public Role* . (Bloomington, IN: Indiana University Press, 1996).

4. Ruth Marshall, "God is not a democrat: Pentecostalism and Democratization in Nigeria", in *The Christian Churches and the Democratization of Africa* ed. Paul Gifford. (Leiden: E. J. Brill, 1995), 239-260.

5. Lamin Sanneh, *Piety and Power: Muslims and Christians in Africa* (Maryknoll, NY: Orbis, 1996); *Turban and Crown: Muslims and West African Pluralism* (Boulder, CO: Westview Press, 1997).

6. Denis Goulet, *The Cruel Choice: A New Concept in the Theory of Development*. (New York: Atheneum, 1973).

7. The *Canadian Journal of African Studies*, 25, (February, 1995) devoted six essays on World Bank reports.

8. See Eboe Hutchful, " Smoke and Mirrors: World Bank's Social Dimension of Adjustment Program, " *Review of African Political Economy*, 62 (1994): 569-584.

9. Dick Berg-Schlosser, "Democratization in Africa: Conditions and Prospects", *Law and State*, 52 (1995): 37-57.

10. Andreas Thimm, "Development, Human Rights and Democracy", *ibid.* : 89-101.

11. Adrian Hastings, *The Faces of God: Reflections on Church and Society*. (Maryknoll, NY: Orbis, 1976).

12. John de Gruchy, " Theological Reflections on the Task of the Church in the Democratization of Africa" In *The Christian Churches and the Democratization of Africa* ed. Paul Gifford (Leiden: EJBrill, 1995): 47ff.

13. John Pobee, *Religion and Politics in Ghana* (Accra: Asempa Publishers, 1991).

14. Paul Felton, "Towards a Charismatic Social Theology", *Theological Renewal*, 8, (1987): 29ff.

Part I

Power and Poverty

Chapter One
The Changing Faces Of Christianity in Africa

1. THE FIRST TIME: EARLY CHRISTIANITY IN NORTH AFRICA

Though the time frame for this analysis is the post-colonial period, many of the readers may not be very familiar with the contours of African encounter with the Jesus movement. The story of the Christian presence in Africa, from early Christianity to decolonisation in the 1960's serves two purposes: first, as the backdrop to our inquiry about how Africans utilized Christian resources in coping with the harsh economic and sociopolitical environments of our contemporary period; second, to show that African Christianity emerged from a creative struggle against the hardware of missionary Christianity. Contrary to the assertions of missionary historiography, Africans had been deeply implicated in the fate of the Jesus movement from the period when it spread out from Palestine into the Graeco-Roman world.It is instructive to observe that God's presence brooded over the African continent at the same time it did in Palestine and in parts of Europe. Thus, from the New Testament nativity accounts to the exigencies of Golgotha, through the event of Pentecost event and the outgrowth of the mission to the Gentiles, Africa was continually mentioned. The focus was on the Maghrib, which shared the Mediterranean and the Red Sea with Europe, Arabia, and Palestine.

Certain factors, of course, assisted in the flowering of the gospel.[1] First, came the Pax Romana (Roman Peace) which welded vastly disparate nations into a vibrant commercial, cultural and political unit. Second, the Greek language and thought provided both a lingua franca and a medium for articulation. Tertullian, (ca AD 155) in his De Praescriptione, may protest against the influence of the Academy on the church:

We want no elaborate disputation after possessing Jesus Christ, no inquisition after enjoying the gospel. With our faith, we desire no further belief.[2]

While Tertullian's protest was not widely shared, it did signal the beginnings of an enduring battle to rescue the simplicity and power of the gospel from the obscurantism of gnosis and sophia (esoteric knowledge and wisdom) especially as a cloud of African witnesses indulged in spoiling the Egyptian, a game of adapting Christianity toGreek and Roman religions.

Third, the ubiquitous Jews whose religion gained the status of religio licita (the only permitted religion),provided ambiguous cover: some opposed the planting of Christianity; but others converted and evangelized. Indeed, they had absorbed so much Greek and Roman culture that conversion to Christianity offered them the opportunity to shift from an ethnic religiosity to a worshiping community in tune with the modern culture of their times. The relationship between Christianity and Judaism remained fraught with ambiguity until separation became inevitable. Ironically, Christianity saved Hellenistic Jews from marginalization.

Inspite of these salient aspects, the North African environment into which Christianity came was, like the Nile, was infested with crocodiles. As Michael Green painted the hostile terrain:

> At whatever level in society it was attempted, evangelism in the early church was a daunting undertaking. It was a task involving social odium, political danger, the charge of treachery to the gods and the state, the insinuation of horrible crimes and calculated opposition from a combination of sources more powerful, perhaps, than at any time since.[3]

Green was referring to the tensile strength of primal religions in the Maghrib environment, especially the mystery cults that underpropped the rich and muscular civilization of ancient Egypt.Moreover, Christianity, fundamentally incomprehensible to the Romans and divergent from their system of ethics, so jarred the dominant political religion that the waves of persecution served as an instrument of social control.

Tertullian's *De Idolatria* argued that the moral collapse of Rome was signaled by the growth of cults even among trade guilds. Yet the gospel seed grew by dint of an evangelistic temper, as every Christian spontaneously served as an apologist. Women played such a large role that Tertullian, in both *Aplogeticum and Ad Uxorem,* used the

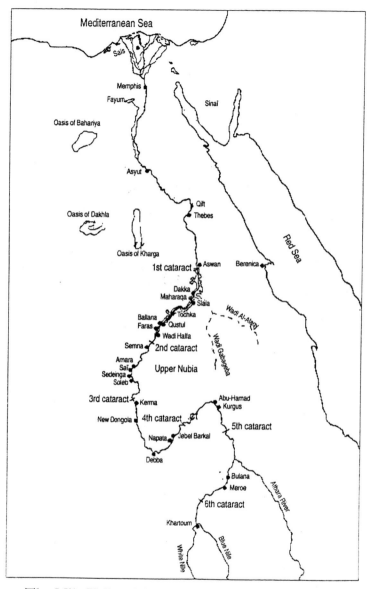

The Nile Valley: Mediterranean to Sixth Cataract

dilemma of a Christian woman married to a pagan man to illustrate
the socioethical constraints created by conversion.

The story of early Christianity in North Africa, therefore, is one
of struggle to grow roots in stony soil, a saga that moved in four
rhythms: before the reign of Emperor Constantine, it was under the
imperial anvil. From that point, sword and spirit cooperated as Caesar
Christian confronted independence. Meanwhile, the wagons of Christian orthodoxies disengaged and formed shorter trains. At first Rome
and Constantinople veered onto differing tracks; later, all efforts to
the contrary, Egyptian Copts disengaged from Eastern Orthodoxy. In
the seventh century AD, the incursion of Islam brought a new dispensation. Therefore, cross and the crescent lived disharmoniously for
centuries with the cross virtually uprooted until the sixteenth century,
when European expansion came to the rescue. Christian remnants
cocooned themselves under tribal covers for survival among the Copts
of Egypt and the Orthodox bastions of Ethiopia.

We shall now examine the patterns of vertical and horizontal
expansion in various parts of the Maghrib. The key question is, to
what extent were Christians able to witness and proclaim the good
news and to confront the spirit at the gates of the various communities that inhabited the Maghrib?

To begin with Egypt, the origin of the Christian mission is
obscure. The brief sojourn of the infant Jesus in Egypt has created a
tradition. Oral tradition in the Coptic church mentions the apostle
Mark as the first of 116 patriarchs of the Coptic church to date.
More pertinent is the rapid growth of Christianity in Egypt both
among the Hellenized as well as the indigenous Coptic population:
The former took a gnostic, philosophical high road, while the latter
appeared to be attracted by the ritual and charismatic elements and
the promise of comfort and solace in the life hereafter.

The indices of growth, argued C. P. Groves, include: (i) the
numerical strength of bishops during church synods. Since each
congregation tended to have a bishop, the attendance of 100 bishops
to the synod of AD 320 and an equally large attendance in AD
343 support the claim of rich branching and flowering; (ii) the fact
that the Bible was central in evangelization and was translated into
various Coptic languages such as sahidic (upper Nile), boharic (Nile
delta) and bashmuric (middle Nile) by the fourth century AD; (iii)
the proliferation of Christian arts and a distinct genre of embellished
art and literature, which indicates both the depth of religious consciousness and popular receptivity; (iv) the explosion of the eremitic

life, which betrays a level of acceptance beyond primary conversion and (v) certain pieces of evidence pointing to a reshaping of culture for example, a tomb excavated at Antinoe in Upper Egypt indicating a radical modification of funerary rites. However, much syncretism clouded this early Christianization as mummification persisted.[4]

Some have surmised that the path of conversion was eased by the primal belief system, especially the Osiris-Isis-Horus saga. First,Christian belief in a saviour who conquered death and resurrected certainly won easy acceptance. Second, a large number of Jews lived in Egypt and converted to Christianity. Third, persecution served as a means of spreading the gospel. Thye church historian Eusebius poured encomia on the faithful witness of the Egyptian Christians especially when a gust of persecution blew under Emperor Septimis Severus. Bishop Dionysius of Alexandria is quoted as saying that his exile into Libya became fruitful.[5] Martyrdom became an effective tool for Christian affirmation, maturity and growth. But soon monastic enclaves became powerful centers for competing theologies and power plays.

Initially, Egypt's enviable catechetical school at Alexandria provided the intellectual strand in rooting Christianity. The Alexandrian school enjoyed the leadership of famous men such as Pantaenus (the founder), Clement,Origen (before his allegorizations frustrated his bishop, Demetrius, and Dionysius, who later became a bishop). Thus, the school and monasteries succored men who endeavored to define and to consolidate Christian practices in a new context. But theological wars and heresies erupted as well as a wide range of prescriptions to find the paths to truth. Personality clashes and vaulting ambition fueled the quest. The greater danger was a speculative theological tradition that ignored the role of the Holy Spirit and failed to attack the real enemy of Christianity.

It has been said that persecution strengthened the early church, while Constantine weakened it. Persecution betrayed the bond between the state and primal religion. Thus, the debate on traditores (those who betrayed the faith by either signing a paper swearing that they had worshipped the emperor or, even worse, surrendered Christian materials to the civil officers) indicated immense sensitivity to Christian ethics. From this perspective, Constantine's relief heralded a period of compromise as the numbers of pretenders bulged, providing opportunities for unbridled intramural warfare and for breeding heresies. Some were pandered by the whims of emperors.

The enduring element in Egypt was the mission to the Copts which was achieved through vernacular translation. When all seemed to give way (since the top soil was thin), the Coptic church stood as the element of continuity. The great controversies left an indelible imprint on the Egyptian Church: the Arian controversy compelled the convocation of the councils at Nicaea and at Chalcedon. In the latter, in 451, Egypt took to monophysite tradition, which reduced the purview of its mission and divided the church. Besides the Mel-kites, there were at least twenty monophysite sects in Egypt alone by the end of the century. Tritheists were perhaps the most pernicious and reductionist of the addicts of the One Nature slogan, finally, drawing the ire of the Byzantine emperor and thereby turning the Copts into a defensive group.

To the west of Egypt were the Roman provinces of Cyrenia, Tripolitania, Africa, Numidia, and the two regions of Mauretania. At Chalcedon, these regions were brought under the jurisdiction of the Alexandrian episcopate. There is scant evidence of Christian origin between Cyrenia and Africa. Simon of Cyrene and the visitors at Pentecost suggest that some of the Jewish population had converted,so the region was not devoid of the light of the gospel. However,there is no indication of a vibrant Christian presence there. Equally shrouded is the date of entry of Christianity into Africa and Numidia. This area had much commercial contact with Italy and was the bread basket of Italy. Agriculture spurred a reasonable Roman demographic presence and mercantile enterprise.

The severe persecution by Septimis Severus belied the impression that Christianity flourished only among the Romans and converted Jews. Indeed, there was a growing African Christian population and the apologetics of Tertullian of Carthage, a metropolis with the highest cluster of churches in Africa, has left an invaluable insight into the battle to consolidate the gospel. As in Egypt, the numerical indices of growth based on the number of bishops showed that by AD 420, there were 700 bishops in this region. However, the Donatist challenge led to indiscriminate ordination of unqualified candidates in the heat of competition. Thus, at the synod of AD 411 there were 386 Catholic bishops and 279 Donatists. Arian Vandals persecuted the Roman bishops, reducing the number to 220 by AD 534; the Islamic scourge reduced them further to 6 by AD 1050. Nonquantitative data point to limited range of evangelized areas outside the Roman military posts. The pervasive use of the Latin language further hindered the impact of mission among the Punic elements and the Berbers.[6]

It was the Donatist party that made inroads into the Berber population for political reasons; nationalist opposition to foreign domination. The wild Circumcellions were in fact rebellious, repressed peasantry. Minimal horizontal growth and Constantine's carrot stick produced the same result as elsewhere. When the Vandals ruled, they used their own Germanic language, engaged in no evangelistic campaigns; and merely sought to establish Arian Christianity. The Byzantine rule from AD 534 bred Caesar Christians. Civil religiosity was rife and lacked deep spiritual roots. Moreover, the Donatist challenge reinforced the penchant for rigorism in African Christianity, and the Montanist not only encrusted a puritan spirituality but nurtured ascetic monasticism. Tertullian, Cyprian, and Augustine, therefore, struggled in a hostile environment to stabilize the enterprise and left valuable legacies, but controversies and military invasions sapped the missionary force.[7]

The southern boundaries of Egypt started from the first cataract of the Nile. The city of Philae was both a ritual and geographical boundary. It hosted the most vibrant shrine to Isis, a cult that dominated Egypt's southern neighbours, the Nubia. This people had four strong kingdoms by the second century AD : the Nobata acted as buffers from the restless Blemmyes of the eastern desert. The Mukurra held the area around the third cataract, Dongola; while the Aloa bestrode the White Nile sporting two ancient centers of civilization, Meroe and Alwa. The Christianization of Nubia has attracted much attention because of its three sources, one that refers to the Meroe kingdom, the other that refers to the intrigues of the Byzantinian Queen Theodora to establish a Monophysite Christianity, and a third to the Chalcedonian stance taken by her husband King Justinian. It is certain that the commercial and cultural contact with Egypt brought Christian influences into Nubia; archeological evidences abound. But it was the enforced unification of Nubian states as new groups moved from the interior to the embattled coastal communities that created the opportunity for Christianity to grow. Nubia's defeat by Islamic forces beginning from around the thirteenth century has attracted attention to the survival of Christian enclaves and to the impact of Roman Catholic and Protestant missionary forces in the eighteenth and nineteenth centuries. Even more intriguing is how the internal history of the Ethiopian Orthodox Church has woven a tapestry that absorbed the Nubian aspects. History books do not often tell this story and may even consider it a spurious weave of myths. It is deliberately privileged here to underscore African Christian initiaves.

Ethiopian and Nubian Christianity

"Hear O Ethiopians, the Lord our God, the Lord is One"

Further up the source of the Nile, beyond the divide of the White and Blue Nile lies Abyssinia which inherited the name for the entire region, Ethiopia. Their relationship with their northern Nubian neighbors was often fraught with hostility. Inscriptions brag of Ethiopia's victories over the Meroites and it is said the constant raids from the south broke the back of the kingdom of Meroe. Here, the story of the Ethiopian Orthodox church claims an existence that spans the roots and branches of the Jesus movement, harking earlier than the birth of Jesus and thereafter. To symbolize this long pedigree, their priests begin every act of worship by first proclaiming an adapted version of Jewish *shema* of Deuteronomy 6:4. Rulers would do so before issuing any public decrees or modifications to the law. There are in fact two voices in the story of Christianity in this region, sometimes converging and other times betraying a gulf of ideological biases.[8]

The history books provide the basis of the introductory overview that is like the voice of the outsider. We must listen to the insider, the Ethiopian Orthodox church. Their story embeds their journey into the Egyptian experience. Thus, the sojourn of the infant Jesus is a shared heritage as the party allegedly crossed the Sinai peninsula by the northern caravan route from Gaza to Raphia to present-day al-Arish; then to al–Farama (Pelusium). Equally shared was the ministry of Mark, the first patriarch of Alexandria whose parents were from Cyrenaica. His charismatic ministry ended when he dared to build a huge church in the suburban part of Alexandria called, Baucalis. The enraged mob of unbelievers attacked him as he was celebrating Easter mass. However, he had already written the gospel known by his name. But the Ethiopian church laid claim to a long history that was not surrogate. Though other historians may place Queen Sheba in Yemen, the Orthodox church's account claims that she resided in Axum, a great city built by a grandson of Ham named, Aksumawi.

Planting the feet firmly in two ancient documents, the Kebra Negast (the glory of the kings) and Fetha Negast (the law of the Kings), it claims that the queen was Medaka whose grand parents reigned from 1076-1026 B.C.E.. Of great beauty and endowed with an inquisitive mind, she was attracted to King Solomon through the stories of Prince Tamrin, a merchant prince, who was supplying Solomon with some of the construction materials for the temple. He organized the trip to visit the King and her six-months stay included long conversations and other forms of discourse and learning. The salacious part of the Kebra Negast (sections 29-32) is about Solomon's wise trickery or old-fashioned seduction that resulted in her pregnancy and the ring that she took back with her. Later, Ebria Hakim, her son and the" son of the wise one" visited the father. Solomon recognized his image and ring as proofs of paternity but failed to persuade the young man to stay and inherit the throne instead of the foolish Rehoboam. He commanded the princes of Dan, Levi and Gad, along with Azariah, the son of Zadok (the priest), to return to Ethiopia with Hakim. More trickery followed as Azariah made a dummy ark and substituted it with the real ark which he stole and took to Ethiopia. Hakim came to the Ethiopian throne with the royal name of Menelik I and proceeded to establish a Judaistic religion.

This explains the heavy dosage of Old Testament aspects of Ethiopian Orthodox spirituality. Matters did not end there: when Christ was born, the claim is that the three magi were all Ethiopians. This disputes other reconstructions claiming that one was the king of Afghanistan, the second the king of Persia and the third, the king of Ethiopia. The oral tradition continues to claim that the Ethiopian eunuch was really from Ethiopia not Nubia inspite of the fact that her title, Kandace,is the Meroitic language for Queen Mother. The Ethiopian tradition claims that her husband was Djan Darada,who was baptized in 34 AD and died in 55AD and that the queen was named, Qarsemot, the fourth Axumite Queen.It further claims that the treasurer's conversion and extensive preaching established Christianity in the kingdom.

Beyond the myth, it is known that the conversion of the Axumite court started in the third century when the Syrian youths,Frumentius and Sidrakos Adesius were captured by the Ethiopians at the Red Sea port of Adulis (Assab in Saba?). The youths arrived there unaware of the controversy between the Ethiopians and the foreign traders from Egypt and South Arabia. The reigning monarchs, King Ala-Amida and Queen Sofya (294-325 AD) engaged them as servants in the court. According to this story line, it was King Ala-Amida who sent a delegation to Rome to congratulate Emperor Constantine on his victories. Upon the king's death the queen named Frumentius as teacher for her sons, Abaraha and Asbeha. They later jointly succeeded to the throne as Ezana and Shaizana and declared Christianity to be the official religion of the state, installed the statues of saints, decorated places of worship with icons, and dedicated the Church of St. Mary of Zion as the location for the ark.

The task was to blend the inheritance from the Levites and the missionary achievements of the famous eunuch into a Christianity that was typically Ethiopian. The rest of the intriguing story centers on the illustrious career of Frumentius who was sent to Nicea in Bithynia, where the council was still in session deliberating over claims made by the Lybian, Arius. From there Frumentius travelled to Egypt, where he was detained and retrained in the Alexandrian School before his ordination as Abba Selama, the Archbishop of Ethiopia in 330 AD. This story line wove Ethiopia into the heritage of the Alexandrian School which was the most prominent place of learning in the early church and served as conservatory of the Monophysite tradition. Moreover, when the Abba Selama returned to Axum in 334AD, he brought back ancient manuscripts such as Greek versions of the Old and New Testaments, Apostolic Canons, Apostolic Traditions, Didascalia, the Didache, and books by the doyens of the school, Pantaneus, Clement, the much-maligned Origen, Dionysius, Didymus (who headed the school during the student days of Frumentius), Alexander, and Athanasius. These would have been like so many drops of water in a bucket compared to the resources Frumentius used in his studies or the number of volumes that survived in King Ptolemy II's (283-246 BCE) smaller library in Alexandria after Julius Caesar's Vandal –like behavior destroyed the larger of the two libraries that housed over half a million volumes and was the wonder of the world.

In this insider's perspective, the crucial position of the royal family in the church is moored with the Fetha Negast which provides that the legal position in the church will be based on their loyalty to the canons and discipline of the church. The power in the church was, therefore, rooted in the combined interactions between the abuna, the king, and heads of monastic houses. Monasticism became significant in the fifth century after the 'Tsad-kan' (just), or Tesseaton Kiddussan (nine saints) arrived. These were Monophysites who escaped from the imperial harassment that followed the Council at Nicea.[9] They evangelized the hinterlands, translated ancient manuscripts into Ge'ez, Amharic, Tegreniya, Gallina, and other indigenous languages; established the eremetic tradition, and domesticated Christian values in Ethiopia beyond the courts. For instance, Abba Aregawi went to Debra Damo, confronted the worship of the python, and established a monastery and schools just as Gerima went to Mettera near Senafe, Afese compromised the worship of fertility gods at Yeha. As they dispersed, so did learning and the inculcation of matured and informed Christianity. The significance is not usually manifest until one looks even farther into the history of Ethiopia.[10] Certain groups from across the Red Sea had come in large numbers into Ethiopia, overawing the indigenous people and establishing themselves at Yeha, Matara, and Asmara in present-day Eritrea; building temples, palace compounds, and covered markets that displayed circles and crescents which signified their gods Mahrem and Almuqah.

Admittedly, Ethiopians migrated into South Arabia and founded communities there but the point is that during this period Christianity was molding these diverse communities into a national entity. Moreover, these new Christian communities came into conflict with Jewish communities that had been established since the exilic period. The Sedaqan also mentored the future leaders of the church such as the most beloved St Ayared, who was educated at the school established beside St. Mary of Zion in Axum, where the ark rested. His compositions of sacred music and hymns dominate Ethiopian liturgy whether it be the kum-zema or the zemane whose melody swings back and forth like a pendulum or the chanted meregde or hand-clapping tsfat, the entire range is like a doctrinal commentary.

Oral tradition has it that the decline of Axum began in the ninth century under Anbessa Waddem when the Felasha queen, Yodit, who was not from the Solomonic line but may have descended from the Queen of Sheba's handmaid, essayed to rout Christianity and install Judaism. She initiated the Zagwe line that ruled from the tenth to the thirteenth century. At about the same time, Muslims successfully took over the Ethiopian communities of South Arabia. Ethiopia lost intimate contact with Egypt and could not secure the appointment of an abuna because of Fatimid rulers who used this ploy to ensure that the people in the south did not unilaterally declare themselves as independent from paying tributes in gold, salt, and frankincense. The story line of the internal history relates that this was the period when the Solomonic line was destroyed, as the new Zagwe rulers moved the capital from Axum in Tegray southwards to Wollo. The spirituality in the Ethiopian communities survived through its concentration on sacramental liturgical worship, the ascetic life, the daily calendar of fasting and feasting, the use of icons and the illustrated handwritten copies of the Old and New Testaments.

Since the Solomonic lineage is the core of the internal story line, Brahan Selassie could declare with glee that,

> in 1270 Atse Yekuno Amlak became Emperor and restored the Solomonic line to power. He held these cords of power until 1285. During his time as Emperor,

> the province of Shoa became the center of the nation,
> and the population underwent a renewal of its political,
> social, legal, educational and religious institutions.[11]

The emperor put one- third of his kingdom in the custody of the monastery at Debra Libanos. This brought to prominence the career of St. Tekla Haimanot (1215-1313), whose evangelistic campaigns and itineration refreshed Christianity throughout the nation. He had studied in the great monasteries, Debra Estifanos and Debra Damo, and had mastered the stories of the lives of Egyptian saints; he could ride rough shod over intramural conflicts and appeal to the masses with a show of sterling credentials of orthodoxy. There is a painting of this saint that depicts him as praying, standing on one leg for so long that the other leg dropped off. To maintain his stance, he had spear points on all four sides of him so that if he became drowsy and fell, the spears would awaken him.[12] He made the monastic life seem attractive, as some sought access to his mystical powers, others pursued the education offered in the monasteries; some of the devotees escaped from their evil past, while for others the allure of power through the endowed cloisters remained strong. The monasteries themselves encompassed a wide variety of personalities ranging from healers, prophets, seers, scribes and scholars, confessors father and mothers, icon painters, musicians, vestment makers, carpenters and masons, chefs and bakers, weavers, farmers, those who lived in solitude for five days a week and would reemerge on Saturdays and Sundays, and so on. Motivation therefore varied.

Seven significant themes serve as a guide through the rich tapestry of the presence of the gospel in Ethiopia and the peoples' responses. These include the relationship between the church and the state especially the significant roles that various monarchs played that determined the expansion of the faith; the level of popular participation and the way the gospel challenged the cultural soil of Ethiopia; theological development as could be perceived in some of the doctrinal debates about a two-day Sabbath; patterns of spirituality and fashioning of liturgical tradition, especially achieved by the distinguished lives of monastic figures; the challenge from Islam; the disastrous attempt to integrate Ethiopian Christianity into the papacy; and the resurgence of Ethiopian Christianity in the twentieth century after some dark days.[13]

As indicated, the fortunes of the church were always tied to the fortunes of the throne and bound to it with legal cords. Thus, the crown practically funded the clergy, founded most monastic houses, and supported them by donating revenues from parts of the kingdom or with the payments from Egypt for using the waters of the Blue Nile. Emperors provided diplomatic cover in the negotiations for the abuna from Egypt and promoted the struggle to have indigenous archbishops. Textbooks mention some of the great kings, but Emperor Lali-bella (1185-1225) was an unusual one who left indelible imprints. He was born in 1140 at Roha in the Lasta (northern Ethiopia) region, and it was said that mysterious signs appeared around him at birth. A thick cloud of bees engulfed the child, and the mother had a revelation that he would be a great king and accordingly named him, the bees know that the child will be a great king! In his youth he sojourned in Jerusalem for twenty-five years, visiting shrines and living an ascetic life. Reputable seers visited this mystic.

Once he ascended the throne, he commissioned eleven churches to be carved out of rock, basing this task on a vision he had. Masons and icon painters were sourced from Nubia, Egypt and all over the country. He named the buildings after a liturgical formula: *Alem* (Savior of the world), *Geneta Mariam* (the paradise of Mary), *Beit Masqul* (house of the cross), *Beit Dengel* (house of the Virgin), *Beit Kiddus Mikael* (house of the archangel Michael), *Beit Golgotha*, and so on. The beauty of the architecture has amazed generations over the centuries. The Muslim invader Ahmad Gran was stunned in disbelief; while the Jesuit missionary Francisco Alvarez, visiting Ethiopia between 1520-27 feared that readers of his Narrative of the Portuguese Embassy to Abyssinia may not believe his description of these churches and religious institutions.[14] After completion of the churches, Lali-bella secured archbishops from Egypt, retired from the throne, and returned to his solitary life of silent prayer in the wilderness.

The kings are largely responsible for expanding the Ethiopian church, for example, when Emperor Kaleb invaded Zafar and Najram in 525 AD in revenge for the massacre of Christians in that region,he established Ethiopian churches in South Arabia, and gave the Ethiopian monarchs the reputation as being great warriors and defenders of the faith in Africa. But sometimes a king would become derailed and face the rebuke of the clergy, for example, when Emperor Amde Zion (1314-1344) became sexually promiscuous. Abba Anorewos, from one the prominent monastic houses confronted him; the king had him whipped in public and persecuted many houses until an incredible fire broke out that stunned him and consumed his palace; he repented and became one the most generous patrons of the church. The kings posed as arbiters in matters of doctrine, convoked debates on doctrinal matters and threw their weight on one side or the other. For instance, Emperor Zera Yacob (1434-68) intervened in the debate over the two-day Sabbath that pitted some of the indigenous heads of monastic houses against the Egyptian archbishops; but the king insisted upon two days to honor the period which Christ spent in the grave before the resurrection day. The emperor therefore summoned the Council of Mitmaq in 1450, where the conflict was resolved.

Zera Yacob, the seed of Jacob, was unusual in the broad range of his reformation of the church. He must have understood that the character of Christianity in his domain was centered around the court and the monasteries, and that the rural dwellers resorted to magicians and sorcerers for solutions to urgent life problems. The challenge was to move beyond a religion of ceremonies and redolent liturgy; a religion that served as a cultural signifier. Indeed, the monastic leaders would occasionally lash out at the prosperous merchants and courtiers who engaged in the slave trade in Nubia and Adal and yet lavishly endowed monasteries as if to bribe God. The emperor strove to ensure that the masses would exchange the covenants with deities such as *Dasek, Dial, Guidale, Tafant, Dino, Maku-uawze* for the Christ; he demanded that Christians wear arm and head bands with biblical affirmations; he revised the church calendars and promoted pilgrimages to the Holy land. It should be noted that while the calendar has many Jewish features it is related to the Julian calendar as used in the Egyptian Orthodox church. The year begins in September, each year is devoted to one of the four evangelists. The leap year is usually attributed to Luke, and nearly every day is named after a saint. According to this calendar, Jesus was born 55501 years after creation.

Above all, Zera Yacob increased Ethiopian contact with Europe and sent a mission to the Council in Florence, 1432-45. It is said that when the Ethiopian delegation was on its way, Pope Eugenia IV moved the meetings to Rome so as to give them an appropriate reception. The pope's hidden agenda was to unite the Byzantine, Armenian and Ethiopian Orthodox Churches with the papacy to shore up his reputation and to mobilize against Muslims. Ethiopian resistance continued for many more years as the contact initiated intrigues by Rome to rein the land of the Qevs, as the Ethiopians called themselves, into the papal ambit.[15] But the exposure attracted a bevy of explorers, ambassadors, soldiers, and Roman Catholic missionaries to the kingdom. After a long period of splendid isolation, Zera Yacob opened Pandora's box.

The pressure from Rome and Portugal dovetailed into the series of Muslim attacks that had intensified since the twelfth century. Various rulers spent enormous military resources to ward off the Muslim hord who gradually consolidated around the coast and forced the capital to be relocated a number of times. Perhaps Emir Almad ibn Ibrahim, nicknamed Ahmed Gran because he was left-handed, conducted one of the most devastating raids in the period between 1527-1578. By 1539, he had destroyed many churches, palaces, and libraries; and carted away national treasures and heirlooms. In desperation, Emperor Lebna Dengel pleaded for Portuguese intervention which came in October 1542 and rescued Ethiopia. The price was to subject the monarch to pressures, through a Jesuit mission to accept papal authority. Forged documents, blandishments, and military attacks were pressed into the service until it boomeranged as the people suspected that their emperor had succumbed and rose up in arms to defend the faith of their fathers. Rumors circulated among the nobility and monastic houses that Emperor Za-Dengel had yielded to the pressures by Pero Pais who arrived in 1603 and made it clear that his mission was to reform Ethiopian spirituality and ensure submission to Rome. Za Selassie led the rebellion that killed the emperor. Matters did not end there as his successor, Emperor Susneyos, was badgered by Pais who died in 1622. Alfonso Mendes took over the task when he became not only the new papal envoy but was brazenly consecrated Patriarch of Ethiopia by Pope Urban VIII. He forced the emperor to swear a formal oath of allegiance to the pope. The cultural history of Ethiopia was electrified as revolt after revolt broke out, and civil wars went on without any hope of abating. The emperor's loyal followers, including his son, began to argue that he break with Rome; his army began to murmur against having to fight fellow Ethiopians. By 1630, the emperor was forced to back down and restore the sovereignty of Ethiopian Christianity.

The civil war may have damaged the fabric of the society more than was apparent because Ethiopia lost its peace throughout the next two centuries as rival princes and theological factions tore the seams apart. One disastrous debate was over the nature of Christ. It should be explained again that the Ethiopian Church held that Christ had two natures before incarnation, but only one after the union; the humanity being absorbed by in the divinity. In the new debate, one side held a conception that was nicknamed, Karra Haimanot meaning, "the belief of the knife as it cuts off the third birth." This was maintained against those who believed that Christ had three births: from God the father, at conception and at baptism from the Holy Spirit.

Worse, Ethiopia could not secure an archbishop from Egypt between 1803 and 1816. The story of the Christian presence at the beginning of the nineteenth century is a gloomy tale. It was as if a desolate wind scorched the efforts of yesteryears. In the Horn of Africa, the decline had been steady with the incursion of Islam beginning in the seventh century. However, the varied policies of different Islamic regimes preserved signs of life among the rural Egyptian Copts; permitted Nubia to remain Christian till the fifteenth century, and left Ethiopian Christianity in splendid isolation,maintaining an image of a muscular church with the character of pristine first -century Christianity, monastic spirituality, explosive creativity in music, fine arts and architecture. However, by the end of the eighteenth century, Ethiopian Christianity was in a traumatized state. Henry Salt painted a sorry picture in Voyages and Travels (1809):

> The nation, with its religion, is fast verging on ruin; the Galla and Mussulman tribes around are daily becoming more powerful; there is reason to fear that, in a short time, the very name of Christianity may be lost among them.[16]

The state structure had grown soft, its boundaries dwindled and internecine theological debates on the Sabbath and nature of Christ created virulent divisions among the court, the leading monastic houses and the abuna. Its ancient liturgy in Ge'ez became less intelligible and less inspiring to Amharic speakers; learning declined as the infrastructure rotted. Indeed, hundreds of churches were destroyed or abandoned amidst scathing violence. Henry Salt referred to the fact that non-Christian Galla communities and Muslims had settled over large areas that were once Christian. This is the period known as zemane mesafint, the era of the princes. This backdrop gave much significance to the regenerating careers of Emperor Tewodros (1855-68) and Emperor Yohannes IV (1872-1889). But this was also a period when a number of foreign interest groups- Jewish, Protestant, and Roman Catholic- discovered Ethiopia. Quite intriguing is the first group of Germans employed by the British-based Church Missionary Society into Tigre, Gondar, and Shoa from 1830. Their goal was ostensibly to purify Ethiopian Christianity rather than to open new mission stations. They deployed evangelical doctrines as the litmus tests on such practices as praying to Mary and the saints, venerating images, kissing the cross, keeping fast and cherishing monasteries. All these would indubitably contest Protestant perceptions and evoke hostile response from the indigenous folk. Around 1842,the missionaries invited the imperial powers of Britain and France to soften the unyielding ground with violence. Equally intriguing is that the Roman Catholic Lazarists who came later appeared to be more culturally sensitize and equipped to operate in such cross-cultural contexst and used the ordination of indigenous priests to gain influence before the contemporary Abuna Salama saw through the insidious project and attacked the Lazarists with as much vehemence as he could muster to preserve Ethiopian identity.

The man who initiated the regeneration of Ethiopia, Kassa Hailu, was born in Qwara, brought up by an uncle and trained in monastic education; but soon he joined a band of bandits, becoming a mighty warrior and one of the princes who held part of the land. His victories over other warlords won him the crown and he took the royal name of Tewodros, King of Kings. He has fascinated historians because of his exceptional energy and activities. First, he was the one who tried to consolidate the Solomonic pretences of the crown by designing the titles and acting it out; he choreographed it from the conflation of myth and history that had always played in the background of Ethiopia's story. He was perhaps driven to this by the enormous efforts the various missionary groups spent in propping up the Falasha, whose Jewish origins were much clearer. Second, he attempted to unify the nation by military conquest. His continued success convinced him that the divine hand was sustaining him, and that he was special. Third, he reformed the church by insisting on monogamy and by down-sizing the number of the clergy so as to enforce stricter discipline. Fourth, he had a deep social conscience and sensitivity towards the masses. His populist agricultural reform included land redistribution that evoked the opposition of the monastic houses, Ethiopia's biggest landowners. Loke other rulers, Tewodros intervened in doctrinal disputes and ruled against the doctrine of three births and commissioned the translation of the Bible into Ahmaric because Ge'ez was becoming incomprehensible to many.

It was his foreign policy that led to his death. The French and the British had tried unsuccessfully to trick him. He subsequently arrested and imprisoned the British representatives, and when diplomacy failed, realizing that he had lost the battle, Tewodros proudly killed himself, a king to the end. The ruler of Tigre, the prominent prince, was crowned in 1872 at Aksum as Yohannes IV, King of Zion of Ethiopia. The flamboyant title was not lost on many observers as he built on the tradition set byTewodros. Yohannes ruled till 1889. The same problems followed him to the grave, namely, national unification, doctrinal uniformity, a viable foreign policy and an adequate response to Islamic insurgence. Military engagement that required a reliance on foreign technological support eased the first problem; the Council of Borumeda tackled the second; an ingenious division of the state into four Coptic bishoprics was equally helpful and even enhanced the Christianization process among the Galla. It was the Madhist revolt that snuffed out his illustrious career. Menelik II (1889-1913) would achieve most of Yohannes's ambitions. The defeat of the Italian imperial greed at Adwa in March 1896 inspired black imagination all over the world and made Abyssinia, the hub of Ethiopia, a name that Western writersused for the whole region inhabited by the sons of Kush. Adrian Hastings put it aptly,

> the years after Adwa were for Ethiopia years of excep-
> tional peace. The authority of Menelik was almost
> unchallenged, the feudal independence of the great
> provinces was quietly diminished. His rule was far more
> a revival of the traditional royal system, the combination
> of a network of great lords, a loyal army, and the church"
> and even more.[17]

Conclusion

African Christianity in this period was vibrant and experienced much growth. It had problems related to the teething stage of a new religion. There were many lively theological debates that left legacies that could assist contemporary African Christianity in articulating Christian ethics, developing a strong spirituality such as was prac-ticed in the monastic tradition, and being a self-sustaining, suffer-ing church, one with a muscular liturgy. Why did it collapse under Islamic insurgence?

Scholars accept a general population figure for Egypt in the year 600 AD of approximately three million persons, a decline from its peak of five million under the Roman Empire.[18] Egypt's once cosmo-politan and connected larger world of affairs had yielded to the rural, the agricultural, and the local. Likewise the pagan had yielded to the Christian, with the leader of the Coptic church in Alexandria in alliance with the Coptic monasteries and Nile communities. Egypt continued to contribute grain to Constantinople, even in the years of the Phocan rebellion (600AD), down to the disruptive dozen years of Persian control of Egypt from 617 AD to 629 AD when the Byzantine ruler,Heraclius regained control of Egypt. But the costs of disruption and dislocation showed in the privatization of many formerly public civic tasks. As in other portions around the Mediterranean, church authorities took on tasks once carried out by local governments.

What was happening to the Churches in these years? Egypt continued to attract Christian pilgrims; Egyptians continued to travel to other parts of the Christian world; and Alexandria appointed the leadership of the Christian communities in Sudan and Ethiopia. It is useful to note the transition of governments included more negotiation than military engagement, with the Persians and the Byzantines concerned more with events in Mesopotamia than with the unfolding drama in Arabia under the Prophet and the Caliphate. A conflict between the Coptic patriarch, Benjamin, and his rival Cyrus divided the church on the eve of the Muslim advance into Egypt. Both factions sought some delay through negotiation with the forces of 'Amr ibn al-'As, the Muslim invader. The eventual Muslim capture of Egypt still raises many questions regarding resistance strategies. The successful advance of Muslim forces into Palestine and Syria made it seem inevitable that Egypt would be next. After initial successes in 640, Muslim advances slowed. But after the death of Heraclius in 641, the leadership of Byzantium fell to a regency government, resulting in confusion in military operations. Some argue that the fall of Egypt to Islam was caused by complicity and capitulation; others perceive a complex of factors involving leadership, exhaustion, and the entirely mistaken hope that Arab control would, like a tide, recede as readily as it had surged into Egypt. Throughout the centuries the Coptic church has remained, honored by its special service to the Holy Family, rooted in the earliest days of the gospel in Egypt, rightfully proud of its contributions to church doctrine from Nicaea to Chalcedon, encouraged by the faithfulness of its early martyrs, and steadfast in its witness into our own time, a new age of martyrs.

However, debate remains about the fate of Christianity in North Africa after the Islamic insurgence. Some have argued that Islam won an easy victory because of its disciplined army composed of good horsemen, imbued with a muscular religious belief that they were engaged in a victory for Allah. Discipline was maintained even after victory because, in these years before the emergence of Damascus as a command center, Muslim forces usually quarantined themselves outside the city walls to avoid mixing with infidels and to remain highly mobile. The expansion of Arabic Islam, as well as the range and speed of the conquest of former Christian states was staggering. How best to explain this rapid expansion and conquest? Some explanations focus on the occupied peoples: the oppressive taxation imposed by the Byzantines had created deep resentment within its client state, which contributed to the people's receptivity to Islam. Similarly, the contests between Persia and Byzantium were at the expense of the Egyptians. Moreover, the Islamic forces engaged less in cultural transformation and more in the expansion of territories. Muslim victories were consolidated by the three options given to captured peoples: to surrender and pay a tribute, to convert to Islam, or to face continued jihadist attack. While the category of dhimma evolved over time, the strategies of Christian (and Jewish) survival emerged much faster. Nubia, thanks to the archers of Dongola, successfully resisted the forces of Islam, which led to a negotiated treaty, the *baqt,* that protected Christian Nubia for several centuries. [19]

African resistance was more evident in Carthage, especially among the Donatists as shown by the Circumcellion raids on the agricultural merchant elite in urban areas who exploited the Maghrib as the bread basket of Europe. Exploitation bred a resistance in Libya, Tunisia, and Algeria. It is alleged that Carthage fell easily because an African commander preferred the Arab incursion to the Byzantine or Roman rule wheras Alexandria held up for three months because a Greek commanded the defense. But Berber nationalism was equally uncomfortable with Roman, Byzantine, or Arab rule. A striking feature of North African Christianity is the prominent strain of hostility toward institutions and imperial governance.[20] The storied prophetess Cuhna (Damia al-Kahena), Queen of the Aures from the hill country near Tunis, illustrates this point. Regardless of its historical accuracy, African memory gloried in her bravery as demonstrated by her victory against the initial Arab attack on Carthage. When the Arabs regrouped, she applied a scorched earth policy to deny them Africa's wealth; she lost the war, she refused to convert to Islam. As long as the Muslims did not insist on forced conversion, their expeditions could be interpreted as liberation.

The collapse of early Christainity in Africa

These realities challenge the simplistic verdict that Christianity in North Africa sat lightly and was easily overawed, for it lacked roots among the indigenous Tuaregs and Kwororaffa; lacked a vernacular Bible; was mired in arid doctrinal disputes and was consequently vulnerable. A defense has been canvased. The first step would be to establish timelines and distinctive strategies among distinct groups, freed from uncritical acceptance of special pleadings in Islamic or Christian narratives. One danger would be to read the later coherence of Islamic rule back into the first half-century of the Islamic expansion. Another danger would be to read later rationalizations back into the first half-century of Christian resistance. It is also important to note changes in strategies. For instance, the Islamic forces did not immediately lash out against Christians. As soon as the Coptic Christians adopted a neutral stance and did not oppose them, the Arabs conciliated by even recalling Patriarch Benjamin.

Similarly, the strategies useful in conquering territories were not necessarily good for governance. Arab conquerors did not have the manpower to govern the large territories, therefore, they used bishops as advisers, ambassadors, governors, and tax collectors. Naturally, they were less concerned with doctrinal differences among the Jacobites, Melchites, Copts, and Nestorians. They pursued pragmatic cooperation by imposing restrictions against Christian public proselytism. The Arabs deployed marriage as a means of expanding their influence: they married Christian women but prevented Christians from marrying Arab women. Other burdens were imposed through time that increased incentives to conversion and increased the costs of resistance.

Moreover, a concern for periodization is important because it would illustrate early Islamic sensitivity to the Prophet's toleration of the "People of the Book" unlike the later Caliphs. The process of migration, Arabization, and new trading patterns took time to emerge. By the end of the first Muslim century, Arabs were found throughout northern Africa, and new caravan trade routes were challenging the ancient river commerce system along the Nile. Internal squabbles among the Muslims had consolidated different regimes and lineages that governed different parts of the new Islamic Empire. Thus, the Ummayyads who consolidated their rule over North Africa by 661AD proved to be more tolerant towards Christians than the Abbassids who overthrew the Ummayyad in 750 AD Similarly, the Fatimids, who were themselves North Africans and not Arab Muslims, showed greater tolerance than their successor Mamlukes from 990 AD. Besides, the Bible had been translated into a number of Coptic dialects, and the rural Copts deployed Christianity as a cultural signifier. However, there is no gainsaying the gradual decline of the Christian presence in the Maghrib. If one were to combine the data from Rodney Stark and Phillip Jenkins, a certain statistical image would read as follows:

Percentage of Christians among the Populations of the Roman Empire and Egypt

Year	Empire	Egypt
239	1.4	0
274	4.2	2.4
278	5.0	10.5
280	5.4	13.5
313	16.2	18.0
315	17.4	18.0

Clearly, Africa was an important center of early Christianity and remained so much longer than the four- volume study on the planting of Christianity in Africa by C.P. Groves would lead us to believe.[21] By 500 AD, argues Jenkins, there were about 8 million Christians in North Africa. This declined to 5 million by 1000 AD, 2.5 million by 1200 AD, and 1.5 million by 1500 AD. The argument is that Christianity grew at certain points in time under Islamic rule, and that the decline accelerated during and after the Crusades. Nonetheless, the Christian presence along the Nile continued to be important till the fifteenth century in Nubia and much later in Ethiopia.

2. SECOND CHANCE: THE IBERIAN CATHOLIC ENTERPRISE AND ITS ENEMIES

Europe responded to the Islamic challenges which included economic monopoly of the Levant route, trade in spices from the Far East, and control of the bread basket in North Africa, and an assertive presence in the Meditarrean. The challenge had cultural and political dimensions, as Arabic scholarship thrived and Muslims controlled much of the Iberian penisula. The military response of the Crusades failed. The *reconquista* project moved with a slow pace. Something happened that would change both the challenge and the course of European history. It was the imagination and scientific endeavor to develope a sea route that would circumscribe the Muslims and open a new sea route to the source of the spices.

Portugal's capture of Ceuta (present-day Morocco) in 1415 signaled the beginning of the European response which ironically was not aimed at reestablishing Christianity in the Maghrib. Iberian missionary enterprise was part and parcel of a variety of motives. C. R. Boxer enumerated four : (i) a crusading zeal against Moors, (ii) the desire for Guinea gold, (iii) the romantic quest for the Christian empire of Prester John and (iv) the search for oriental spices through an alternative route.[22] Christened the quest for ,gold, glory, and God, the admixture of commerce, politics and religion at the root of the enterprise provided an indelible coloring and left the looming question as to which was predominant.

Three pertinent questions relate to the background of the Iberian response, the pattern in the establishment of Portuguese hegemony, and the specific character of missionary presence. From a certain perspective, the inspiring milieu was the Renaissance and the repercussions of the rebirth of learning salted with the daring spirit of experimentation. The personality of Prince Henry the Navigator looms large with the fortunate consolidation of the monarchy in Portugal while others fought wars for thrones; for instance, in England the War of Roses was in progress. The new designs of sails, compasses and other nautical equipment were products of Henry's nautical school at Sagres. It is certain that from Ceuta, Henry heard much about the trans-Saharan gold trade and the possibilities of reaching the Indies.

By the time Henry died in 1460, his men had systematically sailed the Atlantic and discovered the Madeiras, Canaries, Azores, Arguin, Cape Verde Islands and Sierra Leone. In the 1470s they passed the Gold Coast to the Bight of Benin, establishing posts on the Islands of Sao Thome, Fernando Po, and Principe. By the 1480s they reached Loanda, Soyo and Kongo kingdoms, and crossed the Cape of Good Hope in the 1490s to the East African coast, and across the Indian Ocean to Goa (India) by 1499. It was a great feat. The Portuguese Empire was like a long shoestring dotted with coastal and commercial establishments. Only in the Kongo, Zambezi Basin, and India did they endeavor to extend inland. Indeed, till the establishment of St. George's Fort in the Gold Coast in 1482, they traded from their ships, using them as floating bases and later established *feitorias* (factories/forts) at Arguin (south of Cape Blanco) in 1445, Mpinda in 1501, and Mozambique in 1502, all in an effort to tap the trans-Saharan trade of Western Sudan and to wrest the *Estado da India* from the Oman Arab princes and Indian merchants.

The concern here is the evidence that the Portuguese actually set out to convert Africans and the depth and extent of Christian penetration into the lives and cultures of the various African communities. A crusading spirit had suffused Europe and enabled the Iberians to recover from the Islamic incursion into major centers such as Granada in Spain. But the connection between the crusading zeal and the voyages of discovery was made in the papal bulls, *Dum Diversas* (1452), *Romanus Pontifex* (1455), and *Inter Caeteras* (1456) .[23] The second especially is regarded as the blue-print of Henry's motivations. While securing his economic and political monopoly in the New World, he avowed a mission to compel the Saracens and other nonbelievers to convert to Christianity and to build churches, monasteries, and *pia loca*. He had the full authority to send priests who would administer the eucharist in these places. The popes sealed the relationship with Portugal and Spain with agreements known as *padroada* in Portugal and *patronata* in Spain. The agreements combined the political and religious policy of incorporation by permitting state rulers to control the missionary activities and administration of the newly discovered regions. They energized the adventurers with a crusade zeal that captured more African slaves than believers. However, every ship had priests on board who ministered to the shipmates. Shipmasters celebrated the planting of Iberian forts or castle with a religious ceremony; after all, Henry was the Defender of the Faith and Grand Prior of the Order of Christ. At Kilwa, they sang a *Te Deum Laudemus* before they started looting. Iberian Catholicism was a social ornament, a religion of ceremonies and outward show.

To begin with the story of West Africa: Portuguese presence was mainly in the Islands or clustered along the mainland coast. These islands were thinly populated with indigenous people or uninhabited. It was easy to establish prototypical Portuguese colonies. Thus, the Cape Verde Islands served as a refueling depot and a veritable little Portugal. On the Sierra Leone coast, the Portuguese established eight settlements, continued and past the Malagueta coast, four settlements clustered along the Gold Coast. Farther south, Sao Thome served as the principal depot. From here, futile efforts were made to evangelize the Benin Empire, exaggerated in the Western imagination, for instance, inthe map of Africa drawn in 1656 by Groetius. The Oba wanted guns while the Portuguese wanted pepper. Later, the plentiful pepper supply from India made Benin irrelevant while court-alliance ruined the Franciscans. In Warri, the violent reactions of traditionalists blighted the glimmer of hope held by Olu Sebastian, who had been trained in Portugal. Broken images of saints stand as a reminder of these protracted efforts in the seventeenth century.[24]

G. Balandier has argued that Portuguese missionary impact was fleeting, superficial and ill-conceived.[25] Using the data from Richard Gray and Enrique Dussel,[26] a transplanted Catholicism flourished in the islands. In the black towns such as Mbanza Soyo, a *mestizo*

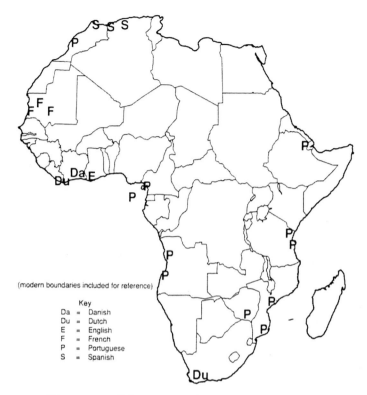

(modern boundaries included for reference)

Key
Da = Danish
Du = Dutch
E = English
F = French
P = Portuguese
S = Spanish

European Discovery of Africa: 1450-1700

Catholicism that emerged through confraternities held sway, while the rural areas witnessed a syncretist form. This emphasized ritual rather than doctrine because rich symbols are ambiguous enough and,when congruent with traditional forms, could serve to facilitate easier grasp and adaptation.It was the Kongo kingdoms that enjoyed the most consistent Christian enterprise on the coast.

The Portuguese enterprise lacked adequate missionary personnel whether white or black. The slave trade, other commercial activities and competitions with fellow Europeans, Arabs, and Indians pre-occupied more attention. The *patronato/padroada* system hindered missions. Nevertheless all these forces worked most visibly in East Africa. The effort to penetrate into Mashonaland, where Mono-mopata ruled, failed; the thirteen little tribes of Madagascar warred relentlessly to undermine the Portuguese adavnce, while the Arabs from Oman reconquered the northern sector of the Eastern Coast.

Africa in the 17th and 18th Centuries

The Jesuit, Jerome Lobo, told the story of the failed effort to turn Ethiopia Orthodox churches into Roman Catholic churches. Here was a church life vibrant in puritanic ethics and lively liturgy that was utilizing indigenous musical instruments, a veritable harbinger to the Zionism of the future.[27] Thus, the Portuguese had very little to show for all their efforts.

By the seventeenth century, Christian presence had reached south of the Sahara but took refuge in about twenty-one forts where neither the trading companies nor the state churches endeavored to maintain regular chaplains. Chaplains were primarily to serve the Europeans in the forts. The companies paid chaplains in trade goods and this tended to compromise them. Two recent studies have used the career of J. E. Capitein, a Ghanaian, to illustrate the dilemma of chaplains.[28] The Protestants made an intriguing effort to employ Africans as chaplains. But Capitein's A Call to the Heathens betrays an ardour to save his people with the gospel. However, he died young in frustration. Indeed, neither Protten nor Philip Quacoo nor William Amo, trained in Europe for service in Africa, had better luck. Neither Portugal nor its enemies had a burden for evangelism. The Africans of the interior were still unreached; but those on the coast were lured into international commerce A second chance to implant Christian presence in Africa was choked by thorns of wordly commercial cares.

3.RESILIENT VISION: THE EVANGELICAL REVIVAL AND ITS FRUITS

God's patience with Africa remained enduring, and the vision to save it for Christ resilient. Weak instruments, flawed strategies, and hostile environment colluded with the slave trade to delay the realization. But in the eighteenth century something inexplicable occurred. There was an outburst of religious enthusiasm, sharpened social conscience, a flow of philanthropy, and evangelicalism in Europe. It took time and conflict before these movements consolidated, gained acceptability and transformed into world mission by the nineetheenth century. In 1892, the American Rufus Anderson preaching from Galatians 4:4, declared that The Time for the World's Conversion (has) Come, because he sensed the public acceptance of a number of theological foundations of the modern missionary movement: an eschatological understanding of the Great Command, piety, an ideology of freedom and a concern for the role of the Holy Spirit in mission. His British copmpatriot,William Carey shared a similar optimism. As in the Iberian period, the relationship between commerce, civilization and Christianity was, according to Fowell Buxton, held indissoluble. But there were crucial differences: (i) a rejection of slave trade and slavery and an advocacy for legitimate trade built on agriculture; (ii) a keener sensitivity towards the poor as illustrated by the Clapham Sect's connection between social awareness at home and the urge to extend the same to crosscultural communities; and (iii) an ambiguous relationship with the secular government. Unlike the patronata structure, missionary bodies were voluntary associations and sought funding from a broader base and a wider band of that social strata.

It is essential to note that either the imperial ardor, improved socioeconomic factors, or international politics stoked evangelical fire.

Many societies formed with the gaol of converting the heathens in far away lands and the urge to serve in missions.But the dominant intellectual tradition emphasized the trusteeship idea that encouraged Europe to partition and govern African communities.[29] As Andrew F. Walls has shown, after a slow start, major shifts during this century included: increased recruitment of missionaries, especially women; vast increase in number of societies; and participating nations; and faiths; and the emergence of a new kind of missionary who was more educated than the godly mechanics.[30] As denominations became more open to the world and strikingly adopted mission, new ideas about the enterprise surfaced as organizational structure supplanted charisma.

The arguemnt here is that industrial revolution provided the basic infrastrcure that would aid crosscultural mission. But the connection between the material revolution, the evangelical revivals, and mission to Africa was abolitionism. As the number of freed slaves increased in Britain, the governement was forced to find a solution. Evangelicals who had drawn attention to the immorality of the trade, seized the opportunity to provide a solution, namely, negotiate treaties with the chiefs which supplied slaves, encourage them to shift to legitimate trade in agricultural products, and use Christianity as an instrument to civilize the communities.Missionaries became locked into the civilizing project and colonial overrule.

Missionary resurgence coincided with the noonday of imperialism. At its heart was racism, sometimes cloaked in scientific garb and hubris. Missionaries were children of their times as the colonial context distorted the missionary vision and scorched the evangelical legacy. They saw Africans, as a blind man saw men, as if they were trees. Imperial jingoism seeped into missionary endeavor and diluted the spiritual emphasis. The matter is not with militant hymns; but a close scrutiny of the candidates'motivation betrays imperial romanticism. But the imperial age offered revolutionary inventions in communication: the steamer, railway, and telegraph. These served as the life-line of missionary enterprise.

However, the finger of God intervened again: the exigencies of the mission field, the quirks of international politics, and the faithfulness of the many sobered hubris and ensured that the gospel spread like the harmattan fire. First,manpower and material resources increased rapidly till the First World War. Thereafter, the impact of the war, rumors of war, the Great Depression, and the Second World War all worked together from 1914 to 1945 to reduce the resource capabilities of the missionary movement in Britain and in Europe.

Only America seemed capable of carrying the torch at the old pace. Second, the mortality rate of missionaries combined with increased manpower shortage to enlarge the roles of indigenous people. Third, the local terrain remained stony, but the pounding of the gospel was more insistent, went beyond the coast into the hinterlands, as the strategies grew more resourceful. For instance, adopting school as a means of evangelization attacked the worldview of the people where it hurt. Much gave way. The embattled gods of the fathers swayed. Much persisted as the African initiative intensified.

To analyze the path of Christian development, we take cognizance of the fact that nationalist historiography objects to predicating African periodization on European events. But there is no gainsaying that the Berlin West African Conference of 1884/5 constituted a significant watershed; so did the First World War, whose shadows persisted into the Second World War. Africa was involved in all these events. As one proverb puts it: the cricket whose son is roasted is a part of the tradition of roasting crickets.Since the competing forces had colonies in Africa, they recruited porters and foot soldiers from the continent to fight on both sides of the conflict.During the First World War, more African porters died than soldiers.

The new crosscultural evangelism started with much spiritual fervor, and this, was the most important qualification for recruitment of a missionary. Before the Berlin Conference precious little was accomplished; indeed, the vision took some time to permeate the established church and elite. In Scotland, the mission field was the Scottish Highlands where recruits were not abundant for a host of reasons. The Church Missionary Society (founded in 1799) utilized volunteers from Europe. The reorganized Roman Catholic machinery required many years to run smoothly. It took much effort to eradicate the slave trade because of ideological, economic, and logistic problems. Daring into many new cultural contexts left many missionaries unprepared and summarily defeated. On the west coast, malaria took a large toll; and on the east coast, The Oman Arabs and Indians vigorously opposed missionary efforts. The exigencies of the mission field forced changes in policy and practice. The net effect was that missionaries held closely to the coasts of the rivers that served as the main mode of transportation and communication. The pace of any foray inland was often determined by security-conscious officials. Moreover, court-alliance, which cramped the missionaries' style, remained the viable method of evangelization. Political considerations led African rulers to welcome or to tolerate the presence of pioneer missionaries.

The Presbyterian missionary leader, Hope Masterton Waddell, rationalized the slow pace as being dictated by the need to build solid foundations. There is no denying that this was achieved and, in some places, the tendency to hug the coastline was broken. Birch Freeman in the Gold Coast, Robert Moffatt among the Ndebele, the Paris Evangelical Missionaries in Basutoland, and the London Missionary Society among the Xhosa all ignored the security factor and planted the mustard seed in the Africa hinterland. Nonetheless,by 1884, much of Africa was unevangelized by 1884. Adrian Hastings characterised the misionary achievement as being full of resolute beginnings but little more.[31]

While the debate may rage to explain the events leading to the Berlin Conference in 1884/5, it chnged the ground rules for colonization, and changed the face of the missionary enterprise. Explantions for European occupation of Africa abound:the doctrine of sphere of influence compelled effective occupation of the hinterlands and forced European governments into the African interior; Africa provided raw materials for european industries and new markets for processed goods. Some have argued that the men-on-the-spot enticed reluctant official minds into the colonial enterprise.Still for others, Britain and France responded to the muscualr nationalist politics of Bismarck's Germany. The net effects were: (i) increased confidence of missionaries; (ii) a shift from court-alliance to mass mobilization for Christ.This meant that the indigenous chiefs lost respect. Paternalism replaced co-operation; (iii) intense rivalry among missionaries ensued; (iv) government intervention and control of quality and curricula in educational institutions increased. They also provided security; and (v) rapid vertical expansion occurred, using education as the key means of evangelization. Other changes followed apace: Christain missions became popular among the Africans, the educated acquired enhanced social status, and native agents became chief mediators of Christianity and Western culture.[32]

To explain these further: Felix Ekechi has explored rivalry as the dominant theme in exploring the growth of mission in Africa. He argued that the direction,pace and strategies for evangelization were determined by the competition among missionary agencies. They used charitable institutions and schools as instruments of rivalry. Meanwhile,local chiefs competed among themselves by exploiting the rival missions.[33]Ekechi ignored the fact that home bases of missions restrained those in the field. In 1888 at Exeter Hall and Edinburgh in 1910, Protestants sought to contain the fury. In the field, delimitations of operational area kept warriors at bay. Rivalry did indeed determine the rapid pace of missionary expansion into the hinterlands. The government increased its role out of concern for order, especially as European international politics continued to be occupied with wars between 1870 and 1945. Thus, the quest for security in the interior hastened the Christianization process. Governments engaged pacification assaults on indigenous communities. Furthermore, the state's use of the carrot and stick through financial aid and inspectorates systems left its indelible imprints in spiritual matters.

Admittedly, the vastness of the continent, and the increased numbers of missionaries, visions and apostolates provide exceptions to any broad generalizations but there was a major shift from the cellular evangelical approach, as signified by Venn's three-selves formula, to a planting strategy in which denominations invested in infrastructure and reproduced themselves. The implications were enormous: the church was imprinted on the African landscape in a Western mold. The ark syndrome bred a Peter Pan syndrome in which Western control of finances and power stultified the roots of the stewardship ethic. Traditions were established that would inevitably stunt dynamic growth.

Biographies of Alston May, Arthur Cripps, and Lester Membe in Central Africa and a revisit to the career of Robinson and Brookes on the Niger Mission (1890-92) reveal evidence of semens of transcendence or those who kept the original vision alive. Till the shock of 1914, the missionary impulse remained vibrant. Brian Stanley's *The Bible and the Flag* indicates a steady growth in missionary recruitment of missionaries.[34] Diminished resources, withdrawal of German missionaries and redistribution of Protestants halted expansion for a few years. From 1914 to the Second World War, missionary resources were hardly enough to meet demands or to cater to heavy investment in infrastructure, charitable institutions, or expansion. Indigenous roles increased as missions turned to local sources for funds. This period laid the golden foundation for the future in bible translation and publication ministry. Translation of the Bible into vernacular languages, especially by Protestant missionaries, catalyzed rapid religious change. For instance, Gustav Aren's study on the Mekane Yesus has shown the invaluable instrument of the Amarinya Bible in reevangelizing Ethiopia and Somalia despite the opposition of the Orthodox church and the violent politics of Egypt in the nineteenth century.[35]

4. AFRICANS AND THE VISION, 1914-1945.

Before the Belgian colonial government jailed him,Simon Kimbangu in 1921 wrote several hymns. One of these exhorted African soldiers of Jesus not lose heart,but to

> Be brave,the kingdom is ours.We have it!They,the whites,
> no longer have it. None of us shall be discouraged.[36]

He was acutely aware of the change of the "baton" or increased tempo of African agency during the period from the First World War to the Second World War, which heralded the process of decolonization. Admittedly, African nationalism reared its head early in the nineteenth century, developed a healthy Africanist ideology, and built a pan-African network in West Africa. "Ethiopianism" was beyond cultural nationalism. The religious concern was significant because blacks from North America and Nova Scotia and scions of recaptives bore the brunt of evangelizing Africa, and wanted to establish a new form of Christianity. Many white missionary organizations recruited black missionaries from the West Indians because the climate daunted white personnel. Soon new interpreters, beneficiaries of western education emerged. As colonial arrogance consolidated in its midday, this class of people became acutely disaffected. The first attack was on the white power in the church that jarred prominently with the Scriptures. This produced a variety of African or Ethiopian church movements. Issues ranged around such African cultural symbols as clothing, names, liturgy, polygamy, and power allocation. This was the root of the indigenization debate of the 1970s. The career of Wilmot Blyden has been used to delineate the contours of this brand of nationalism. But its complexity must be underscored, because some gave voice to indigenous discontent while others took an exit from missionary racist structures. Ethiopianism sought to install an African form of Christian expression and spirituality. Some aspired to creating nondenominational churches.

The post-World War I trends intensified the confident role of Africans. First, as they fought beside whites the mystique of yesteryears vanished. Second, there was a rapid vertical expansion as soon as the logistic and resource constraints of the war ceased. Missionaries hurried back into the affray, staking out boundaries in new villages. Education, white collar jobs, and a new status attracted the indigenes, and growth increased their participation. By the late 1920s, missionaries shifted into consolidation and domestication of Christian values. Christians were to show ethical evidence of their new choice of covenant. Some votaries demurred, but the rush continued for a host of instrumentalist as well as spiritual reasons. It was a painful period. People were restive, for colonialism had removed her gloves: taxation, new administrative system, and judiciary structures were being put in place in the midst of economic disorientation. The new morality inculcated in western schools challenged the old order. Influenza hit Africa in 1918 and in 1925/6. The most sensible diagnosis was that the gods of the fathers were angry. Primary resistance movements took to the ramparts. The church would become a victim when a zealous priestly agent rashly betrayed the secrets of a society or condemned core cultural forms. Nervous colonial law enforcers overreacted and matters escalated. There were numerous examples in the decade bewteen1918 and 1928. In a few places, such as Nigeria, cultural nationalism yielded to nascent political parties such as Herbert Macaulay's National Council of Nigeria and Cameroons, formed in 1920.

But the late 1920s heralded a rapid growth of indigenous spiritual awakening. Years of inculcating the Scriptures betrayed to the natives a deliberate neglect of the pneumatic strand. A people whose precarious worldview was suffused with a keen awareness of the presence of evil and who saw life as the tapping of the resources of good gods against the machinations of evil ones, perceived that the Bible was full of resources to combat disease, poverty, witchcraft and so on. It went beyond the negative: those resources garnered the good things of life too: fertility, prosperity and health.These biblical resources served the same functions as primal religion. In both, the ethical demands also hinged on purity. The rise of *Zionists, Roho, Aladura* (praying) churches before 1945 has been adequately studied. Power and spirituality were at the center of these movements. Power issues emanating from the political, social, and economic spheres found answers in this religious field. Authenticity was not only a cultural matter; rather, it related to faithfulness to the Scriptures. It recaptured the evangelical spirituality that lay at the root of crosscultural mission and became overawed by imperial ethics. There had been an irony that the resilient vision disengaged from secular patronage but was caught by imperial ideology.

The African factor in spreading the gospel had become clear; the new dimension was the recovery of the charismatic element that the Bible posits as the key to the mission of Christ. Prayer, fasting, healing, and deliverance were the characteristics of the new independent churches. Soon they went on mission into culturally contiguous areas, as Nigerians evangelized in Liberia, Sierra Leone, and Gold Coast in a reverse flow from the earlier period when black Baptists

from Liberia, black Anglicans from Sierra Leone and black Methodists from Gold Coast missionalized Nigeria. E. A. Adejobi's Church
of the Lord mission to these places fulfilled Wilmot Blyden's call in
Lagos entitled, *The Return of the Exiles* (1891), which exhorted that
Africans must evangelize Africa.

Quite significant among early purveyors of charismatic ministry,
such as Wade Harris or Garrick Braide, is that their careers lasted for
only two or three years while the inspiration was caught by disciples
and spread like the waves of a river. The emphases constituited a
recovery of the Bible and power-encounter against the spirits that
had ruled the gates of communities. The response often included the
burning of idols and miracles. We shall return to this in a closer study
of the Pentecostal/Charismatic movement in Africa.

The burgeoning literature indicates that early reactions, whether
aspersions and hostility from denominational churches, or the
colonial government's repression failed to halt the growth of these
groups. Equally problematic is the varieties of these groups. Their
fertile breeding and mutations have led many scholars to romanticize
them. But the Bible recommends testing all spirits. Many are not of
God. In 1964, H. W. Turner wrote an intriguing paper entitled, *Pagan
Features in West African Independent Churches*. First, he distinguished
between four types: the healing (nativistic),the eccentric charlatan
prophets who claim to be one or the other of the Trinity (messianic),
the occultic, spiritual groups (vitalistic), and the revivalist forms such
as Reformed Ogboni Fraternity and Godianism. Second, he drew
attention to the Christian elements in the Zionist forms. And third,
he examined the surviving cultic elements especially the secondary
and subordinate cult of angels, symbolism and rituals derived from
the Christo-pagan Sixth and Seventh Books of Moses, the Book of
Mars, the Springfield Books, and cabalistic rituals used in healing
along with elaborate usage of many-shaped candles. He exposed the
fact that many of these groups tap power from familiar spirits in their
liturgies.[37] Some groups shaded off into traditional practices and
made charms encased with scriptural verses.Turner's study deserves
greater attention.

A close study of sacred places, sacred objects, sacred actions,
astral travels, levitation, prossession, trance, outer and inner voices,
and prophesying as practiced by these groups would betray the presence of familiar spirits. Many rituals of cleansing are often occultic
practices. Nationalist historiography in Africa and liberal theology in
the West have combined to remove a litmus test for a Christian typol-

LEFT		RIGHT		
SOLA SCRIPTURA		*SCRIPTURA ET TRADITIONES*		CHRISTIAN
PENTECOSTALS EVANGELICALS (primary & secondary)	PROTESTANTS ETHIOPIANS	ROMAN CATHOLICS (various orders and Apostolates)	ALADURA • evangelical • zionist	
	CHARISMATIC MOVEMENTS			
			JESUS AS THE GREAT DIVIDE	
RUSSELITES			• messianic • revivalistic • vitalistic • nativitistic	NON-CHRISTIAN
				ATR

Testing the Spirits: Typology of Christian Forms

ogy, namely, the centrality of the Bible (used in its fullness) and the place of Jesus Christ as the Great Divide. And yet it should be easy to ask of each group of aladura about their belief in Jesus Christ as the truth, the way, the life. Such rootedness will enable Christianity to foray more creatively into a pluralistic world. Church History must examine the faithfulness of the church in Africa from the perspective of the faithfulness to its calling. However, note that (i) the original aladura stood closer to a biblical tradition. Occultic forms grew later; (ii) their pneumatic emphasis, holistic ministry (which dovetailed into primal worldview); and the increased role of women reminds us of the environment of the early church while their creative liturgy and polity challenge the modern church.

Before 1945, Sabbatharians also appeared on the Christian landscape. They did not owe their existence to Seventh Day Adventists, and they were not mere Hebraists but infact enjoyed a range of typology as wide as that among the Sunday worshippers. It must be noted that the typological spectrum broadened more significantly after our period. But as more Aladura forms appeared to the left of the Roman Catholic position (with greater emphasis on rituals and instruments) stringently biblical Pentecostal groups operated to the right of Evangelicals and Protestants: the Apostolic church groups (indigenous and Welsh) and Faith groups (American and British) became visible in the mid-1930s. At the same time, indigenous groups who had, by themselves, received baptism of the Holy Spirit (e.g., the Church of Jesus Christ, Eastern Nigeria) joined the American Assembles of God church in 1934. Thus, the wave of Pentecostalism in Africa that is erroneously attributed to Americans originated independently and much earlier. African initiative was so vibrant that indigenous entrepreneurs, in West Africa, founded more secondary schools than either the government or the mission. Missionary education had concentrated more on the primary level and on teacher-training than on promoting grammar schools and tertiary education.

Moreover, ecumenical national Christian organizations started an effort to mobilize resources in the 1940s. When T.S. Eliot's shadow enveloped Europe, Africans continued missions. The era, 1930-1950, was characterized by two counterwinds: (i) domestication of Christian values and (ii)self-assertion and innovative confidence of African communities and Christians.An example of these could be found in the Agikuyu custom of circumcision and puberty initiation rituals. This attack dovetailed into the local resentment against white settlers who had alienated enormous acreage of fertile land. The attack on traditional mores added salt to injury and elicited a violent response in the Mau Mau liberation movement. The community split into abolitionists versus traditionalists. The government complicated matters by installing saboteurs as chiefs in a culture that had no chiefs but merely coordinating leaders. The church intensified the affray by expelling the children of traditionalists from its school facilities, using loyalty cards to ferret out rebellion and by buttressing their condemnations based on the coordinated, biased opinions of English medical authorities and racist anthropologists. By the 1930s the freedom fighters responded by opening their own schools. They invited competing churches such as the Orthodox Church and AME Zion (African American groups) to found their own churches. By 1939 they opened a Teachers' College. Underneath this was an articulation of the African antistructural view of Christianity. Must one be white to be a believer? Could one remain a faithful Gikuyu and a Christian? By the 1950s, the Agikuyu became more violent in answering these questions.The violence was unleashed on the collaborators as well as on the whites. Thousands were killed in the Mau Mau uprising, further dividing the Agikuyu political class.

5. WALTZING WITH NATIONALISTS: 1945-1960

This period is characterized by decolonization. Missionaries had many signals but they preferred the colonial project, refused to devolve power, and sought to profile nationalist politics as un-Christian and to produce memoranda on salient political ethics and ideology. Consequently, decolonization took them by surprise as they struggled to turn a rout into a passive revolution. They hoped to retool in such a manner as to retain influence while the indigenous people played surrogate roles.This is passive revolution.

Inspite of the growth in indigenous initiative in Christianity, which was quite evident in this period, the aftermath of the Second World War was still very colonial in all senses. Indeed Christianity was not the dominant form of religion in Africa. Hastings has estimated that there were about twenty-three million Christians in Africa: eleven million Roman Catholics, ten million Protestants, and two million African Independent church devotees.[38] The rapid growth of the last was an irritant to the mainline churches, and the matter grew worse over the years. The mainline churches wielded considerable influence with the aid of the colonial governments. They controlled schools, hospitals, and other instruments of social welfare. The allure of church and education for Africans knew no bounds. White cultural supremacy and administrative control appeared untrammeled. Indeed, the Belgians and Portuguese made no provisions for decolonization. Instead, they used concordats to bind the churches closely to the apronstring of the government. The career of Bishop Jean de Hamptinne, Vicar Apostolic of Katanga, buttressed the loyalist support of the church in Congo.

Similarly, the assimilation policy of the French appeared to be singularly successful in diluting culture as a contested space as could be seen in the artistic and political career of the urbane Leopold Senghor of Senegal. Tutored by the neo-Thomist, liberal Catholics of the stripe of Maritain, he joined the Independants d'Outre Mer and served in the National Assembly, Paris, from 1946. Rabble-rousers were not lacking such as Felix Houphouet of Ivory Coast who hyphenated Boigny (the irresistible force) to his name during his radical, populist career. After the riots of 24 January 1950, he not only narrowly escaped jail but sobered quickly to pull his section of the Rassemblement Democratique Africain from the cloak of the Communists.

Though nationalist politics was in the air all over Africa, our concern is to explore how the churches came through the era of decolonization. We see a shift from cultural nationalism to political nationalism. The relevance and prospects of the church became an issue, making indigenization an option. Nationalists who were suspicious of the complicity and track record of Christianity in the colonial milieu tended to treat the church as the black goat during the political campaigns for political independence. Nkrumah's Convention Peoples' Party was formed in Ghana in 1949; the Richardson Constitution set Nigeria on political fire in 1951; the Kenya Central Association grew wings in the 1940s because of its huge success in the last two decades.

In South Africa, as whites dug their feet deep into apartheid, moderate black politics evaporated into the radical camp. The Maghrib was boiling, belying the calm assurance of postwar colonialism that was preoccupied with Asia instead of Africa. In fact, events in Asia triggered much consequence in Africa. The defeat of France in Vietnam forced decolonization in French colonies. It was the height of the cold war. Former allies who had disbanded into competing camps now used African countries not only as sources for raw materials and markets for industrial goods but also as political foils.

It was a heady period. Some liberal whites within the earshot of Westminster, tried to urge greater, paternalistic care for African welfare, stopping short of political independence. Whites in Southern and Eastern Africa postured God behind their supremacist policy; educated black moderates such as Z.K. Mathews in South Africa, Danquah and Busia in the Gold Coast still sought to weave Western mores into African reality. But the rise of youthful radicals dominated the scene: Mandela, Nkrumah, Nasser, Banda, Kaunda, and Nyerere-all basked in the support of the common man suffering from land-alienation and hostile culture policy. Thus, they would throng out to cheer Nkrumah who won the election while in prison or to fight with Kenyatta in the Mau Mau uprising. With this backdrop, the fate of Christianity appeared ambivalent as the dark clouds of nationalism gathered in the midst of the efforts to consolidate the roots of the faith. For one, the church had few educated indigenous manpower and the population of missionaries remained high. For another, the decolonization gale blew in much earlier than anticipated. Between 1952-1956, Egypt, Libya, Tunisia, Sudan, Morocco, and Algeria became free. The Day of the Jackal betrays the last stance of some French crying over spilled milk. Events were disheveled as Guinea, Mali, Senegal, Ivory Coast; others joined in 1957. More sedate talks followed British Prime Minister Harold Macmillan's *wind of change* policy in British colonies in West Africa. Independence was packaged in constitutional boxes, requiring that the users be able to read and to follow the handbook. It was like equipment that was completely new to the environment. From where would the matured politicians emerge to operate systems designed in foreign climes? Like all aspects of technology there is usually a culture base. T.A. Beetham in his Christianity and the New Africa[39] feared that the nationalist wind might blow fragile Christianity back into the warm embrace of primal religion.

Like any African masquerade dance, the events of these years can best be described from a number of stances. Take the missionaries for instance, they were hopelessly divided. Some taught their converts to eschew rebellious nationalism for a political quest for the kingdom; colonialism was a benevolent structure for the African's good. Others, like William Carey, formerly the Archbishop of Bloemfontein, South Africa were indiscreetly hostile. The irrepressible Michael Scott, the voice of the Herero, represented those who cared for the suffering Africans.African opinion consolidated around the conclusion that they had been left holding the wrong end of the stick. Yet they saw much prospect in the gospel and used this as a mirror to critique the racism of white Christians. South Africa's Albert Luthuli's 1952 speech, which heralded the shift of position, brings out this fact very clearly. He mused aloud:

> How far is it not tragically true that these churches have become distorted symbols? How far is it not tragically true that they stand for an ethic which the whites have brought, preached and refused to practice? How far do these churches represent something alien from the spirit of Christ, a sort of patronizing social service? Do not many Christian ministers talk down to us instead of coming down among us as Christ did and does? White paternalist Christianity-as though whites invented Christian faith-enstranges my people from Christ.[40]

This speech captures much of the emotional turmoil of the period as the engine of nationalism disengaged from missionary Christianity, doubting its capacity to alleviate the continent's political problems and setting the stage for imaging missionary complicity as the source of Africa's woes. This was the staple diet of nationalists who ironically were nurtured in mission schools.

Some nationalists bawdwerzed church hymns or canon; others such as Dr Nnamdi Azikiwe engaged some form of revivalistic religion to popularize his political party; this was long before Osofo Okomfo Damuah started the Afrikania movement in Ghana. [41]The Roman Catholics started a massive ministerial formation of black clergy from 1953. Their emphasis was to understudy which aspects of primal religion could be baptized into Christianity. But the incredible aspect to missionary history is that it never moves in a predictable fashion. The rivalry among missionaries resurfaced as each group urged its lay elite into the new politics and administrative structures so as to protect the denomination. Churches became political pressure groups, and religious rivalry spilled over into the modern political arena and determined the dynamics of the political culture as church and nationalists waltzed. When the Roman Catholics trained the Tanzanian leader Julius Nyerere in Edinburgh and supported the political career of this school teacher, it became clear that the sponsors looked into the seeds of time and planned for the peace and protection of the church in the future. It would remain to be seen whether their calculation proved correct.

A certain scenario emerges in which African Christians gradually immersed themselves into nationalist politics. In some places their role was crucial. For instance, in Uganda three competing power nodes predominated:nationalists wanted independence for the whole country;the Buganda, an ancient society in this new arrangement, feared for its ascendancy and the position of the Kabaka; the Protestants and the Catholics had their interdenominational scores to settle. The Kabaka's supporters formed the Kabaka Yekka (KY), the Uganda People's Congress(UPC), led by Milton Obote was Protestant-based, while Benedicto Kiwanuka led a Roman Catholic organization, Democratic Party(DC). Christianity was in the center of the new politics. The initial good showing by the DP drove the UPC into an alliance with the Kabaka Yekka. Obote triumphed because the Kabaka preferred to deal with a Protestant from the northern region of the country than a Catholic commoner from within his own kingdom.

In the Congo, radical politics emerged from Christianity but this time from the fringes. Simon Kimbangu provided a political twist to religious independency, a factor lacking in most Zionist camps. His messianic portrait of colonialism as a period of African exile with the prospect of restoration was immensely popular. It positioned politics in the heart of charismatic religiosity.[42] Imprisonment followed as night would follow day. But the movement did not die; rather, it wove into the interior of nationalist politics through the career of Kasavubu, who had started his apprenticeship in the cultural politics of the Bankongo. At the death of Kimbangu, Kasavubu let it be known that the spirit of the prophet had taken him over. This explains why Mobutuism of the future would pose him as a prophet too. Other considerations explain the preference of the Belgians, who were hurried into decolonization, for Kasavubu instead of the maverick, leftist, popular politician, Patrick Lumumba. The church's role in Rwanda, first in bolstering the Tutsis and later in promoting the Hutu political ascendancy has been revisited often in the midst of the unending crisis in that country. There is no denying that Gregoire Kayibanda was a protégé of Archbishop Perraudin and the editor of a Catholic newsletter, and that he used the vantage point to found the

Parmehutu, a radical ethnic organization. The story of the Christian contribution in the rise of nationalism in Africa is rich.

The irony is that while waltzing with nationalism, the church had not provided itself with a capacity for taming the power that was being unleashed. The matter of ministerial formation has been mentioned. Increasingly, nationalists postured Christianity as collaborators to imperialist forces and challenged the lack of indigenization of doctrine, polity, liturgy and ethics. Did the church in Africa have the capacity for theologizing its ethics in the new dispensation? Did it possess the financial independence or would it be forever looking to the hands of the metropoles? The failure of mission churches to move from paternalism to partnership and the long period of excessive control bred a legacy of a weak church, suffering from a Peter Pan syndrome.[43] These vestiges of the colonial roots of Christianity would continue to haunt the church as it faced the politics of independence. Matters would be made worse as the nationalists abruptly broke away from the ballroom waltz for *highlife, makosa,* and *congo jazz,* more disorderly and certainly to a different dance beat.

In conclusion, the religious scene at the threshold of independence may be characterized by its diversity and contradictory ways because Africans were engaged in reconstructing Christianity from many fronts: some indigenizers sought to reconcile the new gospel with the requirements of the ancient binding covenants with the gods of the fathers. Religious innovators quested for free expressions of beliefs and practices beyond the restrictions of white missionary control. All wanted to feel and express the true face of Christ and to be rid of the burdens of the vestiges of colonial Christianity, which the missionaries were trying to keep intact in a fit of passive revolution. Meanwhile, other challenges were just as fecund in the excitable resurgent religious landscape. Islam grew with international support; a number of science or theosophic groups invaded Africa, proffering alternative access to the divine in the competitive heavenly race. These turned the issue of pluralism into urgent problems having both religious and political dimensions. Above all, ecological concerns brought sobering realization to the fragility of our earth, its resources, and the connection between the poverty ravaging Africa and ecoethics.

44

Part I: Power and Poverty

Notes

1. Ogbu U. Kalu, "The Golden Age of African Christianity?: Early Christianity in North Africa", *Nsukka Journal of Religious Studies*, 1, 1 (1996): 34-49.

2. Michael Green, *Evangelism in the Early Church* (Grand Rapids: Eerdmans, 1970), 19.

3. *Ibid.*, p. 47.

4. C. P. Groves, *The Planting of Christianity in Africa* vol I (London: Lutherworth Press, 1948), 36ff.

5. Ibid., p. 38.

6. Robert M. Grant, *Augustus to Constantine: The Thrust of the Christian Movement into the Roman World* (New York: Harper & Row, 1970) , 228.

7. Note the counterpoint by I. P. Ellis, "In Defence of Early North African Christianity"In_*New Testament Christianity for Africa and the World: Essays in honor of Harry Sawyer* ed M. Glasswell and E. Fashole -Luke (London: SPCK, 1974):157-165.

8. The insider's view is represented by Brahana Selassie, *Towards a fuller vision* (Leicestershire: Upfront Publishing, 2003).

9. They were: Abba Aregawi, Abba Gerima, Abba Likanos, Abba Pantalewon from Constantinople; Abba Gubba from Cilicia; Abba Afese from Asia Minor; Abba Tsehma from Antioch; Abba Alef from Caesarea, and Abba Yemata from Cooz.

10. Laszlo Tork, *The Kingdom of Kush* (Leiden: E. J. Brill, 1997).

11. Selassie, *Towards a Fuller Vision,* 176.

12. Ephraim Isaac, *The Ethiopian Church* (Boston: Henry N. Sawyer Co., 1967), 24.

13. see Taddesse Tamrat, *Church and State in Ethiopia, 1270-1527* (Oxford: Clarendon Press, 1972).

14. Selassie, *Towards a Fuller Vision,* 176.

15. J. E. Harris, ed. *William Leo Hansberry: African History Notes, vol. II: Africa and Africans as Seen by the Classical Writers* (Washington, DC: Howard University Press, 1981), 9.

16. see Adrian Hastings, *The Church in Africa,* 224.

17. ibid., 238.

18. Walter E. Kaegi, "Egypt on the eve of the Muslim conquest, " in *The Cambridge History of Egypt*, vol. 1, ed. Carl F. Petry(New York: Cambridge University Press, 1998): 34-40.

19. See Roland Werner, William Anderson, and Andrew Wheeler, *Day of Devastation, Day of Contentment:_The History of the Sudanese Church*

*Across 2000 Years (*Nairobi: Paulines Publications Africa, 2000): 40-45.

20. See W. H. C. Frend, *The Donatist Churc (*Oxford: Clarendon Press, 1952):102-105. See also Maureen A. Tilley, *The Bible in Christian North Africa: The Donatist World* (Minneapolis: Fortress, 1997).

21. Rodney Stark, *The Rise of Christianity (*Princeton, NJ:Princeton university Press, 1996): Philip Jenkins, *The Next Christendom: The Coming of Global Chrisiainity(*New York: Oxford University Press, 2002); Charles P. Groves. *The Planting of Christianity in Africa.* 4 vols. London: Lutterworth Press, 1948-1958.

22. C. R. Boxer, *The Portuguese Seaborne Empire, 1415-1825* (London: Hutchinson & Co. Publishing, 1969), 15-38; J. H. Parry, *Europe and a Wider World, 1415-1715* (London: Hutchinson, 1966 ed.).

23. Boxer, *The Portuguese Seaborne Empire*, 24.

24. Lamin Sanneh, *West African Christianity: The Religious Impact* (Maryknoll, NY: Orbis Books, 1983), chap. 3.

25. G. Balandier, *Daily Life in the Kingdom of Kongo from Sixteenth to the Eighteenth Century* (London: 1968), 254-55.

26. i. R. Gray, *Black Christians and White Missionaries* (New Haven: Yale University Press, 1990), 50.

      ii. Enrique Dussel, ed. *The Church in Latin America, 1492-1992 (*London: Burns & Oates, 1992).

27. C. P. Groves, *The Planting of Christianity*, vol. I, 141-142.

28. K. K. Prah, Jacobus Eliza Johnnes Capitein: A critical study of an 18th Century African(Braamfotein: Skotaville Publishers, 1989); D. N. A. Kpobi, Missions in Chains: The Life, Theology and Ministry of Jacobus E. J. Capitein, 1717-1747, (Zoetermeer:Uitgeverij Boekecentrum, 1993).

29. J. D. P. Curtin, *The Image of Africa: British Ideas and Action, 1780-1850* (Madison: University of Wisconsin Press, 1964).

30. Andrew F. Walls – i ,"Protestant Missionary Motivation in the Imperialist Age", *Int. Bulletin Of Missionary Research, 6, 2 (1982):* 60-64.

      ii. *"Missionary Societies and the Fortunate Subversion of the Church", Evangelical Quarerly.,* 88, 2 (1988): 141-155.

      iii "The Legacy of Thomas Fowell Buxton", I*nternational Buletin Of Missionary Research,* 15, 2 (1991): 74-79.

31. see, Adrian Hastings, *African Christianity* (London: Geoffrey Chapman, 1979), 4.

32. Ogbu U. Kalu, "Afrika-Mission in der Koliniazeit: Die Berliner Kon-gokonferenz von 1884/5 und die Entwicklung des Christentums in Westafrika", *Evangelische Mission Jahrbuch* (1985): 94-106.

33. Felix K. Ekechi, *Missionary Enterprise and Rivalry in Igboland:. 1857-1914* (London: Frank Cass, 1971).

34. Brian Stanley, *The Bible and the Flag* (Leicester: Appollos-Inter-Varsity Press, 1990), 80.

35. Gustav Aren, *Evangelical Pioneers: Origins of the Evangelical Church, Mekane Jesus* (Stockholm: Study in Missionalia Uppsaliensa, 82, (1978), 90.

36. see Marie Louise Martin, *Kimbangu* (Oxford: Clarendon Press, 1957).

37. *Practical Anthropology*, 12, 4 (1965): 145-151.

38. Hastings, *African Christianity*, 43.

39. T. A. Beetham, *Christianity and the New Africa*, (London: Pall Mall, 1967), preface.

40. see Hastings, *African Christianity*, 96.

41. Kwame Bediako, *Christianity in Africa*, (Maryknoll, NY: Orbis Books, 1995), chap. 2.

42. Ogbu U. Kalu, "The Politics of Sectarianism in Africa", *West African Religion*, 16, 1 (1975): 16-25.

43. Ogbu U. Kalu, "Peter Pan Syndrome: Church Aid and Selfhood in Africa", *Missiology* 3, 1 (1975): 15-29.

Chapter Two
Ashes on Our Faces: The State, Modernization, and Poverty in Independent Africa

1. THE IMPLOSION OF THE STATE: 1960-1980.

As a backdrop to the challenges of poverty and pluralism in Africa, it is necessary to examine the origin and nature of the modern African states. The implosion of authoritarian states led to poverty and poured ashes on the faces of their people. When Independence came to most of Africa in the 1960s, the stirring forms of music were the Congo *cha- cha-cha* and the *highlife*. In most cities, the church leadership attended the innumerable parties, entertained by the maestros of the two enthralling indigenous African dances. After all, the churches had trimmed their sails to the new conditions and sought to show that they participated in creating the new dispensation. Within a decade, the mellifluous beat turned staccato and the state predatory toward its former ally. We could hear the chief protagonist in Okot p'bitek's *Song of A Prisoner*, declare that *uhuru* (freedom) was far worse than yaws of colonialism. One East African elder put the matter more graphically: our leaders are like lions, they eat their own people. Both sentiments reflect on the strange phenomenon that the music was drowning out, namely, the implosion of the state that would soon attack every other power node in the society, claiming to be the most viable instrument for fulfilling the high hopes of the masses.

The struggles for independence in Africa were fueled by two assumptions, namely, that the land was wellendowed to sustain the populace; and that the leaders, who inherited the mantle from the whites, would mobilize the human and material resources for the welfare and dignity of Africans. But soon the political scene was like a convergence of hunters in a forest on the outskirts of a village. Some of the hunters seemed to have taken control and decided to oust the other hunters. With a change of imagery, the disengagement of the train of the state from the wagon of the churchly ally could best be illustrated with the case of Zaire before posing the questions asking why and how the new structure emerged and water marooned the fluted pumpkin. This country was regarded as the most Christianized of the independent African states. It was predominantly Roman Catholic with a significant dose of the African Independent Kimbaguist church, a messianic movement that inspired anticolonialism and, therefore, was crucial in the birth of the new nation. Skipping over much of the disheveled history of the decolonization process, in October 1971 Mobutu came to power. In an effort to mobilize for national development, he promulgated a *kulturkampf* on 19August1973, declaring that:

> We are now embarking on our cultural liberation, the reconquest of our African soul, Zairian soul. We men of black skin have had imposed on us the mentality of quite a different race. We must become once more authentic Africans, authentic blacks, authentic Zaireans

On 6 November 1974, the tone of the state commissioner of Public Affairs became more menacing:

> The missionaries who came in the name of a certain Jewish child in order to make us know a God who was no different from the one taught to us by our ancestors, have refused to recognize our right to teach God in the name of a son of our country, sent to us by our ancestors.

He soon identified the great prophet to be our wondrous Mobutu Sese Seko who, is shaking us out of our stupor, has delivered us from our mental alienation. Ordinarily, this could be dismissed as one example of the banalities in African politics or as an episode in church-state relations. But here was a sign of a new phenomenon; the rise and growth of the theological state, which imploded within a decade after the installation of various democratic constitutions, whether Westminster or Republican. What was the undergirding ideology behind these constitutions? Why were African states able to turn like lions on their people? And what was the outcome of this new challenge to the church and society? Even more disconcerting is that within two decades, several African states collapsed, embroiled in legitimacy crises and economic ruin and pouring ashes on our faces. Impoverished and traumatized people cried out for a second liberation from those individuals who had claimed to be the fathers of the nation.

An eye to periodization indicates that the period before the second liberation could be divided into two precisely because there was an ideological shift in 1975 that held out some glimmer of hope before the congenital nature of the disease became obvious. Indeed, some have argued that the history of the statist model in Africa could be understood in the progress of four theories that predominated at various times.Before 1980, (i)the modernization theory and (ii) the neo-Marxist and after 1980,(iii) the failure of the state or new political sociology for Africa (NPSA) theory, (iv) and the postmodernist theory.[1] Equally crucial is Y.W.Bradshaw's caution to examine the way events are shaped by the interaction between phenomena at global, national and local events. Thus, the situation in Africa may not be understood only by what the West did or did not do but also by what Africans did to themselves at the national and local cultural levels.[2]

Coincidentally, the post-World War II period was characterized by a belief in rapid progress and stirring changes in European life. This is generally what modernization captured into a theory, reflecting intellectual, political, and economic rebuilding after the wars, rumors of wars, and depression. Basking in the success of the American Marshall Plan and following Keynesian economic theory, modernization models were exported to other ecotheaters. Central to the theory was the role of the state, a belief strongly advocating the state as central to the economic and social development of any nation. There may be questions about the state's specific role and what it could do or not do. Should it be a direct provider of growth or a partner, catalyst, and facilitator? The 1997 World Bank Development report, *The State in A Changing World*, still holds firmly to this theory in spite of i) the end of the cold war and the collapse of command-and-control economies of the former USSR, ii) the fiscal crisis of the welfare states in most of the established industrial states, iii)the important role and sneeze in the miracle economies of East Asia, iv) the collapse of states and the explosion in humanitarian emergencies in several parts of the world. The state here is understood in its widest sense to refer to a set of institutions that possess the means of legitimate coercion exercised over a defined territory and society. It does so through the structure of organized government.

Commentators have also observed that the modernization theory of the 1960s was built on the increasing centralization of the administrative organs of the government. Its tentacles reached down to individuals more than ever before. Recalling those heady days, C. E. Black observed that:

> Then development seemed a more easily surmount-
> able and largely technical-challenge. Good advisers and
> technical experts would formulate good policies, which
> good Governments would then implement for the good
> of society.[3]

State intervention, designed to correct market failures, soon assumed a wider role for the state in various nations and economies. In the process of decolonization, it was assumed that the new states of Africa would be the agents to lead their peoples through Rostow's five stages of economic growth, starting from a preindustrial stage through an industrial take-off stage, to mass -consumption societies. This would strengthen the ties with the former colonial metropoles. Decolonization was a form of restructuring and pruning Western economies with a view to better aligning satellite economies.

Moreover, the emphasis on the modern state and modern market had immense ethical implications: it encrusted Western economic dominance through a new vanguard, namely, multinational companies; it placed economic priority above the well-being of civic society, and this soon led to the militarization of society as a byproduct of national security. At the strategic level, it placed emphasis on the political system and on the transfer of technology. A redefinition of development became imperative so as to shift from aggregative terms to human liberation because at the root of the modernization theory is the structure of the relation of the state to the society. To what extent is the state capable of meeting the welfare needs of its populace? A certain conjecture is that the central roles of the state are i) to provide education, health and infrastructure, thus protecting the vulnerable through insurance and assistance; ii) to make available rules and restraints through an independent judiciary; iii) to ensure a conducive environment for healthy social life and economic pursuit; and iv) to provide voice and partnership through openness and transparency, giving citizens a greater voice in the formulation of policies.[4]

The story of the state in Africa bears little repetition; it is like knowing the result of a boxing match before watching the film. In the midst of the celebration of independence, the new rulers started to change the constitutional structures. By 1984, twenty-three states had military governments, fifteen became one-party states, only six operated competitive political structures, and thirty-four were listed by the World Bank among the low economies of the world. Broadly, three types of states emerged: (i)*fictitious* states were those which existed in the minimal sense that others recognized their sovereignty over a certain territory, whereas in reality bands of adventurers held sway(e.g. in Chad, Equitorial Guinea, etc.);(ii) *prebendary* states were more in number as economic statism aided dominant elites to resort to contesting control and to transforming particular branches of state apparatus into prebends for their personal enrichment and the reward of their followers; (iii) *praetorian* states converted the nationstates into barracks for the military as is the case with Nigeria, where the military has been in power for twenty-eight of its thirty-eight years of independence. The military is virtually a political party consisting of serving and non-serving officers, each with a network of clienteles. Indeed, by mid- 1984, forty-six independent countries of sub-Sahara Africa had suffered at least sixty successful coups. The situation was worse in West Africa, where Ghana and Benin were scarred with six coups, and Nigeria with four. Uganda held the record in eastern Africa, while the Eritrean-Ethiopian war kept the Northern region embroiled. Civil strife in a wide range of countries colluded with famine to complete a dismal equation.

It was in the midst of the cold war, so ideological cleavages emerged: some states as Angola, Mozambique, Benin, Ethiopia, Guinea, Madagascar, Somalia, and Congo took to the neo-Marxist road. Others evolved secular versions of African socialism in the effort to weave a political ideology that would be rooted in primal African models of social organization. Ghana's Nkrumah called his own version consciencism, while Tanzania's Julius Nyerere of on 5 February, 1967 issued the Arusha Declaration, promulgating the Ujaama,a communal, socioeconomic ideology. It brimmed with Christian concepts of social justice and proved a watershed in the economic policies of the new Africa. It shifted from the transformative strategies such as those of Guinea and Ghana, 1962-1966, relying heavily on industrialization to an accomodationist strategy based on agriculture and small-scale industries.[5] These would support rural developmental efforts that would rely as far as possible upon indigenous capabilities. The attention of the West burgeoned the literature and bears little repetition here. Other nations such as Ivory Coast clung to the coattails of France and garnered much economic growth; as our people say, if you follow the big man closely, things will drop out for you. The cost was the avoidance of the intense nationalist rhetoric of the period and the concept of nonalignment in foreign policy, a concept that inspired the cold warring camps to compete in granting huge loans as bribes for allegiance. This is the genesis of the debt burdens of many African countries, which grew out of the debt cycle hypothesis; the theory that developing countries are expected to promote the growth of their economies by means of huge debts.

The modernization theory, intense nationalism, and the emergent neo Marxism all combined to produce mobilization systems and modernizing autocracies that drastically modified the nature of the political parties and the character of the state in African development. The Marxist paradigm notched up the role of the state beyond that of an impartial moderator of conflicting interests. Diagnosing that Africa was controlled by agents of international capital, it proposed national selfreliance, regional cooperation, and the dismantling of class interest as antidotes. Decades ago, Carl Rosberg used the mobilization theory to show how many African leaders dismantled the old political systems and set up highly centralized dictatorships. Declaring development and African identity as the motivation, they systematically changed the nature of the political parties and transformed the indigenous power nodes into networks of personalized power. Parties were merged, arguing that multiparty system was a luxury and expensive to maintain. In its place they sought to install highly integrated and rigorously disciplined action-oriented organizations.

Nkrumah, for instance, practiced an unrestrained exercise of power, driven by a visionary concept of future society, through revolutionary transformation of existing social order. He, therefore, conceived resistance as vestiges of anachronistic past to be countered with a populist legitimacy and a sense of historic mission to liberate Africa from tribalism and other hindrances. From here, developmental economic emphasis was combined with an intent to maximize social welfare and to provide equal opportunity in what was termed *democratic centralism*. To achieve these, opponents were deported, opposition was restrained, and an electoral machinery was created that constantly elected the approved list.[6] There was a preference for no man no vote rather than one man, one vote because of the high value given to unanimous affirmation of the public interest. Autocratic and zero-sum political culture bloomed. The state took over schools, hospitals, the press and disciplined the trade unions, crushed opposition, and humiliated feudal chiefs and intensified the strain between the youthful states and the ancient societies of Africa.

The church stood as a sore finger and as the only viable power node. Some states functioned as modernizing autocracies, rooted in a network of institutional structures and values inherited from the precolonial past. From this perspective, the socialist ideology lacked metaphysical dictates but was employed as populist tactics, designed to obliterate vested interests. Examples abound in the cases of the Parti Democratique de Guinee which was every other thing but democratic, the Union Soudanaise in Mali, and Convention People's Party in Ghana. Within the one-party structures, P. B. Harris has tried to distinguish the push or revolutionary-centralizing party structures in West Africa from the pull or pragmatic, pluralistic types such as Kenyatta's KANU.[7] A contrasting model to the mobilization system is Rosberg's reconciliation system in which competing groups make demands on state policy. As he said:

> The presence of competing centres of power and the voluntary nature of the entire system foster a process of decision-making which is characterized by compromise, adjustment and adaptation between conflicting claims and demands proffered by affiliated organizations.[8]

Rosberg, Apter, and other modernization theorists of the 1960s joined the chorus against the prospects of reconciliation models as in Nigeria, because of the endemic nonintegration factors inbuilt in African political structures, for instance, cultural cleavages, the continuance of cultural and historical differences, uneven rates of socioeconomic development, and fragile consensus. They perceived ethnic parochialism as dangerous to stability. So, from the ivory towers of academia, mobilizing regimes had tacit support.

This sets the stage for understanding why and how statism grew horns in Africa. The first set of explanation focused on the primal roots of African political culture, arguing that ethnicity and authoritarian ethics of power vitiated the potentials for democratic rule in spite of certain elements of republicanism among some African groups. As Hastings quipped:

> The Western democratic constitutions and neutral civil service bestowed upon them as a birthday gift had no indigenous roots to speak of, and even the political parties which had been easily mobilized for the gaining of independence as easily withered when unsustained by any further high raison d'etre. Each became only too easily a new expression of a regional, tribal or family promotion network, despite the high language and ritual demonstrations in the capital.[9]

Katsuyoshi and Markaki's study *Ethnicity and Conflict in the Horn of Africa* has raised the flip-side of the coin, arguing that while it is true that the fluid character of group identities and the salience of ethnicity served as a motivating ideology for conflict, the state was the prime mover in the process by which ethnicity became the mobilizing force. Authoritarian practice of governance, the efforts of autocratic regimes to monopolize national cultural symbols, the state's role in uneven development, its suppression of channels through which populations can demand accountability of leaders- all serve to increase the salience of group identities and create conditions ripe for conflict. As such, regional, ethnic and clan-based movements are best understood in the context of objective political and economic circumstances. In and of itself, goes the argument, ethnicity is not a sufficient cause for conflict. Suffice it to add that left-wing social analysis has arrived at the same conclusion by using class analysis.[10] The state, by monopolizing resources and all avenues of upward mobility, creates a class of vested interest that acts alike despite the different ethnic origins of the members, and exploit ethnic differences for selfish and private gains.

However, much of the political culture is rooted in a primal worldview: the ruler like a chief, breeds personalized and patrimonial ethics; a kinship system undergirds nepotism; ethnicity heightens the tendency for politicians to seek a share of the national cake for their own people. In the novel *A Man Of The People*, Chinua Achebe puts it aptly:

> ...they (the villagers) were not only ignorant but cynical. Tell them that this man (the Minister) had used his position to enrich himself and they would ask you--as my father did--if you thought that a sensible man would spit out the juicy morsel that good fortune placed in his mouth.

It was a short step from here to demand that the minister must do something for his people because one cannot be at the source of a river and soap would enter his eyes. The matter was made worse by the emergence of a new value system that defined the modern sector as the white man's public; one can steal from the white man's public and dance to the big drum in the primal public. This vitiating impact of modernity on the salient values of the old order shall be pursued later. Suffice it to say that personalized political culture bred two genres, the *big man* and the *strong man* leadership types. Each type tried to idolize the leader and thereby bred corruption that enervated the bureaucracy, caused the decay of the political system, and fostered undisciplined political actors. As Anyang Nyong'o has articulated the task, Africa needs a deliberate creation of a democratic ethos that will tame the state as well as civilize political actors.[11] Personalized political culture created an intimacy of power and symbiotic relationship between politicians and the leaders.

Some have argued that the African dilemma was an aspect of the vestiges of colonial experience. For one, the new states were artificial territories, or poly-ethnic collections. Political forms had not evolved organically. Steve Ellis said that African states are like bottles which may contain different liquids while remaining the same shape and form. But mosaic multi-cultural countries have thrived. Others point to the fact that the leaders were not trained or equipped to manage the new structures and colonial capitalism was weak, fragile emergent capitalism. Few countries had even light industries. This background stirred the new nationalist leaders to the desire to catch up with the West and to make education available to everyone--an ambition which collided with the reality of population growth and limited economic growth. There was a gap between the dreams and the capacity. Many countries took to borrowing large amounts of money that was supposed to be development aid. The techniques of aid constitute another complex matter. As Anyang Nyong'o said:

Recent studies by the World Bank advance the argument that the terrible mess that Africa finds herself in now is largely a consequence of the last thirty years of massive amount of technical assistance, inept advice, misguided and institutional destruction. Rather than achieving the lofty goals that technical assistance has as its raison d'etre, that is technological transfer, increase in productivity and wealth creation, so-called technical co-operation between developing and developed countries has led to the under-utilization of existing capacity.[12]

Western powers bolstered the predatory rulers who put ashes on the faces of their people in various ways beyond loans, which forced huge amounts of transfer financial resources back to the aid donors: the donors provided security guards for the rulers at heavy costs, thereby exploiting the insecurity of the political environment. As S. R. Weissman said about the CIA in Africa, they engaged in

> Subsidization of political leaders and parties, military and internal security functionaries and coup-makers; political assassination plots; technical assistance for a presidential bodyguard and security apparatus; provision of a third country foreign military combat and combat support personnel; supply of arms and related equipment.[13]

A new form of imperialism emerged whereby, in pursuit of geopolitical and economic interests, the Western powers did everything possible to succor amenable African leaders. Sandbrook echoed:

> This outside political support magnifies the seamy characteristics of personal rule--the authoritarianism, the recourse to repression, the rampant factionalism, venality and instability.[14]

R. Luckham showed that the French intervened militarily nineteen times in ten African countries within the period from 1960-1980.[15] Dubious Western businessmen colluded with greedy local agents to nurture a debauched political culture with immense moral and economic consequences. DeGruchy concluded that the failure of democracy in Africa was in-built, and that some African countries have done better than East European countries. Imperial rule was not only undemocratic but undermined traditional systems of rule in which mutually balancing segments had been held together. The legacy of independence neither meant genuinely African democracies nor was it founded on strong economic footing. Independence was the Africanization of colonial institutions and economic structures and often the transference of political ineptitude and incompetence.[16] However, African leaders and the political elite bear much of the burden of failure because, as Jean-Francois Bayart would say, they turned the politics of the belly into a systemic political culture.

2. HOT ASHES ON THEIR HEADS: THE POLITICAL ECONOMY OF THE SECOND LIBERATION

By the mid-1980s Western donor agencies, symbolized by the World Bank, became alarmed at the collapse of the Uhuru dream, the debt level, the size of the state and the inefficient policies. The size of the state is measured by the amount of consumption relative to the GDP. It was discovered that, compared to East Asia, governments in Africa had ballooned one and half times and that high government consumption, mostly on public employment and not on investment, caused a drag on growth. Worse, western investors were on the run because of major obstacles:

TABLE 2.1 – AFRICA:Regional Ranking of Business Obstacles (Worst case=1)

OBSTACLES	SUB-SAHARA	NORTH AFRICA
Property rights	1	2
Corruption	5	8
Crime and Theft	8	7
Taxes	2	3
Financing	6	4
Inflation	4	6
Policy instability	7	5
Public investment/ Poor infrastructure	3	1

(Source: *World Development Report, 1997*, 42)

The prevalence of personalism, clientelism, and corruption among authoritarian regimes vitiate economic recovery, deter foreign investors, and blight democratic norms. As the 1992 *World Labor Report* [17] declared, by 1989, the problems of Africa became legion: the debt burden based on the debt/GNP ratio reached 97 % in 1989 for subSaharan Africa; collapse of commodity price, measured by the real world prices for cocoa, coffee, cotton, and tea fell by 50 per cent between 1980-1990; low capital investment- falling by 53% in real per capita terms between 1980-1989 and less investment in people. For instance,in the United Republic of Tanzania expenditure on education and health fell by 52 % between the periods 1979/81 and 1985/87. Figures for Manufacturers' Added Value (MVA) for subSahara Africa in 1997 showed that six countries accounted for 80%, with South Africa alone providing 58%. So, both the agricultural and industrial sectors collapsed at the same time. All these triggered legitimacy crises and concern about the growing pauperization of communities.

Analysts responded with theories of failure of the state. A key aspect of this theory is that it shifted attention from the universalist context to the relativist or specific, local context in understanding the state. A number of backdrops informed this reassessment as to why some states perform better than others: the rapid diffusion of high technology, growing demographic pressures, increased environmental concerns, greater global integration of markets, the shift to democratic forms of government which was heightened by the fall of the Berlin wall and the collapse of the Soviet Union, the sharp decline of sustainable development, and the increase in poverty. Meanwhile, in America, for instance, the pendulum had swung from the state-dominated development model of the 1960s and 1970s to the minimalist state of the 1980s. This backdrop posed a threat of marginalization and irrelevance for African countries . It must be emphasized that there was no shift on the considered role of the state. The vaunted success of East Asia stood as an example. Rather, the quest was how to rebuild the state as an agency of the market economy. It was argued that incentives, under which states and state institutions operate, must be changed in such a manner as to make the state in Africa as capable as that in East Asia.

The 1981 and 1989 *World Bank Reports*, dealt with the problem of accelerated development and the need to shift from crisis to sustainable growth in subSaharan Africa. The mood of pessimism was most noticeable, as if the problems were intractable; to this was added a demonization of the post-colonial elite. The catalogue of woes focused on predatory, statist policies that stifled entrepreneurship and investment, instability caused by incompetent and unpredictable management of the public sector,and a failed legal system. Meanwhile, environmental degradation and abuse of human rights became acute. The 1994 report *Adjustment in Africa: Reforms, Results and the Road Ahead* therefore recommended a number of ideological shifts designed to rebuild the capacity of African states towards good governance. This is measured by the degree of accountability, transparency, and openness in decisionmaking, rule of law and efficient public management, which wpould promote a political and economic liberation, dovetailed and undertaken simultaneously and perceived as mutually supportive. Did this current neoliberal orthodoxy entail a reversal of past liberal thinking that tended to view economic and political development as sequential processes? Scholars greeted the report with hostile reviews, accusing the Bretton Woods organization for being part of the problem; for exhibiting a certain fundamentalist monopoly of the prescriptions and for blatantly purveying misguided policies based on faulty methodology.[18]

John Wiseman added the caveat that there are enormous differences among African states and their experiences in spite of partially shared characteristics such as levels of underdevelopment, social composition of the population, relative balance or imbalance between different ethnic, racial, religious or linguistic groups, styles of political leadership, distinctive historical experiences, and impact of the memories of the past in contemporary politics.[19] In the 1997 report, the World Bank riposted that the rapid change in the global economy required a revisit to old positions and rethinking the role of the state; that its fundamental role is unassailable; in spite of size, ethnic makeup, culture, and political system, the essential difference behind contrasting developments is the effectiveness of the state that should no longer serve as a direct provider and rather become a facilitator, a catalyst, and a partner.

Nothing fails like failure; so the denigration of African politics and the new politics of despair bred a variety of solutions: (i) structural adjustment programs, (ii) mobilization of civil society as a new form of public response, (iii) the explosion of NGOs that would bypass corrupt state apparatus and alleviate poverty at the grass-root level or carry the market economy ideology to the masses, and (iv) the promotion of democratization through embargoes, sanctions, covert military operations, funding of dissidents and aids. The carrot of debt-rescheduling or relief was sometimes waved in the direction of obstinate dictators.

The story of the Structural Adjustment Program (SAP) is based on who is telling it, to whom, and whether one is on the giving or receiving end. On the surface, it is very clear that no economy can consume more than it produces. Thus, the emergence of chronic imbalances between supply and demand must call forth corrective action to ensure that the economy can function on the basis of sustainable transfers from both the rest of the world and future generations and of sustainable utilization of environmental resources. Therefore, SAP moves in two stages: the stabilization phase seeks to rein back demand through increased taxation, cut government spending, and evolve policies aimed at reducing private consumption, especially of imported goods.

The second phase focuses on the supply -side, reorienting the structure of production and consumption, improving allocation of resources across sectors, and increasing the efficiency of investment through institutional reform. The broad goal is to enhance the productive capacity of the economy. It represents the international counterpart of the neocolonial hegemony of supply-side economics in industrialized economies, which presents universal solution to the problems of economic development.[20] The SAP is simply a means of taking over the economies of debtornations and milking the money out of them. IMF and World Bank perform this task on behalf of the six Western nation that control the shareholders. Critics point to the high levels of adjustment lending, draconian stabilization efforts, worsening economic conditions, and only the most fragile evidence of supply-side recovery. Others see potentials of macrolevel improvement but at the terrible expense of the microeconomic level. Of great concern is that the political and social consequences have been disastrous and have increased the pauperization of communities. As Colin Leys argued:

> The time has come to acknowledge that only the analysis
> of the social forces at work in each individual country
> and their political and organizational capacities can
> permit intelligent political choices to be made or alterna-
> tive development strategies to be evolved.[21]

The faces of the poor contort in the rash of liberalizations and removal of subsidies in contexts where social safety net is nonexistent. As they say in Nigeria, "SAP has sapped people." They point accusing fingers to the bias in favor of creditors, decline in imports, unemployment, and the undermining of the survival of the poor. Can democracy work in this climate? Democratization has become a bugbear for two reasons: for one, it does not thrive well among people with empty stomachs. Steve Ellis captured the second aspect aptly:

> Now, five years or more later, doubts have set in. After
> dozens of more or less free elections. It is apparent that
> long-established dictators in Ghana, Kenya, Togo, Benin,
> and elsewhere have proved themselves able to live with
> multi-party politics, and even thrive, without improving
> the quality of governance which aid donors are seeking.[22]

Uganda is practicing an intriguing form of one-party democracy in which all other criteria are met without multiparty provision. Museveni argues strongly that the principles of consultation and the right to choose are safe-guarded.[23] Some smooth transitions have been made such as in Benin in 1995. But a former military strong man has gone through two elections in Ghana and may be giving a tutorial to his Nigerian counterpart. In Kenya, the dictator Arap Moi has won two elections. Democracy has ended wars in South Africa, Mozambique, Namibia, Ethiopia, Eritrea, Liberia, and such-like. Intractable wars have survived in others while coups have reversed situations in Niger, Zaire, Sierra-Leone, and Nigeria. In the Central African Republic, soldiers have staged three rebellions since May 1996 against President Ange-Felix Patasse, whose election in 1993 ended more than a decade of army rule. Even the French have sickened of bolstering his regime with an army. The uneven record will require more analysis, because the instability that is hindering economic growth has continued to create hardship for the people. Chris Allen quipped that:

Multiparty-ism and the rule of law, indeed, even the codification of basic human rights, do not of themselves imply particular representativeness, accountability or transparency. They may be essential to the possibility of reducing inequalities and of removing oppression but do not accomplish this of their own accord. Much more commonly, democracy serves as a system through which class dominance and various forms of systemic inequalities are perpetuated and legitimated. The challenge of those African nations undergoing a process of democratization is to use the space it opens to press for greater justice for the masses of the population.[24]

Where do the people turn for hope if neither SAP nor democracy can subsist? The experience of Nigeria is instructive: four political parties, in 1997, came together and decided to invite the military dictator to change his uniform and become the consensus presidential candidate in the next election, while every other person avoided the hustings. The incumbent dictator would be elected unopposed; so he would not need to face the mass of voters, and he would yet win. Admittedly, it was the dictator who created the parties in response to Western pressures to democratize!

This raises another matter, namely, the positive valuation of civil society as the harbinger of the forces for the rejuvenation of Africa's enfeebled states and politics. This has been occasioned by the resurgence of organized popular protest against incumbent authoritarian regimes, beginning of the 1990s, that have been heralded as the rebirth of political freedom. Arguing that African civil societies have undergone massive transformation and growth since the mid-1980s, Chazan exulted in the pluralization of associational life and the growth of middle rung and intermediate associations based among the urban dwellers and professional associations.

The proliferation of advocacy groups cannot be ignored. But the class content of civil society needs attention. For instance, in Nigeria, the collapse of banks, loss of opportunities for professional groups such as engineers, architects, and other ancillary groups whose earnings were held up in government debts- forced many into politics as the only space for making a living. The military dictator fed on the insecurities of these vulnerable bastions of civil society. Naturally, they capitulated. R. Fatton's typology of civil society enables a proper evaluation of the capable role that this power node can play in wiping away the ashes on the faces of the people. He distinguished between predatory civil society representing the interest of the ruling class, quasi-bourgeois civil society, embodying the aspirations of the middle class and popular civil society, expressing the projects of subordinate classes and groups.[25] Many assert that the middleclass is the backbone of civil society. They are the most active prodemocracy agitators. Yet this is the group that has been decimated by the aftereffect of SAP. The group comprises university students, professionals, civil servants and workers in many countries. Thousands are emigrating to other countries.

As these influential early supporters of democracy experience deterioration rather than improvement in their living standards, they become disillusioned with democracy and politicians and either flee or join the looters. In 1997, only 20% of the electorate bothered to vote in the Nigerian regional election. The military dictator guffawed because the votes could be counted more easily. The fewer, the merrier! The problem that most African countries face is the need to institutionalize democratic organizations and procedures, a process in which all major political actors come to accept the democratic rules of the game. Richard Sandbrook terms the current situation transitions without consolidation, implying that without the consolidating moorings, little hope exists for the endurance of democracy.[26]

This brings us to the proliferation of NGOs, predicated on suspicion of the corrupt state and the view that re-building of state capacity should go along with another policy of avoiding the state apparatus by reinforcing local self-reliance and self-sufficiency. The target is the mobilization of the third group in the class-content of civil society. This should be done by enabling assistance and validating the infrapolitical space in which they articulate their critic of the politics of the rulers. The beam of light is shone into the neon zone of the informal economy that is to be buttressed with formal assistance and used as the core to rebuild the state economy in such a manner that might truly alleviate poverty. The informal sector is where market activities are not regulated by contracts, licenses, and other legal devices. Recently, the International Labor Organization estimated that 59% of the urban labor force in subSaharan Africa is employed within the informal sector. For many years to come, the vast majority of shopkeepers, small-scale entrepreneurs, selfemployed persons and nonunionized workers in Africa will be dependent on the informal sector for their livelihood. Equally recognized is their political potentials, including an uncanny dynamic and the ability to sabotage economic policies.

The World Bank is impressed with the adaptability and innovation of this sector. There are a number of issues involved in all the keen attention: the World Bank is quite aware of the social side-effects of prescribed policies; it does not heedlessly embrace the neo-classical counter revolutionary doctrine of free market and less government as the basic ingredients of third world development. Rather, it operates a variant, which urges market-friendly interventions;for example, by investing in physical and social infrastructure and by providing a suitable climate for private enterprise. This is the root of the rhetoric on poverty alleviation policies directed toward rural development in general and agricultural sector in particular. The 1991 World Bank report even harped on quality of life:

> It encompasses as ends in themselves better education, higher standards of health and nutrition, less poverty, a cleaner environment, more equality of opportunity, greater individual freedom and a richer cultural life.

Supposing a debtor nation cuts public spending in those core areas, the Bretton institutions have no coercive powers to restrain the offender, especially if the cow is providing the milk of debt repayment when due. One resort is the intensification of social movements in the context of socioeconomic deterioration but in such a manner that one does not throw away the baby with the bathwater. Covert dalliance with civil society is a preemptive safeguard; and the use of NGOs has been the dominant response to the challenges posed by this group as well as by the failure of the corrupt state.

This is the heart of the postmodernist theory that shifts focus of economic development from aggregative indices to social indicators such as levels of poverty, inequality, and unemployment. A concern for the development of people rather than for the development of things soon leads to a concern for the analysis of the social system, the so-called noneconomic factors such as values, attitudes, and primal institutions. Ecological concerns loom large in this perspective. Is there a relationship between development and ecology? These issues will be picked up in the next chapter because they are key to reconceptualizing development.

They point to two facets: on the one hand, there is the ambiguous image of NGOs in Africa. They have proliferated so much that in some countries, as Mozambique, they overawe the government. Between 1970-1990, the NGO budget soared from one to five billion dollars. They are engaged in emergency reliefs, child health, women's rights, poverty alleviation programs, environmental protection, rights of indigenous peoples, increasing food production, rural credit to small farmers and local businesses, road building, provision of homes, schools, hospitals, research and water supply. At the

1995Copenhagen Summit, the United States pledged to channel half of its foreign aid to private NGOs. The internal politics is another matter as the case of aid agencies in Rwanda raised disturbing questions.[27] Some have wondered how much of the funds actually get to the target groups. At best, NGOs are part of the social safety net thrown to protect the most vulnerable sectors of the population so as to mitigate the transitional costs of the adjustment programs. This is done in such a manner as to avoid the overextended public sector that has become a major drain on the economy. Subtly, the stage is set for privatizing and rehabilitating the economy. Hostile critics see a political commitment to generate consensus. NGOs are placebo agents; sedating the masses from rioting over the decimating effects of SAP. Their activities raise the problem of poverty in Africa, the ashes on the faces of those who had hoped that independence would bring joy. Do they deal with the roots of the problem or is it that half a loaf of bread is better than none? Beneath the brutal pretensions of the state are the scarred victims.

3.THE FACES OF POVERTY IN AFRICA IN THE 1990S

A number of statistical data reveals the enormity of the poverty syndrome in Africa. Some are typical Western quantitative indicators. For example:

TABLE 2.2 – Economic Indicators of Economic Decline in sub-Saharan Africa: 1980-1990

Economic Indicator	1980	1990	Change %
Per capita output ($billion)	582	335	-42.5
Per capita consumption	465	279	-40.0
Investment % of GDP	20.2	14.2	-29.7
Exports of goods $ billion	48.7	31.9	-34.5
Per capita foods production $	107	94	-12.2
Total external debt $ billion	56.2	147	+162
Poverty % below poverty line	NA	62	-

(Source:United Nations Development Program and World Bank: *African Development Indicators* (New York and Washington, 1992).

But commentators have querried the statistical bases for determining poverty in countries where the generation, storage, and utilization of data may not be as thorough as in the West, especially where the informal and rural sectors of the economy tend to predominate. Other cultural factors determine the level of poverty. People have different concepts of what constitutes poverty. Indigenous languages betray such conceptions and even typologies of poverty. While the debates go on, there is little doubt about the fact that pauperization of the society has become the most urgent problem in all African countries. Beyond a wild rate of emigration as people fraudulently declare themselves as refugees in European countries, the increased levels of social violence betray frustration and a high level of social stress. In recent years both the World Bank and the UNDP have painted a dark canvass of poverty in Africa which shows that most of the population in several countries live below the poverty line even if that line is arbitrarily chosen.

TABLE 2.3 – Africa's Population Living Below the Poverty Line, 1995

Countries	Per capita	Pop.(mill.)	% of poor	Poor (mill.)
Burkina Faso $	300	10.4	35	3.6
Egypt	710	61.9	23	14.2
Ethiopian/ Eritrea	130	56.0	64	35.
Ghana	430	17.5	42	7.4
Kenya	260	28.3	52	14.7
Malawi	140	9.7	82	8.0
Morocco	1150	29.2	37	10.8
Nigeria	280	101.2	40	40.5
Senegal	610	8.3	29	2.4
Sudan	260	28.1	85	23.9
Tanzania	90	28.5	58	16.5
Tunisia	1800	8.9	18	1.6
Uganda	200	21.3	45	9.6
Zambia	350	9.1	64	5.8
All Africa (average)	530	720.0	54	388.8

(Sources: *The World Bank Atlas*, 1996; *UNDP Human Development Report*,1996; *World Bank Development Report*,1996)

These figures call to mind the biblical declaration that those who rule over them make the poor to howl; all the economic policies and advices of yesteryears have merely pauperized African communities to such an extent that 54% of the population is living below poverty line. The countries on the Maghrib have a higher income per capita yet the level of poverty is similar to the level in the subSaharan countries that have a lower income per capita. Huge countries like Nigeria, with its mineral wealth, could not convert the human and mineral resources into healthier environments. The staggering resources of the Congo have produced international competitions and civil wars. Diamond wars have turned Africa's good fortune into doom.Here is the challenge that faces Christian witness, raising certain questions: what is poverty? How do we measure poverty? What are the causes or sources of poverty? Are there alternative models for combating the scourge?

In *The Bible, the Church, and the Poor*, Clodovis Boff and George Pixley refuse to indulge in the involuted sophistry of the academia and defined poverty simply as a label on those who suffer from basic economic need, those who are deprived of the material goods necessary to live with dignity.[28]The authors have avoided the other tendency to spiritualize poverty. Concurring, Bryant Myers of World Vision emphasized that the poor are human beings, made in the image of God and for whom Jesus died; they have names. Therefore, Christians must go beyond the deficit or deprivation model that perceives poverty as resulting from lack of things to a broader perspective of needs:

material: shelter, food, land, money, etc.;

immaterial: knowledge, skill, healthcare, education;

access: opportunities, jobs, participation in sociopolitical life, capacity for self-fulfilment;

empowerment: vulnerability, lack of control over one's affairs, absence of vuilnerability,oppression, andfear of the powerful;

social: healthy relationships, support networks, salient values, moral and religious wholeness.

The dangers are that a deficit model either demeans and postures the victim as a passive recipient of aids or turns the caregiver into a messiah. Indeed, Boff and Pixley reject the moral and natural explanations that point to ignorance, sin, or congenital factors. Poverty is a social phenomenon, unnatural and caused by a perverse economic system; it is against God's design for His people. Myers adds that it is best understood as an aspect of a broken relationship:

Seeing the world in terms of relationships gives us new insights into ...who is doing what to whom...We make people poor when we begin to label them as the other, the outsider, the outcast.[29]

Poverty is endogenous, that is, internal to the system and a natural product of it; caused by the relational or interactional structure of power that a system creates. When those who have power over others use it to benefit themselves, poverty is the result. Poverty- alleviation programs tend to focus on the deficit model, ignoring the poverty-creating nature of power that the economic and political structures weave. Poverty is structural and collective; people are made poor through exploitation by local and transnational operators. The trans-national integration occurs through commerce, investment, techni-cal aid, political and military treaties and alliances. The transnational exploitative class collaborate with local agents. As birds of the same feather, they would fly together, living happily on the sweating faces of the people. At the heart of poverty is the ethics of power; that is, the moral bedrock or undergirding values which control the exercise of power. Some have, however, insisted on a combined aggregate of inherited and un-inherited determinants. This allows a review of cul-tural determinants which impede access to resources and self-care.[30]

Boff and Pixley group the collective Lazaruses into three broad categories: the socioeconomic poor, the sociocultural poor who are discriminated against for color, gender, and ethnicity, and the new urban poor who are emerging in the wake of rapid urbanization in the third world. A closer typology identifies five types:

(i)   the marginalized: excluded from the prevailing economic system, the lords of the informal sector;
(ii) the unemployed or partially unemployed (urban industrial workers, wage earners, the working poor);
(iii) the rural workers: small holders, settlers, tenant farmers;
(iv) the wretched: the sick,beggars, street kids, prostitutes, and the abandoned; refugees, ostracized, those who are bereft of kin group.
(v)   those living under violent, unhealthy moral and social environ-ments.

The relationship between power and poverty exposes the sources or causes as asymmetrical power relations in society, institutional-ized injustice, oppressive dehumanizing power, violence through the militarization of the society, the politics of exclusion and corruption. Fear and insecurity, abuse of human rights, and dictatorial exer-cise of authority impoverish communities. Julio de Santa Ana lays much emphasis on the ideology of materialism, a certain economic worldview that places things above the welfare of the people. He calls it the irrationality of the rationality of the current economic system; the absurd insistence of reducing economic processes simply to profit-making; a Faustian spirit recognizing no limits, cultivating the market in order to obtain the most advantages. He says that this system is like a spiritual entity that has cast a spell on the devotees; they operate around a center to which accumulation gravitates and power is concentrated.[31] Meanwhile, their victims writhe in two hungers, says the Cuban poet Roberto Retamar: one for bread, which can be satisfied; and the other for beauty, which is insatiable.[32] When one breaks the spell of the system and reimagines the economic order differently from a countersystem and ethical consciousness, poverty is not about want; rather it is a model of living. Social sinfulness has entrapped people into a certain mode of life that can only be changed when the victims exerting a liberating power. Leonardo Boff insists that:

> It is not the churches that free the poor, nor a beneficent
> state, nor the classes that assist them. These can be allies
> of the poor, provided they do not take their protagonism
> and hegemony from them.[33]

The church's role would be to see, judge, decipher the causes that engender suffering, seek their cultural roots and tentacles in the ideology of power, and act in solidarity, protest, and denunciation.

The secularist approach to the problem often recognizes the need to reconceptualize development as an attack on the chief evils of the world today, namely, malnutrition, disease, illiteracy, slums, unemployment, and inequality. Measured in aggregative terms, one would lose sight of justice. This has produced the quest for alternative indicators or measurements for development and poverty. However, theorization tends toward variants of the deprivation model. This model has changed its assumption. Some have abandoned the use of subsistence index-food, healthcare, and shelter. Others have resorted to the CPM or Capability of Poverty Measure that focuses on basic needs. It differentiates between absolute and relative poverty. The former refers to the number of people who are unable to command sufficient resources to satisfy basic needs. Counted as the total number living below a specified minimum level of real income, an imaginary line is drawn for a year and a figure inserted for calcualtion. For instance, one could employ the purchaisng power for 1985 in the United States and use 275 dollars as a basis.

Based on these indices, poverty-focused policies try to locate poverty, specify the extent and characteristics. It draws a distinction between absolute or abject inability to access basic needs and poverty-line people who may have legal rights to housing but are unable to access enough food to live a healthy life with basic education. A variant of this is the Human Development Index based on life expectancy (longevity),adult literacy (knowledge), real per capita income (standard of living), and infant mortality. On these social indicators, Africa's image is gloomy:

TABLE 2.4 – Africa's Human Development Index:,1992 (0>1=lowest to highest)

Country	HDI	GNP (US $)	Global Ranking
Guinea	0.191	500	173
Ethiopia	0.249	410	161
Nigeria	0.348	350	139
Kenya	0.434	340	125
Egypt	0.551	610	110
South Africa	0.650	2,540	93

Source:UNDP, *Human Development Report* (New York, New York University Press, 1994): 129-131

All these aggregative indices have limited usefulness, saccharined of blood and flesh. Indeed, these select data give a glimpse of the imperative for plumbing the essence of development to represent the whole gamut of change by which an entire social system is transformed to seek the diverse basic needs and desires of individuals and social groups within that system. There should be a shift from merely dealing with conditions considered unsatisfactory towards conditions of life regarded as materially and spiritually better and truly human. From this perspective, development has a new and an inner meaning: sustenance, self-esteem, freedom. Sustenance is the ability to meet basic needs; self-esteem suggests a sense of worth, self-respect, and an unwillingness to be used as a tool by others for their own ends. People need to be able to choose, to have an expanded range of choices and emancipation from alienating material conditions of life.

In conclusion, the failure of the state in Africa is beyond economic explanation. Much of it is a amtter of ethics; realting to the ethics of power, because some people have monopolized power and colluded with Western entrepreneurs to rob their people of both material resources and dignity. Admittedly, some of the arsenal were borrowed from primal cultural values. But this was achieved by bawderizing the salient, countervailing norms. At the national level, the quest for revolutionary transformation and recovery from the indignities of the past was scorched by the weak legacies of colonialism. After all, decolonization was not undertaken for the love of the colonized but rather as a restructuring of European economy, reducing the overhead costs for greater efficiency of a liberal market economy. This ideology promoted the implosion of the state. Ironically, the competing command-control economy intensified the role of the state. In the hands of African leaders, the power was used to predate on the populace. As lions, the leaders ate their own people. The current recovery measures pose even worse threats to the people: SAP has sapped the abilities of communities to live decent lives. This is to put the matter mildly. The increased use of NGOs has the singular weakness of a faulted theoretical base. A deficit model of understanding poverty cannot empower the poor to liberate themselves:

> For Christians, liberation is not confined to the social
> sphere; it has spiritual and eschatological dimensions as
> well. This establishes the qualitative difference between
> the classical Marxist conception of liberation and the
> Christian.[34]

At the core of the challenge for Christian theology and history is a recognition that the prevalent political theology must address questions of relationship-the relationship of God to the oikumene (the whole inhabited earth) relationships of power between those conferred with authority and the people. The economic structure may appear confusing as experts wade from the macro to the micro levels, but the bottom line is, Who is exploiting whom? The church needs to search the primal roots of exploitation and show a certain type of solidarity that avoids paternalism so as to be the allies of the poor. The poor may include the materially poor and the rich who are spiritually poor. Evangelizing the rich for wholesome practice of stewardship is a key table. The church must engage in objective, collective, practical and participatory action to transform the economic and political structure of the continent. But first of all, it must build the relevant data for meaningful intervention. Key to this information is the relationship between the ecology, the worldview, and the political economy. This we shall pursue in the next chapter and later explore the various ways in which the church in Africa has theologized and practiced their understanding of the questions of power and poverty.

Notes

1. Goran Hayden, "Rethinking Theories of the State: An Africanist Perspective", *African Insight*, 26, 1 (1996): 26-35; Dickson Eyoh, "From Economic Crisis to Political Liberalization: Pitfalls of the New Political Sociology for Africa, " *African Studies Review*, 39, 3 (1996): 43-80.
2. Y. W. Bradshaw et als., Rethinking Theoretical and Methodological Approaches to the Study of African Development, *African Studies Review*, 38, 2 (1995): 39-65.
3. World Bank, *The State in a Changing World* (Washington, DC: World Bank, 1997): introduction; C. E. Black, *The Dynamics of Modernization*, (New York: Harper & Row, 1966), Chap 3.
4. Compare the predominantly economic criteria in R. Sandbrook, *The Politics of Africa's Economic Stagnation* (Cambridge: Cambridge University Press, 1984), 33.
5. The two concepts are discussed fully in J. Cartwright, *Political Leadership in Africa* (New York: St. Martin's Press, 1983), Chap 4.
6. Carl.G.Rosberg, *Democracy and the New Africa* (New York: 1963).
7. P. B. Harris, *Studies in African Politics*. (London: Hutchinson & Co. Publishers, 1970).
8. Rosberg, *Democracy*, 39.
9. A. Hastings, *The History of African Christianity, 1950-1975* (Cambridge: Cambridge University Press, 1979), 47.
10. F. Katsuyoshi and J. Markaki's (eds) *Ethnicity and Conflict in the Horn of Africa. (London: James Currey: 1994); Musa I. M. Abutudu, The State, Civil Society and the Democratization Process in Nigeria* (Dakar: Codesria Monograph 1/95, January, 1995).
11. Peter Anyang Nyong'o, *State and Democracy in Africa*, AAPS, no. 13, (1993).
12. Ibid., "Aid Doesn't Benefit Africa", *Nation*. (Kenya), July 27, 1997, 19; Steve Ellis, "The Strange Life of African States", *African Insight*, 26, 1 (1996): 2-4.
13. S. R. Wissman, "CIA Covert Actions in Zaire and Angola: Patterns and Consequences", *Political Science Quarterly.*, 94, 2 (1979): 285.
14. Sandbrook, *The Politics of Africa's Economic Stagnation*, iii.
15. R. Luckham, "French Militarism in Africa", *Review of African Political Economy*, 24 (1982): 55-84.

16. J. W. De Gruchy, *Christianity and Democracy* (Cambridge: Cambridge University Press, 1995), 167-168.

17. J. F. Bayart, *The State in Africa: The Politics of the Belly* (London: Longman, 1993).

18. See, *Canadian Journal of African Studies*, 29, 2, (1995) for reviews by six scholars; John Mihevic, *The Market Tells Them So.* (Penang: Third World Network, 1995*)*.

19. J. Wiseman, *Democracy and Political Change in Sub-Saharan Africa* (London: Routledge, 1995).

20. Compare "Tribunal or the Policies of the IMF and the World Bank", *International Journal of Health Services*, 20, 2 (1990): 329-347 with (a) the collection of academic papers edited by R.van der Hoeven and F. Van der Kraaij, *Structural Adjustment and Beyond in Sub-Saharan Africa (*London: James Currey, 1994); and (b) the rosy account by Saleh M. Nsouli, Assistant Director, IMF Middle East Department, in Colin Leys, "Structural Adjustment in Sub-Sahara Africa", *Finance and Development* (September 1993): 20-23.

21. D. E. Apter and C. G. Rosberg, eds., *Political Development and the New Realism in Sub-Saharan Africa.* (Charlottesville: University of Virginia Press, 1994), 228. See chapter by Colin Leys.

22. Ellis, "The Strange Life of African States", 2.

23. (M. Karlstrom, "Democracy Uganda Style", *Africa*, 66, 4 (1996): 485-505.; B. Coplan and T. Quinlan, "Nation vs. State in Lesotho", *Africa*, 67, 1 (1997): 27-60.

24. Chris Allen et al., "Surviving Democracy" *Review of African Political Economy* (ROAPE) 54 (1992): 10; see also Edward A. Alpers, "Africa Reconfigured" *Africa* 67, 1 (1997): 27-60.

25. R. Fatton, "Africa in the Age of Democratization: The Civic Limitations of Civil Society", *Africa Studies Review* 38, 2 (1995),: 67-99; N. Chazan, "Associational Life in Sub-Saharan Africa", In *State Power and Social Forces* eds. J. Migdal et al. (Cambridge: Cambridge University Press, 1994).

26. R. Sandbrook, "Transitions without Consolidation: Democratization in Six African Cases", *Third World Quarterly*, 17, 1 (1996): 69-87.

27. Hugh McCullum, *The Angels Have Left Us: The Rawanda Tragedy and the Church* (Geneva: World Council of Churches, 1996).

28. Clodovis Boff and G. V. Pixley eds., *The Bible, the Church and the Poor* (Maryknoll, NY: Orbis Books, 1989), 1.

29. Bryant Myers, "What Is Poverty Anyway?" *MARC Newsletter*, 97, 1 (1997): 3-4.

30. See Gunnar Myrdal, *Challenge of World Poverty* (New York: Random House, 1970), 101-114 for a discussion of inherited and uninherited determinants.

31. In Leonardo Boff and Virgil Elizando eds., *Ecology and Poverty : The Cry of the Earth, Cry of the Poor* (Maryknoll, NY: Orbis Books, 1995), chap 1.

32. Ibid., 71.

33. *Ibid.*, 72.

34. *ibid.*, 236.

Chapter Three
Sacred Eggs On Sacred Faces:
Worldview, Ecology, and Development

1. THE BACKDROP: DEVELOPMENT FAILURE

The relationship between church history and ecological ethics needs to be spelled out because in the effort to give the discipline a methodological identity, ecoethics is crucial. People live and are nurtured by the resources of the environment. Indeed, cultures are hewn from the rocks of challenges that the ecological system poses for a community. This chapter makes two points:first, the reconstruction of the story of the gospel in Africa should start from a recosntruction of the ecology-environment,culture, and worldview of African communities.This is the context into which the gospel enters and challenges.A church history that starts from the home bases of the gospel bearers runs the risk of clothing African Christianity with a foreign garb. Second,it is becoming axiomatic that the roots of the current ecological disasters are spiritual. The nurture, mobilization, and utilization of a community's resources for the enhancement of life are all dependent on the core values embedded in the worldview of the people and especially the ecological ethics emanating from that worldview. If, for instance, there is a shift from anthropocentric view of the world into a more organic one that perceives the ecosystem as a shared psychic space, the purview, questions and method in doing history will change.History will cease to be an interpretation of the human past but an interpretation of the relationships of humans to themselves as well as to animals and other beings sentient or nonsentient.

For church history, ecology is core to the biblical definition and task of the church and determines the pattern of reception and domestication of the Christian gospel. In recent times, many books have appeared on conversion. Hardly any considers the import of

ecological ethics on the patterns of conversion. Yet the patterns of
vertical and horizontal expansion of the gospel are determined by
ecological factors.Geography, values, and culture of a community
not only are challenged by the power of the gospel but they, too,
affect the community's response to the gospel. The history of the
church is the story of the ways that communities struggle to harness
the resources of the gospel to meet their needs.The human problems
that compel the diaconic response of the church emerge from environmental challenges. Thus, both the rootedness of African Christianity in the worldview and the fact that the major challenges to
the church's faithful witness arise from both the worldview and the
ecology compell the historian to start from these core aspects. They
open the window to the reasons for people's responses to the challenges of life. The African worldview is a religious cosmology that
determines the responses to new religious agents, either as extension
of the innate spiritual desires and hopes of the people or as challenges. New religious movements source their problematics, idioms,
and answers from this fountain. Moreover, development, understood
as liberation from dehumanizing forces, depends on the ecological
ethics of the people. The neglect of this fact and resort to predatory
ecoethics court developmental failure. All the new states announce
development as their goal, and all have failed because little attention was paid to the well-being of the environment in which human
beings live and eke out their living.

Commentators argue that the ecoethics of world religions hold
answers to the degradation of the human environment and the con-
sequent threats to the earth,to the future of humans, and to other
living beings. So, the concern of this chapter is to point the churches
in Africa to a new form of historical existence. This exigency enlarges
their public role, because it is a major political and policy issue. Initially there is the argument that worldviews should be the beginning
of any reconstruction of a community's encounter with the gospel.
Admittedly there are many worldviews among the varied peoples of
this huge continent, but there is a deep spiritual structure to religion that may remain the same even when the religion itself changes
and the divine names and symbols are replaced by other names and
forms. Such deep structures or existential meanings tie together a
wide range of folk practices in different subculture theaters. Despite
the variety of names and forms, African traditional religions do
genuinely exhibit an astonishing uniformity of emphasis that makes
of them merely local variations on a few axiomatic themes to a much
greater degree than we find in Christianity or Hinduism. The his-

torian should plumb the indigenous knowledge of the people and build into it the resources of the gospel's ethics to enrich the capacity for a truly human living. When this is ignored, the consequences can be disastrous as some examples have shown.

In 1996, a state government in Southeastern Nigeria sought to combat the devastating collapse of agroindustrial projects in the rural communities. The state acquired some irrigation pumps through the Federal Ministry of Agriculture, aided by a World Bank loan scheme. But when workers entered the farmlands of a certain community, Amanuke, to dig trenches, the entire community descended on the workers wielding machetes, spears, and dane guns. The hapless workers tried to persuade the irate villagers that the irrigation would enable them to crop all year round. But the villagers complained that the forest adjoining the farmland housed their epical ancestral shrine. Besides, if the ancestral progenitors wanted them to crop all year round, they would have caused the springs that coursed underground to burst to the surface. Ancestors are very loving and usually careful about such things.

Obviously, the project officers had ignored the people during the project design and were both insensitive and inattentive to what the people felt and desired socially, economically and spiritually. Posing as messiahs to the poor, they ignored the axiom that a people's culture, worldview, and religion affect their perception of development. Currently, much of Africa is plagued by development failure, which, in turn, has bred legitimacy crises, economic collapse, environmental degradation, and human rights abuse. It is therefore difficult to engage in any meaningful scholarship that does not address these problems. The calamity at Amanuke has replayed itself in myriad of contexts all over Africa. Did the primal worldview of the Amanuke people cause the failure of the agroindustrial project? Can we avoid the romanticization of primal worldviews and still advocate salient traditionalization of change agents?

The perspective here is from a theory of directed culture change that stresses the understanding of how existing indigenous institutions can provide the basis for development models, based on a consideration of the environment, the use of local human and natural resources, and the belief systems.[1] Arthuro Escobar notes the current requirement by agencies such as USAID that the project implementation be preceded by a social soundness analysis which assesses the feasibility of development projects and their relevance to the socioeconomic environment.[2] This often does not go deeply enough.

There has been a tendency to attribute development failure to certain notions about non-Western primal communities. It is assumed that indigenous cultures constrain their mobility towards economic and technological development; that they slow down agricultural change, and that they contain destructive aspects and retarding features to be eliminated.[3] Some say that their behaviors are not wellthought out, being guided by complex social and cultural factors. From these shibboleths have emerged advocacy for replacing local strategies with Western models,[4] misreading of the African landscape, and the enculturation of the non-Western attitude as prerequisite to development. It is as if the goal is to adapt traditional modes to modern technology and systems.[5]

But underlying the jaundiced perceptions is a clash of worldviews that informs the definition of development. The Western enlightenment worldview tended to define development in aggregative terms. Thus, the colonial ideal was socioeconomic progress or modernization, attainable through successive stages of economic growth. This conceptwas separated from religion. Indeed, it was hoped that religion and ethnicity would disappear.[6] The eradication of religion has not occurred however. Rather, there is a decline in the belief that science and public life are based on objective rational assumptions that have nothing to do with belief, be it personal or communal. The questions are raised once again: can religious activities be separated from development? Are they compatible? Does the implementation of one enhance or hinder the effectiveness of the other? How do beliefs and ideologies influence resource management? How can Africans reconceptualize development so as to escape from the theories of the past that have inscribed so much pain on our faces?

There has been a paradigm shift towards a holistic concept of development and sustainability. It recognizes the integration of economic, cultural, religious, and ecological aspects into the change process. There is a growing recognition of cultural diversity and local processes as core aspects of global reality as opposed to the assumption of increasing homogenization found in the modernization theory. For us in Africa, the paradigm shift in the theory of knowledge is crucial, because the failure of the agricultural sector in the continent combined with horrendous scale of environmental degradation pose a threat. Worse is the lack of an ecological policy. The paradigm shift should enable us to return to the drawing board for a development strategy that would be inclusive, more sensitive to the full range of social realities, and conscious of the method, context, and content of the change process. Tension is inherent in cultural exchanges. Indeed,

Iyam argues with a fascinating study of the Biase of the Cross River Basin that:

> Local circumstances also embody important cultural elements and practices that discourage development initiatives by both external and local agents and constrain the realization of desirable changes in rural communities.[7]

There is, therefore, no attempt to romanticize primal cultures. The question pulsates, to what extent are development failures caused by the indigenous worldview and the coping mechanism that they legitimate? As Murray Bookchin would argue, to advocate a return to rustic simplicity is unrealistic and naive.[8] Indeed, urban dwellers often endeavor to coax villagers to preserve primal cultures while the latter lust after industrial goods. This suggests a search for factors within particular societies that promote either antinature or friendly attitudes. Many in the West blame environmental abuse to human arrogance in the exploitation of natural resources. This may well be in some cases; but it could also arise from vulnerability caused by ignorance, of a technological incapacity for taming nature, and a deeply religious perception of nature.

Sensitivity to such wider vistas of the problem enables us to see development as a liberating effort to supplement indigenous knowledge and institutions. It involves a modification of both material and non-material factors. It occurs when a community initiates an adjustment of the ideational and attitudinal components of culture so that enhancing factors are activated for improving an existing state of affairs.[9]

It would involve a cognitive disposition by the community to modify their affairs and a mobilization/utilization of their entire populace- men and women. They must be willing to reassess traditional rights and privileges. Here the gender issue is raised cogently because many have connected environmental abuse with abuse of women and children.[10] From this perspective, the development process runs along a certain groove, utilizing the adaptive nontechnological cultural elements that influence the economic process of communities. The shift from perceiving peasants as tradition-bound to imaging them as rational beings opens the way to modifications of their worldviews in such a manner that closed systems open to the imperatives and possibilities of changes. This is what Robin Horton called the open predicament.

2. THE SACRED EGG: ANATOMY OF A WORLDVIEW

Indigenous cultures are underpinned by worldviews that serve as reservoirs of indigenous knowledge. They are stored in proverbs and folk myths. Myths of origin abound, explaining how the world came into existence. One of these myths imagine the world as a sacred egg, at once fragile, enfolding and nurturing. Its sacred origin imbues it with a sacral order that, when understood and followed, would ensure a miracle as this seemingly fragile frame has the capacity to sustain so many and so much activity. We shall return to this precarious vision anon.[11]

From such myths people begin to construct reasons as to how and why things are the way they are. Explanation aids prediction of space-time events and this, in turn, enables control. Myths of origin are, therefore, the vehicles of worldviews and differ among the ethnic groups who inhabit West Africa. A common structure underlies all of them, and they share a deep-level meaning. Each is couched in religious, numinous terms: creation was the act of a Supreme Being utilizing the services of subaltern gods. The divine origin confers a sacred shroud on the created beings and the social order.

People, therefore, construct a world order with a certain rhythm in order to explain, predict, and control life- situations in their eco-system. A wise student defined a worldview as how people view their world. It is a mental construct that empowers action and endows both rhythm and meaning to life processes. It is the foundation of customs, social norms and law. Worldviews are embedded in the peoples experience and then expressed or reenacted in their cultures. This can be illustrated with one cultural feature, namely, masquerades. These are very important in the rituals, festivals, aesthetics, and plastic arts. Masqueraders of semisavannah, grassland communities tend to be clothed in dry grass. Some look like moving bundles of grass. Among the forest-zone dwellers, the masqueraders leap out of the bushes as followers caparison with leaves and branches. In the Owu Festival of the riverine communities of the Niger Delta, the masqueraders arrive in canoes with masks depicting various kinds of fishes. The community dances to the waterfront, welcoming and leading them with a chorus into the village, and the celebration begins. At dusk, the masqueraders are led back to the beach; as they paddle off, the people wave and cry for the departing ancestors. That is the crux of the cultural form: the masqueraders are ancestors; they are the gods as guests to the human world. With their arrival,

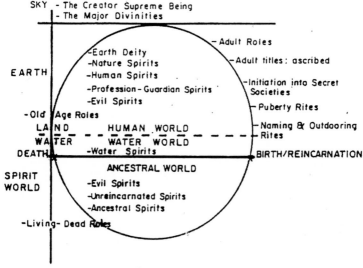

African Worldview

the seen and the unseen worlds meet; the living and the living-dead reunite even if for a brief period. The Owu cultural festival (in the riverine region of southeastern Nigeria) is a celebration of a certain worldview explaining the moral order of a riverine community.

The environment poses a challenge and the community constructs a world view that unravels the riddle of the universe. It must address and reflect the specific nature of the challenge by probing their inner experience. People forge culture in the encounter with and effort to tame their environment and harness its resources for the nurture of that community. Worldviews underpin the culture. As culture is the powerful expression of the creativity of the human spirit, the engine that moves civilization and the substance of history, worldview is the hermeneutic, the cultural lens through which human experience is viewed.[12]

Unlike church historians contemporary anthropology has been more attentive to the relationship between worldviews and modes of local appropriation of the gospel message. Various anthropologists have sought to capture the nuances of worldview: some call it mind world, and explore the differences between Western and non-Western mind worlds. The ethnologist, Edward Sapir, termed it:

the unconscious patterning of behaviour in society...
the way a people characteristically look outward on the
universe.

He noted that patterns of thought, attitude towards life, conceptions
of time, a mental picture of what ought to be, a people's understanding of their relationship to unseen things and to the order of
things, and their view of self and of others-all these are included in
a people's worldview. He might be inelegant in the attempt to be
comprehensive.[13]Paul G. Hiebert organizes the content of worldview
into three categories--cognitive, affective and evaluative.[14] These
refer to the abstract ideas,interpersonal structures, and ethical values.
Charles Kraft underscores the place of values in a worldview as:

the culturally structured assumptions, values and com-
mitments underlying a people's perception of reality;...
deep level bases from which people generate surface-
level behavior.[15]

Therefore, concludes Marguerite Kraft, worldviews:

Affects how people perceive self, the in-group to which
they belong, outsiders, nature around them and non-
human world...(and) makes it possible for people to
feel comfortable in their environment....Worldview is
a picture of what is and ought to be, and it provides
the motivation for behaviour and gives meaning to the
environment.[16]

It is, indeed, as John Grim puts it:

a story of the world which informs all aspects of life
among a people, giving subsistence practices, artistic
creation, ritual play and military endeavour a significant
content.[17]

Like other aspects of culture, it can be unconsciously learned but
deliberately transmitted. It could become encrusted into customs safe
in the womblike warmth of the sacred egg. But, however resistant to
the battering waves of change, the crusts chip away as the process of
reconfiguration and reconstruction begins.Worldview determines how
a community expreinces and expresses a sense of the supernatural.

One problem in African church historiography is that Western-
trained historians function with Western worldvies and thereby
distort the story of gospel encounters with nonWestern peoples.
Robin Horton argued that though they are large areas of resonance

between Western and African thought patterns, differences persist because of the nature of worldviews; he characterizes a worldview to be like theory- building and, therefore, a

> quest for the unity underlying apparent diversity; for the
> simplicity underlying apparent complexity and for order
> underlying disorder; for the regularity underlying appar-
> ent anomaly.[18]

It does more as it brings into causal relationship wider vistas of reality and everyday life. He demonstrated with the Kalabari world-view, showing that the fears and hopes and religious ardor of the Kalabari could easily be understood by a close look at three basic kinds of forces: ancestors, heroes and water spirits. Appreciating the idiom of their mystical thinking may not only solve the riddle of the primitive mentality which bothered Levy-Bruhl but explain the factors at the mental matrix of the community that help them to survive in their ecosystem. They could link events in the visible, tangible (natural effects) to their antecedents in the same world (natural causes).

Are worldview constructs fantasy? In his study of the theories of the individual and his relationship to society among the Tallensi (Ghana), Meyer Fortes demurs. He takes the multiple soul beliefs of the Tallensi and places them in everyday thought and behavior as a Westerner would link psychological imperatives and sociological imperatives.[19] The activities of gods and spirits celebrated in rituals and in festivals play out in the social space much of the concerns of daily living. This is what Peter Berger calls the cosmization of the social world.[20] It is also palpable that both culture and worldview are not static. Indeed, some have surmised the existence of three publics in African social analysis: the primal setting where the gods of our fathers hold sway, the intrusive Western public, and the emergent public forged in the encounter between the two. Nigeria's Fela Ransome-Kuti, the Afro-jazz maestro, characterizes the emergent public as *shakara,* a hybridized or creolized culture that is neither African nor European. In his album, *Authority Stealing* he explores the moral implications of these cultural shifts, satirizing the noveaux riches who would steal money from the western public and dance to the big drum in the indigenous public. The emergent culture erodes the salient values of the indigenous culture without adequately replacing it, thereby creating tension and indiscipline. This elite class perceives the Western public as other than theirs and behave in a manner that could not be tolerated in the primary public. There is a certain sense of moral anomy. The trouble arises when the same people assume leadership roles in their villages; they become bearers of unwholesome values that, like a virus, destroy the traditional value systems. The palate for American junk culture among the youths in the emergent public puts an enervating pressure on traditional institutions.

The impact of new worldviews within indigenous cultures constitutes one aspect of the task of this chapter. The broader goal is, as J.B.Callicott put it:

> The revival and deliberate construction of environmental
> ethics from the raw materials of indigenous, traditional
> and contemporary cultures.[21]

As argued earlier, to plumb the worldview is to understand the forces that challenge the existence of the church. Leaders derive power from the primal culture to deal with the problems posed by the ecology. The church borrows its idiom from the same fountain to respond and to advocate for a reimagined world. An authentic story of Africa's encounter with gospel must start from a profile of African culture and worldview.

3. ANTHILL IN THE MARSH: THE AFRICAN'S PRECARIOUS VISION OF THE WORLD

It has been argued that underneath the varieties of cultures in Africa is a core worldview structure (illustrated in the diagram). Details may vary even within an ethnic group. Crucial are the concepts of Time and Space. Mircea Eliade has argued that among traditional societies there is a predominant construction of the concept of time around the movement of the agricultural season.[22] Time is cyclical, moving from planting to harvesting, followed by a repeat of the eternal cycle. The myth of eternal return is woven with this fabric. Life follows the pattern of nature, moving from birth through accession to various roles, rights, and duties, and symbolized by membership in one sodality or the other, till death. Matters do not end there; a new stage of living would begin as the personality soul of the individual begins a journey through the spirit world until reincarnation.

To fill in the details: rites of passage celebrate the various stages of life. At birth, the out-dooring ceremony not only provides an opportunity to declare who has returned to the family, it covenants the individual to the land, to the community. Eight days earlier, the child's umbilical cord would have been put in a calabash and sprinkled with herbs and after some pronouncements buried under a tree at the back of the house. The child is rooted to the land with which it shares an everlasting bond. Through open and secret societies, the community would teach the child the salient values and coping mechanisms for harnessing nurture from the ecosystem. In the *isi ji* ceremony among the Afikpo-Edda culture complex, adolescent boys are initiated by sending them off to the bush to fend for themselves without parental aid for weeks. They live off the resources of the ecosystem that are regarded as sufficient for all their needs. They are initiated into the secrets of the natural and symbiotic relationship between them and nature. This is also common among communities on the Zambezi coastland.[23] Among the Biase, Ejagham, and Igbo groups on the banks of the Cross River, the *akang* secret society serves the same function and the initiation ceremony is similar. The *poro*, which enjoys wide provenance in West Africa, contains elements affirming an identical ecological ideology.

The relationship between the child and the ecosystem is reinforced by the creation myth. In spite of variations, the account in the Ifa corpus appears in most: the Supreme Being who delegated some gods to create the earth, gave one of them the task of forming the body from clay. But he himself breathed the soul into human beings. Still another deity was chosen by the unborn child as the guardian of its destiny. In Nigerai,the Igbo call this guardian *chi*, and the Yoruba refer to this as *Ori*. As an Ifa verse puts it:

> *Ori,* I salute you.
> *Ori,* nicknamed atete niran.
> He who first blesses a man before any other orisa
> No divinity blesses a man without the consent of his *Ori.*
> *Ori,* I salute you.
> You allow children to be born alive.
> A person whose sacrifices are accepted by his *Ori* should rejoice.[24]

At a certain point, the individual accedes to decision-making roles, and when death comes the unity of the seen and unseen worlds become clear in the funerary rites. J. S. Mbiti in his *African Religion and Philosophy*, Christian Gaba in his analysis of the *Sacred Utterances and Prayers of Anlo People* (Ghana) have emphasized that the human world is a replica of the spirit world.[25] This explains the ritual of burying a slave alive so that he can continue to serve the achieved person through the journey. For one, people retain the status they had in the human world, for another, passage through the spirit world is referred to as a journey. The return is reincarnation, reserved for those, who lived honest lives and did not die from inexplicable diseases or from lightning-a punishment from the gods for a secret offense. As an *Ifa odu* or verse puts it,all the good things of life that a man has, if he lacks good character, they belong to someone else. The person will not be able to join his earthly family to enjoy the legacy. Even as the personality soul sojourns in the ancestral world, he remains a part of his family, endowed with spiritual powers to aid them more. Thus, the ancestor is referred to as a living dead.

Our interest is not to mine the depths of this worldview but to focus on its core structure with its predominantly religious and ecology-sensitive character. The various names for God reflect His presence in response to the challenges of the ecosystem. Jan Plat-voet has argued that a major trait of African indigenous religions is environmental and cultural concerns; they differ markedly after the specific economic use that a society makes of the food resources of its environment for its livelihood.[26] As Tumai Nyajeka has argued, with data from among the Shona, the circle as a shape can be said to accurately symbolize the nature of the world, defying the search for a beginning and an end and a hierarchical structure. Life is an organic web. The living and the dead are united; the spiritual and the manifest worlds flow together in a circle.[27]

Though there are three dimensions of space, the sky, earth (land and water), and the ancestral worlds are all united. R. S. Rattray in 1927 described the Ashanti world as an alive universe. Indeed, the sky was once very near to the earth. When women who were pounding meals constantly hit the sky with their pestles, the Supreme God lifted the sky a little higher out of their way. Aetiological myths soon yield to historical consciousness in the pursuit of the unity of the cosmos by imbuing each space with powerful forces. The sky gods, usually male, manifest as Sun, Lightning, Thunder, and the like. Among them is the Moon in full beauty, female and inspiring aesthetics, creativity, giving its own light, which evokes songs and dances. Otherwise, the sky gods serve as judges, oracles and arbiters. People swear by them. The Sun carries sacrifices to the Supreme Being above and mediates blessings.

Earth consists of land and water. It is said that after the gods finished creation, forming land out the anthill in the marsh, they stayed back inhabiting various features of the earth-mountains, rocks, rivers, and streams. Land is the heart of the matter. It is under the guardianship of the Earth goddess, whose shrine is prominent in many communities. The Mbari Museum in southeastern Nigeria is, perhaps, the most elaborate in West Africa. Many of the earthen

Table 3.1 – Covenanting Deities: Distribution in Igboland, Nigeria

Nature of Deity	%	CULTURE-AREA DISTRIBUTION										Total
		North	North-E	North-W	West	Ceentral I	Ceentral II	Central III	South	South-W	East	
1. Earth	9.59	3	3	1	·	16	·13	7	12	1	2	59
2. Nature	9.91	14	9	11	1	2	4	5	9	2	4	61
3. Water	21.18	5	12	16	8	10	34	25	10	7	7	134
4. Guardian Patron	12.35	9	5	6	3	6	18	12	8	2	7	76
5. Oracular	2.76	2	2	-	-	2	1	4	3	-	3	17
6. Spirit Force	24.45	14	18	28	6	5	21	3	20	4	32	151
7. Ancestral	18.86	21	8	5	4	15	25	14	14	1	9	116

figures show how the Earth deity nurtures the communities with her fertility. However, she is more revered in subculture theaters with acute land shortage or endowed with significant land features. G. A. Ojo draws attention to the fact that many African communities regard various features of Earth as their protectors and revere them. For some, hills are protectors; thus, people in savannah zones tend to use the hills as shrines for sending messages to the Supreme God. They name their children after the hills. For others, land is so sacred that people swear by her, and her powerful allure is the source of tribalism in politics.[28]

Trees are often reverenced, as they are imbued with spirits. Massive trunks and buttresses, such as silk cotton (Eriodendron orientale), iroko (Chlorophora excelsa), boabab (Andansonia digitata) in deciduous forest areas attract religious ardor. It is believed that the *newboldia laevis* (akoko) is inhabited by mischievous spirits which come as babies but soon return to the spirit world, breaking the hearts of families. Satin wood is found to be useful because it is inhabited by a munificent spirit. The *cordia milleni* is good for making drums and must be inhabited by a musical-minded spirit. Abnormal trees, for instance, a palm tree with seven trunks or with sixteen branches attract dreadful reverence. At Gbarnga, Liberia, a trunk from which the community had harvested firewood suddenly rose again with life inspite of the marks of the axe cuts. The indigenes cordoned it off with palm-fronds, as it was deemed sacred.

Usually there are some specific trees on the road to a village that are alleged to be protectors standing at the gates of communities. Such trees are linked to trees in the market squares. Shrubs or trees in the market are sacred, and communal sacrifices are made at their feet for the well-being of the entire community and to attract the patronage of neighboring villages to that market. Market days are sacred and farming activities are forbidden on those days. Age grades are assigned to sweep and clean the market square; meanwhile taboos hedge the market square as the abode of benevolent spirits. Fighting and stealing are considered heinous crimes. Production, exchange and distribution are sacralized. One District Officer quipped about the West African that:

> the towering vegetation silently growing and overwhelming his huts and cultivation, shutting him in, must have filled him with a sense of awe and impotence and fear.[29]

Little did he realize that the worldview served for conservation ethics to ensure the sustenance and protection of the land.

Just as the marketplace was sacred, so was the farmland. Contact with it was hedged with taboos supervised by various deities under the Earth goddess, for instance:

i.   Communities must perform fertility rituals before land distribution begins.

ii. People must wait for everyone to commence bush clearing before setting fires.

iii. Harvesting may not begin until the yams grown at the fertility deity's shrine have been harvested.

iv. People are prohibited from processing certain kinds of food in the village. Cassava processing must be done outside the village and by the river-possibly for hygienic and health reasons so as to remove the cyanide acid effectively and to protect goats from eating these harmful chemicals.

v.   Sexual intercourse in the bush, especially on farmland, is severely prohibited:for one, it may be illicit; and for another, it is an abomination committed on the face of the Earth goddess.

vi. Fighting and especially threatening someone with a farm implement is prohibited.

vii. People are prohibited from going to any farm to fetch firewood on a market day. This avoids the temptation to steal from another person's property.

viii. The Yam god will kill those who steal from other people's barns or steal from agricultural products heaped on the roadside.

ix. Harvesting another person's hunting trap or fishing trap will incur the wrath of the patron deity, who might evoke the good services of the Thunder or Lightning deity.

These taboos and many more ensure an orderly utilization of nature's resources.The control is left to the gods. For instance, the Yam deity indicates, through a diviner, the areas of the farmland to be farmed each year. Crop rotation and preservation of the soil through fallow is given sacred sanction.

Many animals are protected in a similar manner. Humans are social and relational beings and often sociality involves a high sensitivity to the world of animals, and human relationship with them. This may be inner reality of what anthropologists call totemism when humans recognize their complex, intimate, reciprocal, personal and ambivalent relationship with animals. In some cases, humans recognize a kinship relationship whose roots stretch into the distant past. They perceive certain animals as ancestors. James Frazer who wrote *The Golden* Bough was mystified by the tenedency among hunter-gatherers to venerate and deify animals.Some communities regard the monkey as an embodiment of the ancestors; others as the embodiment of dead twins. In drier parts of tropical Africa, vultures are perceived to be reincarnated ancestors.Pythons and many other animals are revered as totem animals among African communities. People are prohibited from killing such animals. Many African communities recognize that spirits operate in the human world through the following animals, birds, and fishes:

1. Air: (a) birds--owl, crow, vulture, bat;
               (b) insects--fly, bee, soldier ant;
2. Land: (a) lower animals--lizard, tortoise,
                   chameleon, snake;
               (b) higher animals--rat, monkey,dog, cat, leopard,
                   lion, tiger, chicken, and reptiles;
               (c) human being as an embodied being;
3. Water: (a) reptiles:crocodile, water snake;
               (b) fish: electric fish, gold fish.

M. Jackson discussed the attitude to elephants among the Kuranko of the Sierra Leone, where some people claim that they can turn into elephants to take revenge upon their enemies.[30] The interesting aspect is that the category of sacred animals is selected from the three dimensions of space, further imbuing the whole universe with sacred quality.Equally interesting is the attitude towards domestic animals: it is strictly forbidden to kill a pregnant goat or disturb a sheep or a goat during parturation. In some villages, such animals should be tethered and their droppings used for manure in the garden.

    Land is so sacred that it is regarded as the guardian of morality: interpersonal offenses are perceived as pollution of its sanctity; secrecy and covenanting bonds are sealed by swearing by her. In decision-making processes, matters are sealed by knocking the staff of authority on the ground. The Earth and the ancestors unite in creating a theory of obligation in communities where there is no secular theory of obligation. Ancestors are buried in the Earth's womb and libations are used to placate and invoke intervention into human affairs. In certain communities, the chief would occasionally perform a ceremony in which he inquires, through the priest of Earth deity, whether he still enjoys her support. This evaluation exercise keeps the ethics of power from becoming oppressive. Ancestors and the Earth deity are crucial in the social control models--in socialization, restriction, punishment, and reward.[31]

A close taxonomy of deities would show that some communities perceive their waters as daughters of the Earth deity. Spirits inhabit water and rivers that run through long courses have shrines installed at various spots. Ifi Amadiume has provided a rich cameo of this. Marine spirits are usually characterized as female and give wealth, fertility, beauty, and political influence.[32] They inspire musicians and balladiers. Several marine cults feature in ethnographic studies of Africa and bear little repetition. Elaborate festivals are held in honor of rivers that are the protectors of communities. Springs are also hedged with taboos and sacrifices so as to ensure that they neither dry up nor are polluted, and that drought does not plague the people.[33]

A research project entitled, *Gods of our fathers: a taxonomy of Igbo deities*[34] experimented with a methodology for studying worldview, focussing on the names, gender, nature, function, provenance ,sacrifice and gender of the priest of each deity. The assumption is that the worship of deities emanates from the spiritual depth of individuals and communities. The deities were distributed according to subculture theaters. Using a sample of 615 deities, it was possible to show the organic nature of the worldview and how the religious emphases in each culture-area are related to the predominant ecological challenges. For instance, though the Earth deity is said to be so important, she is given less elaborate attention by riverine communities. The culture areas prioritized the seven archetypes according to their needs: oracular, earth, nature, water, guardian/patron, ancestral, and spirit force.[35] It is expected that a similar pattern would be true for the wider African environment. Some communities engaged in long distance trade, and therefore risked their worldview to wider perspectives. In others, secret societies predominated as the guardians of indigenous knowledge; some developed pictographic writing, but the severe ambits of secrecy prevented the skill from developing.

In African communities, there is an emphasis on tapping spiritual forces to facilitate coping abilities. This is because existence is precarious. In one liturgy, the votary gives oblation to both the munificent and the malevolent gods, saying that he came to the world and found them at loggerhead. He is ignorant of the cause but would rather be left out of the controversy. This is easier said than done. According to Ifa texts, the Yoruba believe that there are two pantheons of gods who compete for the domination of the universe. The good gods number four hundred,while the hostile ones are two hundred.Between them and the Supreme Being is Eshu, a capricious deity who can aid or harm, depending on the sacrifice given. It is a cosmos in which the good gods want to bless while the evil ones want to thwart personal and societal goals. This precarious vision induces an ethic of stewardship, caution, and attention to the unity of all creation. The world is a sacred egg; humans weave covenants with the good gods so as to ward off the machinations of the evil gods. A covenantal understanding of this worldview is crucial. Festivals are sacred moments for reenergizing and renewing of the covenants with the gods in the sky, land, water, and ancestral world. Jacob Olupona has examined the political implications in the use of festivals to legitimate the sacralized political order.[36] Taboos hedge the bounds of behavior while the boundary of the sacred and the profane collapses. For Peter Berger the sacred means:

> a quality of mysterious and awesome power, other than man and yet related to him, which is believed to reside in certain objects of experience. This quality may be attributed to natural or artificial objects, to animals or to men...The sacred cosmos is confronted by man as an immensely powerful reality other than himself. Yet this reality addresses itself to him and locates his life in an ultimately meaningful order.[37]

Since this order was created from the anthill in the marsh, darkness ever threatens. Nature is at once nurturing yet mysterious, wild, uncontrollable, and unpredictable. Human beings are hardly the masters. Rae Eleanor pursues the implications of this for gender ideology.[38]

This order requires salient moral values for its maintenance. The Ifa corpus which is found in many parts of West Africa including Nigeria, Benin, Togo and especially among the Yoruba, Fon, Igbo, Edo,and Ewe teaches a number of these including hard work, self-help, good character and maintenance of nature through sacrifice. Sacrifice is the weapon that brings about resolution and tranquility in a universe in which conflict is the order of the day.[39]Ifa teaches deep reverence for nature. Thus, libations, spells, incantations and chants are used as modes of communication. When a herbalist sets out for the forest, he pours libation to the patron deity and,within the forest, he uses chants and incantation, to arouse the healing herbs to draw attention to themselves. He calls them by their secret names and they respond. Efficacy of pharmacopoeia is achieved through ritual. They are addressed as human beings. For instance, the mountain is addressed as:

> The old immortal man on top of a locust bean tree: if the locust bean tree does not fall down, the fat old man will

> not descend there from. Good health and immortality
> are the attributes of the mountain.[40]

Nyajeka, concludes that among the Shona, the cosmology is nonan-
thropocentric but at the same time celebrates as unique the experience of being human in the universe.[41]

In Africa, much of the religious ardor is spent on environmental
matters because as Sara Mvududu shows with data from Zimbabwe,
environmental changes tend to have severe effects on families: de-
afforestation vitiates the energy supply, drought and soil degradation
ruin the food sources, and there are no synthetic alternatives as in
the West.[42] Patterns of spirituality preserve fragile and vulnerable elements in human-nature relationship. As the old priestess said, the
world is like an egg which can easily break; and, if it does, we are
ruined; therefore we regularly give eggs to the gods in sacrifice so that
they may remember and gently preserve us.

4. THE OPEN PREDICAMENT: PRIMAL KNOWLEDGE AND DEVELOPMENT

Inspite of the sacralization of the ecology the question still
remains whether the primal cultures of Africa have promoted healthy
ecological ethics. How do beliefs and ideology influence resource
management? The backdrop is perhaps captured by D.U. Iyam when
he points to three contemporary trends:

i.   the capacity of indigenous practices to manage rural social orga-
      nization has become overwhelmed by the demands of new cul-
      tural elements generated from within and outside the society;
ii.   the resulting reconfiguration of indigenous institutions has ren-
      dered them less effective for communal management;
iii. as a consequence, a weakened array of cultural conventions and
      institutions has become minimally able to influence rural socio-
      economic relations and has created disadvantageous conditions
      for economic growth.[43]

The internal source of the weakening process could be related
to the fact that primal cultures have responded to the challenges of
nature in a vulnerable manner. Vulnerability is the inability to control
one's response to challenges. Does veneration constitute stewardship?
Veneration as a coping mechanism is a vulnerable response that has
not been supplemented with resource management. There has been
little evidence of the ethic of replenishment. The tendency has been
to tap the resources of nature but to leave it to the gods to replenish
the earth. For instance, if one wanted to use satin wood, one would

go to the tree with a pot of palm oil and entice the spirit inhabiting the tree to come down for a meal. During the interval the tricky man would fell the tree. But there was no cult of tree planting. Population pressure and intensification of land use were met with abandonment or resettlement. Thus, new settlements grew up in farmlands;these are usually identifiable by names indicating that they are new out-growths of old settlements. G.D. Stone has therefore contrasted the yeoman with the entrepreneurial attitudes in landuse.[44] Primal ethic was environmental-friendly at the core but lacked sustainability, and this raises the question as to how that ethic can be utilized in a more entrepreneurial manner.

An analysis of the obstacles that indigenous worldviews inflict upon on ecological development would include seven crucial areas:

i.   Environmental changes.Although they are sometimes caused by natural sources, much could be explained by examining the det-rimental effects of intensified and insensitve land use,unplanned habitat structure, road-building, procuring laterite for house construction and other practices that intensify soil leeching. Pol-lution of rivers often caused silting of waterways without the benefit of dredging technology.

ii.   Sociocultural factors. Kinship lineages and landholding patterns could affect availability of arable land for the community. When authority structures were strong, the wisdom of the elders could be harnessed to obviate the obstructionist tendencies.

iii.   Agricultural practices. Bush burning denudes top-soil nutrients and affects the quality of the yield. The lack of storage facili-ties for surplus, and poor distribution networks through fixed market days combine to keep production at a subsistence level.

iv.   Poor infrastructural facilities. Inaccessibility compounds matters for many communities. Lack of adequate healthcare delivery, water supply, and education vitiates opportunities and encour-ages urban migration that spirals into mobilization of a new power node and purveyors of a new worldview.

v.   Gender ideology. Although women are the primary entrepre-neurs, they are constrained by cultural factors from maximizing market opportunities. Patriarchy diminishes the role of men in production and reproduction. Thus, the full labor force is not mobilized; meanwhile the men lose respect and power in their families, which affects the capacity of the political system to mobilize the entire populace towards an identifiable social goal.

vi. Breakdown of social control models caused by emergent values. The growing challenge to traditional beliefs and practices, says Iyam, has resulted in a highly diminished sense of awe and reverence for traditional belief systems.[45] The absence of any visible supernatural retribution as a punishment for violating proscriptive rules has demystified the deities and elders, and many community members have become unwilling to cooperate on locally initiated projects. The power that moves the alive universe is weakening.

vii. Festivals of waste. Certain festivals, especially related to communal ancestral rites, which tend to last for months or even a year, are wasteful in terms of time and material goods because they obstruct capital accumulation.

These obstacles are not barriers; rather, they merely raise what Robin Horton called the open predicament models of configurating closed systems into open ones. It is clear that the so-called closed systems are not closed inflexibly. Much to the contrary, for as primal societies changed so did the highly dynamic and adaptable religions that were unencumbered with fixed canonical scripture. There was a built-in adaptability partially resultant from loose articulation of beliefs and from the fact that certain cults were attached to institutions and sets of social relations and therefore liable to change. Some years ago, an Association of African Earthkeeping Churches was formed in Zimbabwe, committed to healing the groaning creation. The interesting aspect is that it emerged from among the indigenous African churches. These utilize ingredients of African culture in reconstructing the faith.[46] They engage in conservation of wildlife, water, and afforestation by establishing environmental hospitals and dispensaries and by holding tree-planting eucharists. They tap the salient aspects of indigenous knowledge and add the missing element-conscious proactive conservation. They translate indigenous knowledge into the Christian idiom. For development ethics, they suggest listening, learning, and translating. Projects should be fitted into the worldview or scariscape of the community, empowering them to move further with as little disruption as possible into a new level of human development.

We end with the case that we started with: the Amanuke community claimed that their forefathers moved across the Niger and Anambra rivers and settled on a certain spot. The ancestral shrine was built on the southern edge of a large tract of land. By balancing the types of crops, rotation, and the reservation of large tract of virgin forest, the community has managed, for over a century, to keep themselves well-fed. Inaccessibility has protected them. Then came the government with an irrigation project designed to enrich arable land for many communities. One possibility was that as soon as the pumps started to churn, the state could have used the Land Use Decree as basis to declare the entire tract as government property and could parcel out portions to the Amanuke farmers, who would become tenants in their own land. The prospective loss of control soured the offer of assistance, just as the emotional attachment to the shrine was acute. The community's greatest need was not irrigation. They were not resistant to change, indeed, they had built a secondary school at their own cost. The proposed project merely divided the community and left them vulnerable to outside change-agents. Their sense of development was more holistic, recognizing the implication for all areas of their life. It was rooted in their primal belief and experience of the ecosystem. The tension betrayed the gap between the urban elite and the rural opinionmoulders. An eloquent leader soon stirred the community by reminding them of their glorious past and the threat looming in their future. The recitation was electrifying as some of the progovernment councillors were declared to be saboteurs.

Rural communities possess instruments of change that could be tapped for environmental healing and development. Beyond the web of kinship are age-grades, women's societies, and secret societies. These evoke powerful loyalties. When traditional loyalties collapse under the anvil of modernity, these bastions of the rural worldview could still be employed. People dread the losing face which is the penalty for failing to fulfil obligation to one's age-grade. A joking relationship is a powerful instrument for shaming such renegades. The urban elite cannot be easily ignored. The village's Improvement Union has become a modern pressure group. They can serve as the bridge or as the agent or catalyst. They are the priests, sanitizing the emergent culture; or as interpreters of modernity to their root cultures. This informs the title of Wole Sonyinka's novel, *The Interpreters*. He explores their dilemma, too.

5. CONCLUSION: SEEING THE FUTURE THROUGH A REARVIEW MIRROR

The contention here is that though change brings tension – the traditional worldview is embattled- by listening carefully to the calabash of wisdom, the path through the seven obstacles would become apparent; our folktales contain precedents describing the instances when our ancestors went through seven forests to establish thriving communities. This is a call for a sense of transcendence in the midst of a culture of deconstruction; for a directed change and an engineered worldview that does not damage the community. Northrop Frye, the Canadian literary critic, writes that the only guide to the future was a rearview mirror. The challenge for our times is to address the problem of development failure in a new way: by reaching back to our oldest values of community and responsibility, by inspiring a greater respect and stewardship for the land and the resources.

The Amanuke case underscores certain principles for building an alternative development paradigm: (i) self-determination – shaping development strategies from inside rather than from outside the region; (ii) participation- encouraging broad-based involvement of the people in defining and implementing alternative strategies; (iii) self-reliance- building on local structures and capabilities to enable the region to redress its dependence on goods, resources, and assistance from outside the region, (iv) equity- fairly distributing the assets, resources, and other benefits of development among the various social groups, genders, and generations; (v) sustainability- grounding alternative development strategies in a sound, secure environment and in consideration of the local human capacity; (vi)holism- promoting policies that give as much priority to social policy as to economics, and that are attentive to the cultural and political needs of people.

Some measure of resonance in Christian and African worldviews suggests that there is a capacity for practicing a new and salient ethic. For instance, African societies would share the Christian genesis story that in the beginning God made the *oikumene*,the whole inhabited earth, and that His spirit brooded over it as the hen would brood over her eggs. Added to this, is the fact that there are enormous resources within the Christian tradition for developing an environmental-friendly ethic. The structure and promises of the covenant are embedded with the sacral understanding of nature. When misused the earth will cry out and groan for liberation. Ecological disasters become an aspect of social sin, and social sin has catastrophic consequences on the ecological sphere. Poverty has ecological roots in many ways. A sensitive approach to environment, in spite of the misused dominion passage, is by biblical directive.[47] In Africa the matter has immense implications because of the effects of the decline of the agricultural sector of the economy and the increase in health issues. It is estimated by the 1992 World Bank Report that tropical deforestation occurred at the rate of 0.1 % annually during the 1980s in subSahara Africa.[48] There has been a loss of watershed protection, local climatic changes, lost coastal protection and fishing grounds.

Ironically, there is an inverse relationship between environmental protection and reduction of poverty; yet poverty is both a cause and an effect of environmental problems. For instance, the debt burden, the SAP, and the collapse of the economy have made it impossible for African countries to spend on environmental preservation. The population is exposed to diseases. The modernization strategies have caused air, water, and land pollution. The population growth has intensified land use and wrecked the quality of soil and forest. There is, therefore, an acute need to respond to the dire relationship between poverty and environmental degradation and the possibility of achieving development with an environmental-friendly strategy. It is imperative for the church to address these matter directly.

Notes

1. D. U. Iyam, *The Broken Hoe: Cultural Reconfiguration in Biase Southern Nigeria* (Chicago:University of Chicago Press, 1995), 205.

2. Arturo Escobar, "Anthropology and the Development Encounter" *American Ethnologist,* 18, 4 (1991):658-82.

3. C. Ramirez-Faria, *The Origins of Economic Inequality Between Nations*, (Cambridge, Mass: Unwin-Hyman, 1991).

4. E. L. Shiawoya, "Small-Scale Farmers, Local Governments and Traditional Rulers in Agricultural Production" In *The Role of Traditional Rulers and Local Governments in Nigerian Agriculture* eds. A Akinbode et als (Ilorin: ARMTI, 1986).

5. Escobar,"Anthropology and the Development Encounter". .

6. W. Van Geest, "Development and Other Religious Activities," *Together: A Journal of the World Vision Partnership* 55 (July-September, 1997): 1-8.

7. Iyam, The *Broken Hoe,* 7.

8. D. Kinsley, *Ecology and Religion: Ecological Spirituality in Cross Cultural Perspective* (New York: Prentice-Hall, 1995), 212.

9. Iyam, *The Broken Hoe,* 12.

10. (i) Eleanor Rae, Wo*men, The Earth, The Divine*, (Maryknoll, New York: Orbis Books, 1994).

    (ii) R. R. Ruether, *Women, Healing Earth: Third World Women on Ecology, Feminism and Religion,* (Maryknoll, New York: Orbis Books, 1996).

11. O. U. Kalu, "Precarious Vision: The African's Perception of His World" O. U. Kalu, ed., *Readings in_African Humanities* (Enugu: Fourth Dimensions Publishers, 1978), chap. 3.

12. M. G. Kraft, *Worldview and the Communication of the Gospel,* (Pasadena, CA: William Carey Library, 1995), 20.

13. D. G. Mandelbaum, ed.*Selected Writings of Edward Sapir in Language, Culture and Personality* (Berkeley: University of California, 1958), 548.

14. P. G. Hiebert, *Anthropological Insights for Missionaries,* (Grand Rapids, MI: Baker Books, 1985), 46.

15. Charles H. Kraft,, *Christianity with Power,* (Ann Arbor, MI.: Vine Books, 1989), 20, 182.

16. Kraft, *Worldview and the Communication,* 21.

17. M. E. Tucker and J. A. Grim, eds., *Worldview and Ecology* (Lewisburgh,PA: Bucknell University Press, 1993), 42.

18. Robin Horton, *Patterns of Thought in Africa and the West* (Cambridge: Cambridge Universtiy Press, 1993).

19. Meyer Fortes, *The Web of Kinship Among the Tallensi,* (London: Oxford University Press, 1949); *Oedipus and Job in West African Religion* (Cambridge: Cambridge University Press, 1959).

20. Peter Berger, *The Sacred Canopy* (New York: Doubleday, 1967): 24-28.

21. Tucker and Grim, *Worldview and Ecology,* 32.

22. Mircea Eliade, *The Sacred and The Profane: The Nature of Religion* (New York: Harcourt, Brace and Jovanich, 1959).

23. Simon Ottenberg, *Leadership and Authority in an African Society,* (Seattle: University of Washington Press, 1971); see Brian Morris, *Animals and Ancestors:an Ethnography* (Oxford: Oxford International Publishers, 2000), chap. 3 and 4 on rituals of childhood.

24. W. Abimbola, "Ifa – A West African Cosmological System", In *Religion in Africa: The Experience and Expression.* Blakeley, van Beek and Thomson eds., (London: James Currey, 1994): 101-116; see, 112.

25. J. S. Mbiti, *Religion and Philosophy,* (London: Heinemann, 1969); C. Gaba, *Scriptures of an African People* (New York: NOK Publishers, 1974).

26. J. Platvoet, "Religions of Africa in their Historical Order", *The Study of Religions in Africa,* Platvoet, Cox and Olupona, eds., (Cambridge: Roots and Branches, 1996), 46-102, esp. 52.

27. Ruether, *Women, Healing Earth,,* 135.

28. G. J. A. Ojo, *Yoruba Culture: A Geographical Analysis* (London: University of London Press, 1966), 150.

29. Ibid., 106.

30. M. Jackson, *Barawa and the Ways Birds Fly in the Sky* (Washington,DC: Smithsonian Institute Press, 1986); Brian Morris, *The Power of Animals:*

An Ethnography (Oxford: Berg,1998) and his *Animals and Ancestors* (Oxford: Berg, 2000) are based on Malawi.

31. O. U. Kalu, "Gods as Policemen: Religion and Social Control in Igboland", *Religious Plurality in Africa*. Olupona and Nyang eds., (Berlin and New York: Mouton de Gruyter, 1993): 109-131.

32. Ifi Amadiume, *Female Husbands and Male Daughters* (London: Zed Press, 1988); *Re-inventing Africa: Matriarchy, Religion and Culture* (New York: St. Martin's Press, 1998).

33. O. U. Kalu, "Gender Ideology in Igbo Religion"*Africa*, 46, 2 (1991): 184-202.

34. Ibid., *Embattled Gods*, (Trenton: NJ: Africa World Press,2003), chap 2.

35. Ibid.,"Nsibidi, Pictographic Communication in Pre-Colonial Cross River Basin Societies", *Cahiers d'Etudes des Religions Africaines* 12, 23/4 (1978): 97-116.

36. J. K. Olupona, *Kingship, Religion and Rituals in a Nigerian Community*. (Stockholm: Almqvist and Wiksell International, 1991).

37. P. Berger, *Sacred Canopy*, 24.

38. Rae, *Women: The Earth, The Divine*.

39. Abimbola, "Ifa Corpus", 106.

40. Ibid., 115.

41. In Ruether, *Women, The Healing Earth*, 138.

42. *Ibid.*, 143-160.

43. Iyam, *Broken Hoe*, 2.

44. G. D. Stone, *Settlement and Ecology*. (Tuscon,AR: Arizona State University Press, 1996).

45. Iyam, *Broken Hoe*, 209.

46. M.L. Daneel, "African Independent Churches Face the Challenge of Environmental Ethics"*Missionalia* 21, 3 (1993): 311-332.

47. Leornado Boff and Virgil Elizondo, eds., *Ecology and Poverty*. (Maryknoll,NY: Orbis Books, 1995).

48. V. U. James, *Environment and Economic Dilemmas of Developing Countries* (Westport, CT: Praeger, 1994):69-80.

Part II

Poverty and Prayer

Chapter Four
Tools of Hope: Stagnation and Political Theology: 1960-1996

1. UNDERSTANDING POLITICAL THEOLOGY: PROBLEM AND CONTEXT

A human rights advocate from an African country was confronted by a Western supporter with the query; if the African in the street wants democracy, why are there no riots in the streets, mass actions that would drive the dictator away from the seat? The hapless, embarrassed activist tried gamely to explain that many countries in the continent did not experience political transition and decolonization through violence. Then it occurred to him that the real reason might be that the populace has lost interest and become apathetic and hopeless because all the institutions of recourse have been vitiated. The judiciary, the universities, the civil service, the youth, and the debauched politicians have all been corrupted by the dictators. Taming the state may have been easier if only the political class was disciplined and trustworthy. In many countries there are youths paid to mobilize others to hold rallies on behalf of dictators when, ordinarily, this would be the sector of the populace prone to oppose tyranny. The question soon got to the church. What has the church done? The advocate scratched his head and muttered that the complexity would first include the size, number, and types of Christianity in Africa; and second, the varied forms of churchly interventions in the political arena. Here we shall skip the head-scratching and resort to the medieval formula: *ubi Christus ibi ekklesia*, where Christ is, there the church.

The face of Christianity in Africa has changed tremendously through the years. It should, therefore, be useful to look at the political theology of some broad types of Christianity. The first focus will be the mainline churches that arose from the evangelical revival and missionary impulse. There are two core assumptions here: first, that all missionary efforts to Africa failed before the evangelical surge of the nineteenth century. The character and motivation in that surge have received much scholarly commentary and bear no repetition here. The implication is that the contemporary mainline churches are, therefore, products of evangelicalism and exhibit the trends of evangelical political theology. Admittedly, evangelicalism runs in different grooves, producing varied political stances, often affected by the traditions of different countries, and has mutated through time and in response to the challenges of various mission contexts. As applied here, evangelicalism is not a denominational designation but a spirit that pervaded among Roman Catholics as well as among Protestants. It was basically an impulse to share one's faith; it was the engine that moved the modern missionary movement.

Second, the missionary movement of the nineteenth century helped to lay the groundwork for a certain global ideology that bound large areas of the world's people socially, economically, and politically. Indeed, the relationship between Christianity and globalism runs through the quest for catholicity in the early church, as ssen in the ecumenical and missionary movements, in the information on world religions, in the interfaith dialogue; linking young churches to international metropoles and to the struggle for justice. But it is the collusion with the theory of modernization that is our take-off point because the end-products were the slave trade, slavery, culture iconoclasm, radication of the divinity of the market and the crushing debt burden. And so, even as communication and the flow of information become more sophisticated and create a global village, Africa is out of the scene – too poor to afford the costumes for the Halloween party. Africa is the Cinderella of the modern world. The only news from Africa is about war, famine, hunger, refugees, and other disasters. In the midst of the chaos, where is the goodspell? Where is the church? Can its political theology save Africa from the Frankenstein it created? It has been suggested that missionary ideology drank from Enlightenment cistern. This means that a viable African option could only emerge from a critique of that tradition, recovering a more organic perception of institutions in the pursuit of the well-being of the people.

The burden here is to examine the various ways in which the mainline churches have responded to the aftereffects of the rise of the state, poverty, and environmental degradation. How have they reflected critically on the meaning of being a church in these situations and the responsibility to practice justice? It is assumed that religion is an integral dynamic element of any given historical period, at once influenced by the surrounding culture and creatively shaping the sociopolitical and ideological matrix. Even more cogent, when the Ecumenical Association of Third World Theologians (EATWOT) met at Bahia,the communique *The Road to Damascus* severely indicted third world churches:

> We Christians have often been deaf to God's voice and blind to God's presence in the people. We have often been silent instead of denouncing injustices and oppression.(article 44)

Article 62 branded this posture as an aspect of unbelief, idolatry, and heresy defined as selecting some part of the message and rejecting other parts.

The first task here is to clarify an understanding of political theology. Second, we will examine the period, 1960-1985, which was dominated by the theory of modernization. How did the mainline churches perceive and practice political stewardship? Did they serve as tools of hope? At a third remove, the Second Liberation, 1986-1996, witnessed an enlarged political space for Christianity, the strident voice of women theologians, and the explosion of Pentecostal and charismatic spirituality. The responses to poverty, pluralism, and legitimacy crises by the last two phenomena have received less attention than deserved. What manner of political theology do they offer Africa? These are large matters deserving deeper treatment; in two different chapters; so, suffice it here to explore the roles played by the mainline churches in the quest for democratization and wiping away the tears from the faces of the people.

Fourth, in the midst of new forms of ecumenism, has Christianity matured into a civil society capable of mobilizing the people to exercise liberative power and reimagine their socioeconomic order, given the resources of their indigenous knowledge and the power of the Pentecost? According to Elochukwu Uzukwu, is the church in Africa, a listening church, one that reflects critically on the wounded face of Africa and the apparent hopelessness shared by friends and foes?[1] In a recent comparison between Christianity and Islam, Lamin Sanneh argued that Islam tends to take command of prominent centers of public life and from there proceeds to extend its sway over the rest of society. He pointed to comments by Al-Bakri and Ibn Khaldun, who observed that Christianity does not embrace religion as a state idea, and that without the state religious truth lacks the necessary political instrument to establish and maintain itself.[2] And yet Christianity harbors a global view at its core. This ambivalence about politics is imaged in the ambiguous doctrine of Two Kingdoms, one controlled by the sword and the other by the power of the spirit. The boundaries and relationship of one to the other remain unclarified and fraught with conflict and pragmatic adjustments. The ancestry of the idea itself is equally contentious; some point to Paul and others to Luther and to Augustine. Matters became worse with the collapse of the concept of Christendom.

Political theologizing is, however, unavoidable because it is the discourse of our public life and reflects our perception of the meaning of Jesus in the midst of our chaotic conditions. In Africa, the political is beyond what elites do or say but is about the fears and hopes of the common person, the *wananchi*. Indeed, there is a distinction between *selikari*, the state, represented by the wealthy and powerful and *wananchi*,(swahili word meaning, *nonentity*), the world of the marginalized and the excluded. Therefore, reflection on the governance of the polis is a process of discerning of the move of God in changing life circumstances and in the midst of the oppression of the rich against the poor. This means that our focus should not be on the communiques and pronouncements of church leaders on behalf of the institution. These are often for the consumption of foreign allies. Rather, the emphasis should be on the practice of prophetic role by the church.

A definition of the church as the people of God means that the articulation and coping strategies of people constitute the content of political theology in any context. It is a crucial aspect of the theology of life. That is, if theology is human reflection on the relationship of God to human beings and nature (Greek: *oikumene*), much political theologizing is oral, as people invoke the fingers and eyes of the creator onto the events of daily living – either seeking protection from oppressive powers or pleading for God to punish the predators. At the core of the political is power and the allocation of power. The questions of power are: who holds power? For whom? And to what end? Theocratic, erastian (elitist), and democratic conceptions of power have emerged in answer to these questions. They evoke the undergirding ethics of power and the differing understanding of the responsibility of power. At the core, politics and governance are matters of values and morality. The predominantly economic discourse in modernization tends to hide this fact. Timothy Njoya pointed to this in his politically-loaded sermon, which caused an uproar in Nairobi on 5 October,1986:

If human development in economics, politics and education were able to satisfy man in everything without moral values, we Kenyans would by now be free from the crimes of educated lawyers, bankers, judges, clergymen and rulers who are caught breaking the law or stealing money entrusted to them by their clients. In Habbakuk, justice derives from faithfulness to God and to one another and from being satisfied to serve God in one's nation.[3]

And yet, argues Jurgen Moltmann, political theology is not simply political ethics but the political consciousness of theology, designating the environment in which Christian theology should be articulated. It is a hermeneutic category that refuses to repress the historicity of the sociopolitical conditions into privatized religion. Responsible theology must engage in institutional criticism, as it reflects on the place of churches in the life of society. Political theology

> would like to try to interpret the dangerous memory of the messianic message of Christ within the conditions of contemporary society in order to free man practically from the coercions of this society and to prepare the way for the eschatological freedom of the new man.[4]

Implicit in the eschatological message are two aspects. First, a sharp awareness of the idolatory in human systems, economic, and political. This means that the peace the state can give may not necessarily be the peace of God. This ruins the civil religious enterprise, using religion to legitimate political ideology or indulging in the worship of the gods of the state (Greek :*politiken*). We may, however, see the signs of the kingdom in certain structures such as those which promote freedom. Second, the coming of the kingdom for the poor is a much greater attack against the religiously deified state. The political forces are deprived of direct religious justification from above, leaving the poor with the option of reimagining their reality according to the gracious promises of God. Such knowledge is commitment to action as the focus of the Christian life becomes the future of the hopeless.

Thus, the focus returns to infrapolitics, the space in which the subordinates who have been excluded articulate their God-talk on their own conditions and the pretenses of the rulers. For instance, when governments launch the *Operation Feed the Nation* (OFN), the people know the real meaning to be *operation fool the nation*, because the budget would be spent without an increase in food production. As Moltmann also cautions, political theology does not want to dissolve Christian faith into politics nor replace Christianity with humanism.[5] Rather, the commitment is to bring Christians as liberators to the place where they are being waited upon by the crucified one. In the suffering of the wretched ones of the earth Christianity is waiting upon its own and for their presence.

Christian ambivalence to the power of the state is predicated on two aspects of Christian worldview. God not only created the *oikumene* but is involved in its history. Despite the Fall which enabled Satan to cast a pall of control over the *oikumene*, God has, through Christ, and in love initiated the redemption of his creation from the world order (*kosmos*) created by Satan and his cohorts and bedecked with embellishments (*kosmetikos*) that allure, dazzle, and draw people away from the counsel and purposes of God. There is a tension for Christians as to who should be in the world but not of it. Christians should seek to influence her values without being conformed because friendship with the kosmos is enmity with God. This ambience is further confirmed in the New Testament worldview (see diagram) in which eternity has intruded into human history from the birth of Christ. Thus, as the present age (the here-and-now period) is moving to a close, eternity (the not-yet period) enlarges its presence. Eternity also represents God's reign. The resources of the reign of God are here among human beings but its fullness has not completely manifested. Some may interpret this worldview with apolitical, other-worldly emphasis. Others posit the doctrine of two kingdoms, separating the spiritual and worldly concerns. But a theology of engagement or transformation arises from the centre of the gospel. It interprets the presence of the reign of God as an empowerment to share the kingdom resources, to fulfil the messianic hope of justice, and to share the new life that Christ brings through the power of the Holy Spirit. In *The Way of Jesus Christ*, Jurgen Moltmann argued that the Christian focus on conversion should mean turning around, turning from violence to justice, from isolation to community, from death to life.[6]It should be a dissatisfaction with the status quo, a source of judgment on the present world, and the challenge to Christians to participate in the redemptive work of God. There is a keen awareness that while the state could serve some common good, it could also become a domination system under rulers imbued with power from Satan.

However, the focus here is on political praxis rather than on reflective theology precisely because there is a difference between what the Bible prescribes, the church leaders' perceptions of, and how both the sheep and shepherd should live out their faiths in concrete political situations. As De Gruchy has argued, the church, as the people of God, has a mandate to engage in politics for certain purposes, namely, for consensus-building, peace-making, reconciliation;

for nurturing a culture of salient values, of clear social teaching, of challenge to unjust economic policies, and to be a prophetic witness. The church can do these effectively by mobilizing reliable information and expertise, by ecumenical action, and by practising justice within its walls. There is no dearth of theological grounds: creation, liberation, eschatological motifs, the Trinity, *imago Dei*, doctrine of sin, which informs a perception of the state and the individual, a certain understanding of *koinonia* which highlights values of the base community against the divisions of patriarchy and hierarchy. The doctrines of the common good and the covenant of the local context, all these dovetail into a keen awareness of the sovereignty of God, who rules over all the nations of the earth. The relation of the local church to the universal church checks the abuses at the national contexts: First, it requires that the church resists nationalization as much as it resists privatization, and affirm its universality even as it seeks to be critically and creatively engaged in its particular context. Second, the church serves as a means to curb destructive nationalism and national policies which are globally detrimental (such as those relating to the environment); and third,the church serves to protect weak nations from the aggression and from the interference of more powerful nations. The church must work together with the policies and structures of international control mechanisms. [7]

The church, has, throughout history, provided the matrix, analogies, antecedents, key concepts, and practical examples for a wholesome world order – locally and globally. The eschatological message of prophets, their concrete utopianism, their social vision as the *shalom* of God and the perception of the *oikumene* as a relational concept that extends from the fellowship of Christians to the human community are only a few ways in which the Bible has crafted tools of hope for the powerless. The question for the African church,then is whether it possesses the theological conscientization, the capacity for information, tools for combat, and adequate ecumenical and missionary impulse. Could it arise above debilitating poverty and the militarization of society by repressive and predatory state? The dark side of globalization has been the triumph of liberal economics of the market. As the technological and information resources of Europe grow, as the debt burden weighs down African states engendering virulent competition, political instability, and psychological disquiet, people quest for sources that can offer a religion for stabilizing hope.

2. TOOLS OF HOPE: CHRISTIANITY AND THE POLITICS OF MODERNIZATION, 1960-1985

To return to political praxis: even as the firecrackers herald-
ing political independence flared, and nationalism suffused the air,
African understanding of the church's role and relationship with the
state was based on its colonial experience. As Adrian Hastings has
argued the church-state relationship in Africa is complex because
of the size of the continent, the number of European structures
that were reproduced, and the variety of religious groups involved.[8]
Broadly, Islamic-dominated countries, especially in Northern Africa,
tend to operate shariat-controlled states, hostile to other religions.
There are mixed-religious zones such as Nigeria, where Christians
and Moslems form groups large enough to cause much conflict in
the political sphere. There are many countries south of the Sahara
where the competition is between primal religions and Christianity, with the latter in political ascendance. Only in the Republic of
Benin was there an attempt to make voodoo the national religion.
The experiment failed as Soglo lost the election in 1996. It should be
stated that in many African countries votaries of primal religion are
in the majority.

Hastings posits certain determining indices for the type of relationship that might prevail: the size and ecclesiastical organization,
the vertical spread and social quality of the adherents, the inherited
pattern of colonial relationship, theological emphasis and international relations, and such like. For instance, in Anglophone countries,
the Roman Catholics and Anglicans have so much clout (financial,
structural, international) that the state cannot ignore them. This is
the case in Liberia, Ghana, Nigeria, Kenya, Uganda, Zimbabwe,
Zambia, Sierra Leone. In Tanzania, the Lutherans in Malawi, the
Presbyterians in Francophone countries, the Roman Catholics enjoy
similar powers. There is a tendency towards partnership, cooperation, covert competition, and insulation from the raw side of repressive states. Crises do occur but hardly deteriorates to thelevel of Idi
Amin's butchery.

In summary, state-religion structures in Africa break into five
patterns:

i)   Moslem states run with the shariat theocratic laws.
ii)   Mixed states characterized by interventionism and conflict,where
      religion is used as expedient and partisan force. The state is a
      competitor for the moral ground, and its intervention becomes
      an aspect of political conflict.

iii) Socialist states characterized by secularism and conflict. The leviathan national state combats all irrational forces especially organized religion.

iv) Secular state with a Christian bias; noninterventionists against non-Christians, tendency towards coopting religion.

v) Neutral secular state with a liberal democratic tendency, freedom of religion, strictly noninterventionist.

Thus, periodization may be attempted, depending on how the churches have perceived the needs of the people, the society, and the state as an institution: the vestiges of the colonial syndrome dominated the period from 1960-1975 especially as the church attempted to adjust to the growing implosion of the state. The period from 1975-80 was very bumpy because of the large number of military governments and chaotic economies. The period of second liberation, 1985-95, restored many churches to the political center, creating enormous challenges. In spite of the enlarged space, there is some doubt whether a new political theology emerged in any African country outside South Africa during the last decade.

A certain Peter Pan Syndrome or dependency on Western traditions predominated in the African church. Nowhere is this more pervasive as in political theology.[9] Missionaries, in the colonial period, may criticize the state as in Mongo Beti's *Poor Christ of Bomba*; they may be embarrassed by the crudity of traders but the three groups constituted the bastion of civilization-bearers. Fowell Buxton's African Slave Trade and Its Remedy joined them, an unholy trinity who set out for Gold, Glory and God. Internal conflicts may rage but a politics of collusion predominated rooted in shared ideology and, soon, in concession to modernity.

Lamin Sanneh attributes the concession to modernity, criticism, science and good tone to a tradition of enlightened worldliness, typical of the eighteenth century, and based on bland piety, self-satisfied and prosperous reasonableness, honest conviction that churches must after all move with the times. This soon bred the notion of religion as a social ornament. By the imperial era, religion as cultural helix was corkscrewed into official submission, with the cultural coil guiding the religious axis.[10] Sanneh argues that when the church entered confidently and uncritically upon the heritage of its secular captors, it gave up its autonomy as the price for being included in the affairs of state. This, he said, created a peculiar situation, as the church appropriated the national cultural enterprise as a devout vocation.

In Africa, this model, entrenched in the colonial era, continued into independence period because the churches take their cue from their overseas metropoles. For instances, if we look at ecumenical political thought as the index, the pattern of church-state relationships would become palpable. When the International Missionary Conference (IMC)met at Oxford in1937, the dominant perception was a balanced view of the state as a historical reality serving the common good. However, the increasing concentration of power and monopoly as a means of coercion made it potentially an instrument of evil. It was necessary, therefore, to restate that the state is not the ultimate source of law. God is; the state is not a guarantor but servant of justice.When the IMC met in 1948, at Amsterdam, a slight shift focused on *Responsible Society*, where the people would control state power through legitimate, peaceful, reformist changes. They alluded to a number of sustaining chapters and verses of the Bible. These postures meant that in the colonial field, the church devoted itself to charitable institutions and to binding the wounds of those injured by the system. Admittedly, these institutions – schools, hospitals, artisan workshops – served as a means of evangelization and nurtured those elites who carried the nationalist flags. But in the atmosphere of denominational rivalry, the colonial government manipulated the churches effectively as these propagated Victorian mores.

When independence came, many churches devoted their energies to deep-seated collusion, namely, to get their people into power as a protective clout in the competition with other religious bodies. The relationship between mission and nationalism has been debated; so has the supposed support for political independence. The shift of ideological gear may have encouraged the decolonization ideal. Suffice it to say that the church-state relationship in Africa, 1960-1985, shows five patterns:

i)   Ghana and Kenya, where Nkrumah and Kenyatta were consistent in their negative attitude toward Christianity. They did not owe the church any debt of gratitude in their ascendancy to power. Rather, both had the distinction of winning elections when in prison and naturally perceived the colluding church with the same lens as the colonial government.

ii) In Zaire, Cameroon, and Rwanda, the *volte-face* of the new states shocked their religious patrons. This was also the experience in countries such as Angola and Mozambique, where the close contact between the state and the church made the socialists very antagonistic.

iii) The emasculation of the church was worse in Liberia for the American-Liberians who ruled combined the church with the state apparatus. For instance, President WilliamTubman was also the President of the Methodist church; his successor, President Tolbert was the chairman of the Baptist church, his Vice President was the presiding Methodist bishop while the moderator of the Presbyterian church was the chairman of the ruling True Wing Party. As Gifford concluded:

> When one examines the role of the churches in the history of Liberia, a clear picture emerges. Christianity was part of the structures of dominance. Professing Christianity was like speaking formal English – it identified one as belonging to the dominant class. Alongside the True Whig Party and Freemasonry, Christianity was the third pillar on which the whole oppressive structure was built.[11]

iv) In Kamazu Banda's Malawi, the support of his Presbyterians forced the minority Catholics into acquiescence. It was a good case of divide and rule as the Life President installed his Malawi Peoples Congress as the only voice. His repressive measures enjoyed the greatest support in the Nkhono Synod, made up of churches founded by the Dutch Reformed Christian Mission.

v) Zimbabwe represents a case study for churches that had the additional problem of healing the social wounds of guerrilla warfare. Here, the Roman Catholic church, like the World Council of Churches, had a major shift in political praxis and supported Mugabe and the freedom fighters. Meanwhile, Muzorewa compromised the Zimbabwe Christian Council by his moderate attitude to Ian Smith. First,the new government sought to dismantle the support base of Muzorewa especially as his Lutheran church was badly divided. The Anglican church equally reflected the fragmentation of the society. Second, as the internal battle raged between the Shona and the Matabele, between Mugabe and Nkomo, the Protestants became incapable of speaking prophetically because of the ethnic divide. Third, by the mid-1980s most churches found it impossible to resist the government's development ideology. It was only the Roman Catholic church that had the boldness to criticize the repression of Matabeleland in 1982-1983. The NGOization of the church constitutes a fifth model that would become more pervasive in the future.

All the five patterns produced the same effect of enervating the church in the political arena or turning it into a legitimating force. This produced acquiescence for national ideologies which declared that the states were secular states. For instance, in Nigeria, the church supported a constitutional declaration that the country was a secular state while the Moslems protested vehemently. It was not only the permeation of liberalism within churches but that church leaders shared much in common with the political elite – education, lifestyle and views. This *big man* subculture created an intimacy of power and blunted the prophetic witness of the church. The church elites were, as the political elites, ineffective modernist brokers to their people, drawn into the orbit of Western heritage though lacking meaningful roots in it precisely because of the relatively superficial nature of the assimilation.[12] Meanwhile they began to lose contact with their own societies and became like salt that had lost its saltiness. The state grew untrammelled; corruption infested the body politic and injustice paraded at noon.

Between 1966-1971 two crucial shifts occurred: first, the new states removed their gloves and moved to authoritarian models. Socialist ideologies sprouted, attacking church control of education and social welfare and throwing their allies into a spin. In Mozambique, Machel nationalized church properties. Second, as has been argued, in Geneva (1966) and in Uppsala (1968), ecumenical political theology shifted from the reformist base to advocate a redistribution of political power and the pursuit of justice through support of armed guerillas. Tension arose within the World Council of Churches. But the matter was settled in Nairobi 1975. Among Evangelicals (the Lausanne group), political activism such as support for communist-inspired armed resistance caused much disquiet.[13] But among Catholics, Vatican II (1966) was very important in liberating the people of God in the pursuit of the dignity of human life. The debate on liberation theology that sprouted in Latin America pointed to the limits of the openness advocated. In the United States, black theology opened a new front for black activism. The impact of these heady events was more important for Southern Africa than for the rest. Indeed, African theology, which grew horns between 1973 - 19 83 tended to devote its energies to cultural theologizing. The issue of identity was important, but the neglect of the political realities rankled among the blacks under the anvil of apartheid regimes. As an aside, the distance between Geneva and Lausanne in the political stance was reflected in Africa: the mainline Evangelicals such as the Sudan Interior Mission, the Sudan United Mission and the Dutch Reformed Christian Mission and such-like tended to be apolitical in their posture. They engaged in cellular missionary strategy, tracting, radio ministry, ministerial formation, medical and healthcare delivery, and other forms of charitable services. They eschewed heavy investment in West Africa's infrastructure and concentrated on saving souls through strenuous evangelism and espousal of a Scofield-type dispensationalism. The government soon challenged the monopoly of healthcare and radio services by the churches.

However in order to deal with the first crucial shift, the new states in Africa moved to capture the church, to enclave it, and to become a metaphysical state. In their practice of the doctrine of two kingdoms, the state used the edge of the sword to dominate, pretending to be a *defensor fidei* (defender of the faith).This could be could be illustrated with the examples of both Portuguese Angola and Mozambique. It was Portugal's dictator Salazar who adroitly set the ball in motion with the Concordat of 1940, recognizing the Catholic church as the official institution to promote the national and colonial aims of the state in the overseas territories. The state funded the church and, in return, became involved in ecclesiastical appointments. In both Angola and Mozambique, the high profile of the church boomeranged with the success of left-wing revolutions, which ultimately bulldozed both Catholics and Protestants. In Angola, the secretary of the ruling party's central committee, Lucio Lara, declared that any activities that placed faith or religious belief in opposition to the revolutionary transformation of society would be punishable.[14] In many African countries, the political vocabulary borrowed and secularized Christian ones – national redemption, economic salvation, political justification, national regeneration, sanctity of the state, supreme law of the state, political kingdom – indications of the state takeover of religion.

In Ethiopia, the state takeover of the Orthodox church was crucial to its survival in the dark days of Muslim domination of the Maghrib (as described in the first chapter). Emperor Haile Selassie used the Revised Constitution of 1955, the Penal Code of 1957 and Civil Code of 1960 to consolidate the bonds. The emperor became sacred and the *abuna* (archbishop) sat on the Council of Regency and Crown Council. The fall of one meant the collapse of the other, for in 1974 a competing religion, Marxism, won the day. In these matters the rule is that the winner will take all. The statist snake swallowed the others.

In Zaire, the rise of the big elephant, doctor, conqueror, teacher, natural miracle, General Seseko Mobutu, putatively a Christian, augured an attack on the church. His messianic slogans, call to African authenticity combined a virulent nationalism with a religious myth to whip up a major political force. He fooled the emasculated academia to chorus these slogans in their academic journals and kept the church-governmental affairs under orchestrated control.

On the west coast, Ghana's Nkrumah, whom the propagandists declared would never die, pursued the tight-rope walks between liberal democracy and communist socialism. Like Kenyatta, he never disguised his negative feelings toward Christianity. The church came under massive attack as its catechism and creeds were bowdlerized.[15] In the Cameroon, President Ahidjo, a Muslin from the northern region, monopolized powers so completely that the church became silent while the northern minority Muslims had a field day.

In retreat, the churches clamorously voiced some protests, which turned more into moral and ethical discourse and tonurturing their denominational identities. The problem was that nationalists made them appear as votaries of a strange God,as collaborators with fallen imperialists. But in Kenya,the little bird and veteran politician, Oginga Odinga sang that it was *not yet uhuru*(freedom has not come!).

Thomas H. Moore has tried to schematize the pattern of Christian political ethics in Africa. He argued that the cry of the French Revolution for Liberty, Equality, and Fraternity actually derived from Christian roots and hijacked into Western imagination and political thought; that these ideals could be detected in missionary political, and social emphases in Africa. The colonial period witnessed a missionary, concern to offer missionalised cultures some liberties from the dehumanizing elements of their cultures. Moore used the work of James Dennis, which chronicled *Christian Mission and Social Progress* (1897), to buttress the argument that Christianity is a supreme force in the social regeneration and elevation of the human race. Dennis inventoried the rescue operation from forty-nine evils grouped into seven categories, arguing first that there was a shift from early pietism, and then that social policy focused on individual charitable efforts, supplemented by a range of voluntary societies engaged in philanthropy, moral crusades, mass movements of opposition to particular social evils.

Charles Dickens' acerbic wit dealt with this trend in *Bleak House*. But soon, social gospel began to enthrall between 1880-1920s in a desire to reconstruct the whole of society on Christian basis. Admitting the charge of paternalism, social gospel focused on the social structures of inequality as responsible for human misery; but between 1920-1960, such social activism was denounced as a distraction from the proper work of saving souls. In the postmodern period,

Christian political ideology has shifted to the notion of fraternity or interdependent relationships in a pluralistic environment. This is the core of globalism.[16]

The churches in Africa, until recently, subscribed to the reigning ideology of European metropoles without a significant critique. Therefore, their political practice followed two patterns: an emphasis on ethical liberation of believers from primal ethics and social welfare projects; and the occasional challenge on corruption in state exercise of power. The churches in most of Africa failed to appropriate the political resources of the gospel. Rather, they bound wounds, gave education and, through knighting the elite, and issuing declaratory communiques tried to influence the political culture. Yet as Sabar-Friedman has shown with data from the Church of the Province of Kenya (Anglican), the church possessed a wide network and capacity for political subversion. For instance, the CPK had urban church councils, church armies, information boards, a Protestant Medical Association, diocesan mission associations, a Mothers' Union, an Anglican youth organizations, parishes, and village churches. She concluded that without entering the arena as a political party, these structures and services could transform the CPK from a purely religious body to an extraparliamentary institution that would seek to cater to the basic needs of Kenyan society politically.[17] The same could be said for other church bodies, especially the Roman Catholic church whose NGOs included, Pax Christi, Caritas, Justice and Peace, and CIDSE.

The silence of the churches allowed the political leadership to define politics and the meaning of political involvement as well as the legitimate modalities of both the exercise and limits of power. The notion of the church as the conscience of the society was overawed by the implosion of the autocratic state until the 1980s in Kenya. Arap Moi succeeded in limiting the scope of political discourse and defined and enforced an ever narrowing realm of politics.

A qualifier exists because in some countries, individuals and certain denominations sometimes shocked the state with trenchant criticism that was unexpected and disarming. In Mozambique, various pastoral letters criticized the socialist state in a country where people were very attached to the church. Indeed, the opposition, RENAMO, hid under the cassock of the church. Similarly, in Kenya, there was a shift from attacking the corruption of the state operators to challenging the legitimacy of the one-party structure in the mid-1980s. John Pobee has traced the united voice of the church against

Ghana's regimes,from Nkrumah to Rawlings.[18] In 1972, Catholic
bishops in Tanzania published *Peace and Mutual Understanding* as
a critique of Ujamaa and humanistic socialism.It was obvious that
Nyerere wanted to improve the lot of the peasants, and wanted to
design a political strucure and culture derived from African worldview and roots. But it was equally obvious that his enforced Ujamaa
program was being resisted at the grassroots by peasants because it
flouted core traditional values such as a religious attachment to the
land of one's birth where the umblical cord is buried. James Scott
used Nyerere's dilemma to theorize on the clash between indigenous
values and *thinking like a modern state*. Nyerere was *seeing like a
state*[19].Instead of establishing cooperation at the village level, he gave
the famous order that everybody must be villagized. Some say that he
immitated the Israeli's kibbutz model overriding all the anthropolgi-
cal and environmental research on Tanzania.Similarly, church resistance in Zambia against Marxist ideology was considerable between
1976-1982. In some countries, Nigeria, for example,secularist
Human rights groups emerged in the 1980s; the problem was how to
arouse the churches to cooperate with these groups. In most places,
the forces of ethnicity, religion, fear, and the militarization of the
society fragmented the opposition and created niches that dictators
exploited with ease. But gradually, the legitimacy crises created a void
in the political arena.

3.TAMING THE PREDATORS: MAINLINE CHURCHES AND THE SECOND LIBERATION OF AFRICA, 1986-1996

Both Paul Gifford and Kwame Bediako observed rightly that in
the 1980s, there was a noticeable enlargement of the political field
for religious leaders in Africa. The backdrop, as has been argued,
is that the World Bank/IMF decided to align political freedom to
economic policy in the wake of the collapse of Soviet Union in the
1980s. Moreover, the constraints of the cold war and the attendant
competition vanished. Readjustment of international relations with
the Third World could be safely prosecuted without former caution.
As the French President Francois Mitterand declared his support
at La Baule, in 1990, linking aids to democratization, conferences
started in Africa to oust dictators and to pour hot ashes on their
heads. Political associations proliferated: 250 emerged in Zaire, 100
in Congo, 68 in Cameroon, 25 in Burkina Faso, 33 in Nigeria, and
so on. Leaders started to manoeuver in the whirlpool. Some lost;
others manipulated votes (in Cameroon, Togo). Paul Biya, the Cam-

eroun dictator,was reelected over Ni John Fru Ndi by a slight margin
of 119,000 votes. Foreign observers declared the election rigged. In
Zaire, Mobutu held tight until 1996; in Nigeria the military played
a sleight of hand; and in Rwanda, Burundi, and Somalia, civil wars
broke out. In Ghana, Rawlings changed his stripes, a trick that he
learnt from Sergeant Doe of Liberia, and that the leader of Gambia
successfully emulated.

In these conferences and crises, church leaders played major
roles in Togo, Benin, Gabon, Congo, Ghana, Nigeria, Liberia,
Kenya, South Africa, Madagascar, Zaire, Malawi, Zambia, Rwanda,
and Tanzania. Before 1990 there were ten multiparty states in Africa.
Between 1991-1993, twenty-two more states joined. However, at
issue is whether the enlarged role was a function of a new political
theology or whether circumstances foisted the onus on the church.
Nevertheless,the potential role of the church has always been
acknowledged. Mwai Kibaki, then minister of education, Kenya,
told the National Council of Churches in Kenya (NCCK) that:

> A modern church is expected to be outspoken because
> other groups in society must be cautions. We must have
> at least some organization which speaks up for the right
> of the men regardless of what happens tomorrow...an
> active organization which speaks for our problems which
> we face today. I cannot think of any other organization
> or better placed than the church to play the role.[20]

As repression decimated civil society, little did the state realize
that it was playing into the hands of its age-old competitor. The
church was the only institution to which people could turn. In
Mozambique, as soon as the accord was signed between the Frelimo
and Renamo (brokered completely by the church), many churches
mediated the reconciliation process. The churches began to serve as
agencies for rehabilitation or healing the social wounds of the war.
This is called the NGOization of the church. As Western powers
either distrusted official state or, in opposition, wanted to mount
pressure on them by establishing alternative groups, church leaders,
in spite of their previous records of lackluster politics, became veritable agencies for intervention. They served as good covers for the
pretense that the democratization programs were home-grown. As
large international church organizations such as the WCC or the
Vatican mobilized to aid democratization, their churches become
NGOized. The marginalization of churches in the earlier period gave
them fresh, untainted public image.

Paul Gifford also drew attention to the dark side effects: as governments try to coopt mainline churches, their image in the public eye may be compromised. The elitist big- man model of leadership might intensify in the church thereby creating a gap in social perception. The problem of credulity looms large. The career of Archbishop Okogie in Nigeria is one sad example of the danger that lurks in the new dispensation. The Nigerian government spread the rumor that it had paid the cleric's medical bills in a foreign country. Similar examples come from Tolbert's Liberia and Mobutu's Zaire, where there were deliberate efforts to compromise the church.

The most glaring example is, perhaps, the Catholic church in Rwanda. Ian Linden stressed the strength of the church and argued that it was much rooted in Rwandese society. It was certainly the biggest economic force in the country after the state and, therefore, a visible actor on the political scene during the early 1990s. When a church such as the Catholic church exercises extensive power in all sectors of society and all over the country in the social, political, and economic realms, it will tend to elicit a response in which people maintain a mere institutional link, while lacking any intensive power. The Catholic church in Rwanda-Urundi suffered this syndrome. Indeed,it became so implicated in the ethnic and political conflict that by the end of 1994, the priestly cadre was split. It was not only that many priests had been killed, or that the church building (e.g., at Kigali) was the scene of the ugliest massacre ;but that in fact, the group known as Africa Rights produced reports to show that a Catholic priest was involved in the Hutu slaughter of the Tutsi. The collusion of the church hierarchy with French and Belgian authorities has become a sore point as the Vatican struggles to retrieve a modicum of credibility for the church in Rwanda. Matters have not been eased by the squabble between the priests who stayed and those who went into the refugee camps with the people. Thus, the success of yesteryears first threw the church into the hot waters of national politics and scalded it into coma. Virtually all commentators accuse the Roman Catholic church of being responsible for manufacturing ethnicity in a community where people traced their ancestry to the same eponymous progenitor.[21]

However, there is little doubt that the mainline churches possess enormous clout due to longevity, evangelization with social and charitable institutions, some period of control of education, and close contact with ruling groups unless when ideologically at polar ends. Their declarations could influence ethos, their pulpits could be used to educate the members about particular issues. Church lobby or pressure- group tactics could be quite effective. Churches have been known either to support particular candidates for office or even to become a democratic political party. Civil disobedience and participation in revolution are exemplified in the careers of some churches in Africa. The Lutherans in Namibia were solidly behind the mobilization of support for the liberation fighters, the SWAPO.

A certain pattern appeared in the responses of the church to the state in the 1990s:

i)   In some places, as in Malawi, one denomination bit the bullet and initiated the attack on the predatory state.

ii) In others, an individual churchman would catalyze the change process. Such was the case of the Camerounian Baptist minister Simon Bolivar Njami who wrote Biya a candid letter dated 30 August 1983.

iii) Christian ecumenical groups mobilized in Benin, Nigeria, Mozambique, and Kenya, to name but a few, to pursue the democratic cause.

iv) Pluralistic, interfaith groups also sprouted in the heat of the struggle in Kenya and Malawi.

iv) Pentecostal/Evangelical groups who saw great openings for social activism in former socialist countries intensified their activities in Guinea, Sudan, Angola, and Mozambique.

These patterns are not ironclad; much to the contrary, as a case would start with one pattern and slide through a number of other configurations. For instance, in Malawi, the Roman Catholic Bishops' Pastoral Letter that called for a multiparty system in Lent 1992, shocked both the ruling party and the Life President. The official reaction was to mobilize the goodwill of the Protestants against the Catholics, especially against Bishop John Roche. But the Presbyterians demurred and by October, the Public Affairs Committee emerged as an ecumenical organization. Other faiths joined, and the committee became a multifaith pressure group.[22]

Two cases from Kenya and South Africa further buttress these claims. First is the data from Kenya. Recent studies have focused on the role of the Church of the Province of Kenya (Anglican, CPK). It was the official church of British colonial power and enjoyed a relatively privileged position buttressed by a physical presence in people's everyday life. It acquired a powerful material base and a tremendous organizational capacity. Even when Bishop Henry Okullu in his *Church and Politics in East Africa* (1974) advocated a democratic power structure, the official theology still prescribed a constructive collaboration with the powers that rule. Controversy surfaced more visibly under Arap Moi in 1982 after the coup attempt. A coercive centralizing process began. Repressive state surveillance and crack-downs followed apace. Varied forms of popular protest emerged among the *wananchi,*but Moi insisted on destroying all forms of opposition. As he warned in 1984:

> I call on all ministers, assistant ministers and every other person to sing like parrots...If I put a full stop, you should also put a full stop. This is how this country will move forward.[23]

Moi claimed to have played this role under his mentor Mzee Jomo Kenyatta. This is how willy-nilly the onus of opposition was foisted upon the church. Matters started with Dr. Timothy Njoya's sermons, which saw corruption as only the leaves of a tree; the roots were in the lack of salient values in the political culture.The preda-tory power structure was invested in a one-party system. He called for its dismantling. Officials responded with wild hostility. Nairobi's daily newspaper Weekly Review, blazoned a front-pager, *Njoya at it again* (January 12, 1990):

> Faced with Njoya's unprecedented assault, senior gov-ernment and KANU leaders nationwide, led by the Vice-President, Professor George Saitoti, sprung to the defence of the one-party system, arguing that it cannot be reasonably compared with the crumbling totalitarian-ism in Eastern Europe. It is a reflection of officialdom's current mood that the minister of Livestock Develop-ment, Elijah Mwangale, demanded that those who make statements such as Njoya's, even from the pulpit should be detained without trial.

The Presbyterian Church warned against the use of pulpits for politi-cal motives. Pulpits are for goodnews, obviously construed as unal-loyed support for the President. More sermons followed and it was the President's turn to respond. According to another daily newspa-per *Kenya Times* (9 May 1991):

> President Moi yesterday criticized Dr Timothy Njoya, saying the churchman was inciting the public against the government so that if he is arrested he can attract sympathy abroad by claiming that Christians are being persecuted. He said that anti-government elements were hiding behind the human rights masks and he said the government would not spare them. Religious leaders

> should be on the forefront of upholding the law...Would
> more parties bring more economic development in
> the country? Will they give Kenyans more food, better
> schools and health? Political pluralism would breed more
> tribalism and sectionalism in the country.

Countering the redherring of tribalism, Njoya declared that God created tribes in His infinite wisdom, and that there was nothing wrong with tribes; what mattered was whether power was wielded in such a manner as to ensure the healthy development of all tribes. Parliament collectively jumped to its feet to debate the sermon and to chorus the sentiments of the President. An enthusiastic assistant minister for Public Works, Ngumbu Njuriri, revealed to Parliament that Njoya comes from a family with a history of mental problems. This was said inspite of the fact that Njoya received a doctorate degree from Princeton! At this point, the Moderator of the Presbyterian church summoned Njoya, and after an abusive confrontation announced that Njoya has been defrocked. The Member of Parliament for Mbooni constituency thanked the Presbyterian Church of East Africa for defrocking the prelate.

Many factors explain this attention to Njoya's case. It betrays the political culture that shields the ruler with the sycophant political class. Insulated, he can use a personalized, clientele system in vitiating moral imperatives in the exercise of power. The role of the Presbyterian church is instructive. It abandoned its minister with a doctrine of obedience to political authority. Old habits and the chains of bondage kept the church intolerant of criticism against the political dictator. The real issues in the political whirlpool became clearer. It was not just corruption. Central were a critique of the structure of power, advocating a shift from one-party to a multisystem polity and the politics of transition, which raised to the fore the issue of pauperization, the byproduct of Structural Adjustment Program. Other church bodies woke up to the danger to the public weal. This is where the huge resources of the Anglicans became important, especially the role of Dr. David Gitari,the bishop of Kirinyaga. Equally interesting is that while the president was declaring the Christian Council as enemy number One, other Christian bodies such as the Roman Catholic church joined the affray and nonChristians weighed in anchor into a multifaith protest body. A mass movement formed in response to the economic hardship. As President Moi anticipated, the opposition sought assistance from foreign countries including Canada. Space constrains the rest of the analysis of the contours of public debate till the formation of a multiparty structure in Kenya.

The roles of the ruling elite, the press, the fact of ethnicity combined to complicate the scene. Gitari's sermons, *In Season and Out of Season: Sermons to a Nation* serve as examples of homiletical form of doing political theology. It is a strategy made famous by South Africans such as Desmond Tutu and Allan Boesak, whose resp[ective works *The Finger of God* and *Walking On Thorns* stimulated much political passion through the decades of the 1970s – 1980s. Between 1991-1993, the NCCK produced eleven books, raising the issues of the debt yoke (1991), women and voting (1992), responsible citizenship, economic justice, the challenges of democratic governance quest for democracy, a voting handbook, a new Parliamentary agenda, the proceedings of the Workshop on Structural Adjustment and the multiparty electoral processes (1993). The argument here is that the use of public enlightenment on such a widescale enabled the mobilization of the church's counterpower. Information is a crucial tool. In the end, however, ethnic conflicts within the churches and political immaturity complicated the squabble among the opposition to give Moi two opportunities to retain power in the changed circumstances.

Explanations of the transformation of Christian political praxis refer to the growth of Christianity in contemporary Africa and the emergence of a new political ethos of engagement. The pressures of the times and the lack of a viable alternative cannot be ignored. Gifford argues another source, namely, that in Africa, Christian involvement in development is enormous not just in traditional areas of schools and hospitals but in digging wells, housing projects, farming or weaving cooperatives and emanates from a certain understanding of the meaning of salvation.[24] In countries hit by drought or civil war, local churches were involved with projects designed to assist displaced people or former refugees to rebuild. Quite often these churches lacked adequate resources and are by-passed by NGOs which tend to work independently, prescribing for the people what they believed is good for them. It may therefore be argued that in spite of obvious lack of political conscientization, the same church that the state treated with the carrot and the stick sometimes found itself as the only institution that could give voice to the cry of the people. It was not because many of them had not compromised and lived the same life as the elite; it was not because they practiced democracy in their internal affairs. Indeed, it is doubted that many churches are educating their people on the politics of transition. Many have no informed response to the problems of poverty and environmental degradation. Overseas aid agencies work with much frustration to inspire local churches to be more caring. Human rights and other social activist projects in many churches are inspired and funded from outside. This raises ideological problems that will surface in the future. After all, the problem of selfhood and aid was the staple diet of missiological discourse in the early 1970s after colonial bouts of philanthropy. It created an identity crisis that led to debates on indigenization and moratorium.

It was only in South Africa where the church could articulate and practice a viable political theology. For others, their protests were often as the noise of cans tied to the tail of a cat. The centrality of political theology in this region is historical. The Boers evoked biblical metaphors of power and covenant in the process of land-grabbing and in the conquest of Africa, adding their survival from perfidious Albion, the English. Assiduous church-going and theological legitimation of apartheid succoured them to the modern period.

Their victims also took to the Christian high road as Ethiopianism gave a cultural nationalist interpretation to black hopes in the nineteenth century. The African Americans who evangelized Southern Africa till the 1920s provided the taproot to black Christian response and evoked a white onslaught. Black response to white political Protestantism grew into a pneumatic groundswell – the Bantu prophets. Zionism was a quest for belonging, a spiritual survival strategy. It played a crucial role in the political expression of unresolved issues, ill-concealed by the fabric of normal politics and not articulated by political institutions.[25] But as Lyn Graybill has argued, there were at least four Christian political theologies articulated with religious rhetoric and fervor – the universal vision of Luthuli and the African national Congress (ANC); the antiwhite position of Sobukwe and the Pan African Congress (PAC); the black theology of Steve Biko and the Black Consciousness Movement (BCM); and the nonviolent ideology of Desmond Tutu and the United Democratic Front (UDC). Albert Luthuli and Desmond Tutu's position emerged from a prophetic/transcendent view of Christianity in that they perceived a central message in the Bible, which the doctrine of apartheid violated. Albert, Sobukwe, and Biko perceived Christianity as utilitarian instrument, to harness the ultimate for one's immediate purpose. Biko was quite impressed by the violent reaction of Jesus to those who trafficked in money – the image of the oppressor – in His Father's house. This incident

> shifts the emphasis from petty sins – stealing food when hungry, working without a pass, lying to the police – to the major sin – allowing an evil system to exist.[26]

Christianity is relevant only when applicable to people when it has meaning for them in their given situation. This prophetic posture saw Christianity as an instrument of change and differed from the priestly ideology of those whites who used Christianity to sanctify the exclusivist position of the government.

The final stretch of the march against apartheid was character-ized by ambiguity, as various forms of Christian political theologies clashed. At one level was reformed protestant theology used by Afri-kaners to build a quasi-theocracy characterized by much spiritually and politically conservative ideals and ideas. Opposed to it was the liberationist theology fed by both Latin American liberation theol-ogy and Black theology of the African Americans. Black theology raised a new hermeneutic and an alternative vision that empowers the reversal of the conservative alliance of the church with the domi-nant powers and for the identification of the mission of the church with those involved in a revolutionary struggle against oppression. As Boesak put it

> the work of Christ and his kingdom is discernible in the
> secular, social and political revolutions of our time, and
> that the Church's function is to discern and to witness
> to it and to participate in God's work in a changing
> world.[27]

At the root of this theology are first, the shift from the modern-ization theory to the underdevelopment theorization of the African condition; second, the impetus of liberal theology in the West with an emphasis on activist/engagement in issues of social justice and a new economic order. As liberal theology and neoMarxist analysis tangoed; a conservative, evangelical Protestant theology rose in opposition. They have been stigmatized as fundamentalists or better known as either American Religious Right or The Moral Majority. Studies of the implosion of this political ideology into Africa tend to portray them as agents of American geopolitical and economic interests in Africa.[28] They are seen as a deliberate effort to rescue embattled South African whites and as a counterinsurgence to Black theology and to the World Council of Churches' influence and support for freedom fighters. Karla Poewe and Hexham have disagreed very strongly from their own data from South Africa.[29] Ian Linden's review of Gifford's *New Crusaders* made the salient point that in spite of the ideology of conservative political theology of the American evangelicals and charismatics, it cannot be said that American intelligence officers deliberately fostered this form of religiosity in Africa.

However, Gifford's concern was about the persistence of ideological religion which legitimates the existing social order, defends the dominant values, enhances the authority of the dominant group and preserves the existing social order. He contrasted this with the concrete utopian counterpart that reveals the limitations of the existing order, questions and challenges the authority of the dominant group and their values, and seeks to improve the cause of the vulnerable poor. This political theology suffused the *Kairos Document*, a key catalyst of revolutionary Christian posture in the South African saga.

South Africa, in the postapartheid context, is unique by encrusting a cardinal Christian principle in the business of governance. The Truth and Reconciliation Commission may encounter enormous problems from various constituencies but posits the paradigm of confession, forgiveness, and reconciliation as essential for healing social wounds. It is an affirmation that underpinning the political sphere is a moral order and principle. Robert Schreiter, has brought this out most clearly. First, he differentiates between conflict resolution (requiring administrative skill by a facilitator) and reconciliation. Reconciliation is a spiritual process that includes forgiveness and repentance. Reconciliation is grounded in profound experiences of consciousness-raising and social transformation. Second, it demands that people are willing to re-read their history and redefine their identity, a process that makes them confront the wounds received and the wounds inflicted, recognize the narrative of the lie in their past, and directs them to practice forgiveness, repentance, and restitution. Third, reconciliation transforms all parties involved; it resituates them in the world, it modifies their power relations, it renews their social identities, and it enables them to tell the history of their interrelations, freed from the lie in a common story acceptable to all.[30]

To those who ask, where is justice if those who killed Steve Biko are given amnesty?, the answer is in the profound fact that they have come out to confess. As Donald Shriver has argued, the classical age had long recognized that justice alone is not sufficient to assure social peace in the city. It may create resentment in some sector and future conflict. City judges resorted to amnesty and to other forms of absolution. This is the true meaning of shalom.[31] There is a haunting jingle that punctuates television programs in Pretoria: *Si-mu-nye-e-e,* We are one!. *Simunye* is a Zulu word breathing the hope for the future, anxious for the return of love for one nation.

Finally, the 1990s has witnessed a pulsating urge to move the church into the void in the political space as both the predatory spite and debauched political class have bred cynicism. The Christian Association of Nigeria is an example of how a certain ecumenism has become imperative in the face of these forces as well as world-wide Islamic resurgence. The Circle of Concerned African Women Theologians has also enlarged its activities; not as feminists in the Western tradition, but in order to bring women's voice to the issues of the political sphere. Certain groups among the African Independent Churches, especially in Southern Africa, are pointing the way to a Christian response to ecological issues that are central to human survival. They are still providing the succour and community but the rise of Pentecostals has introduced new elements.

The political space is now filled with religious actors of various hues. A new Christian political theology of engagement has emerged, providing spiritual tools of hope. It neither ignores the African's worldview nor our needs; it confronts the unwholesome spirits behind the demonic structures created by those who have poured ashes on our faces. These matters will be pursued in the next chapters. Suffice it to say that the rise of charismatic movements within the church will soon create a need to connect spiritual renewal and radical politics and to source the power of the gospel in creating new human beings. There is an obvious need for the church in Africa to reflect and to act on the moral roots of a modernization model of development and to be a church that is sensitive to the poor. Such sensitivity is not measured in charitable activities but in being,doing, and saying prophetically in contending with the undergirding values in the exercise of power.[32] Only a prophetic church that is spiritual and alive could serve as a tool of hope amidst the political stagnation that has befallen Africa.

Notes

1. Elochukwu E. Uzukwu, *A Listening Church: Autonomy and Communion in African Churches*. (Maryknoll, NY: Orbis Books, 1996), 2.

2. Lamin Sanneh, *Piety and Power: Muslims and Christians in West Africa*. (Maryknoll,NY: Orbis, 1996), 10-13.

3. Timothy Njoya, *Out of Silence: A Collection of Sermons* (Nairobi, Kenya: Beyond Magazine, 1987), 64.

4. Jurgen Moltmann, "Political Theology" *Theology Today*, 28, 1. (April 1971): 6-23, esp. 8.

5. *Ibid.*, 22-23.

6. Jurgen Moltmann, *The Way of Jesus Christ: Christology in Messianic Dimensions* (London: SCM Press, 1990), 102.

7. J. W. De Gruchy, *Christianity and Democracy* (Cambridge: Cambridge University Press, 1995), 262-63.

8. Adrian Hastings, *History of African Christianity,1950-1975* (Cambridge, Cambridge University Press, 1979); *The Faces of God: Reflections on Church and Society* (Maryknoll, NY: Orbis Books, 1976); *The Church in Africa, 1450-1950.* (Oxford: Clarendon Press, 1994); "The Churches and Democracy: Reviewing a Relationship." *The Christian Churches and the Democratization of Africa.* ed. P. Gifford (Leiden, E. J. Brill, 1995): 36-46.

9. O. U. Kalu, "Peter Pan Syndrome: Church Aid and Selfhood in Africa" *Missiology.* 3, 1 (1975): 15-29;

   "Theological Ethics and Development in an African Context" *Missiology*, 4, 4 (1976): 455-464.

10. Sanneh, *Piety and Power*, 132-135.

11. Paul Gifford, *Christianity in Doe's Liberia* (Cambridge:Cambridge University Press, 1993), 57.

12. Sanneh, *Piety and Power*, 95.

13. V. R. Stevernagel, "Social Concerns and Evangelization: The Journey of the Lausanne Movement" *International Bulletin of Missionary Research* 15, (1991): 53-6.

14. Alex Vines and Ken Wilson, "Churches and the Peace Process in Mozambique"*Christianity and the Democratization of Africa* ed.Paul Gifford(Leiden: E.J.Brill,1995):130-147 show the limits of the concordat, the inefficient nationalization, and the dire consequences for FRELIMO;K. W. Henderson*, The Church in Angola: A River of Many Currents* (Cleveland TN: The Pilgrim Press,1992)

15. See, John Pobee, *Religion and Politics in Ghana* (Accra: Asempa Publishers, 1991).

16. T. H. Moore, "Human Rights and Christian Missions in the Emerging Global Culture",*Missiology*, 24, 2 (April, 1996): 201-22. Bebbington disagrees with Moore; see his contribution in G. A. Rawlyk and M. Noll, eds., *Amazing Grace.* (Montreal: McGill-Queen's University Press, 1995), 195.

17. G. Sabar-Friedman, "Politics and Power in the Kenyan Public Discourse and Recent Events: The Church of the Province of Kenya" *Canadian Journal of African Studies*, 29, 2 (1995): 429-453.

18. John Pobee, *Religion and Politics in Ghana* (Accra: Asemga Press, 1991).

19. James C.Scott, *Seeing Like a State* (New Haven,CT:Yale University Press,1998).

20. Paul Gifford, ed., *The Christian Churches and the Democratization of Africa* (Leiden: E.J. Brill, 1995);Sabar-Friedman, "Politics and Power in the Kenyan Public Discourse", *Canadian Journal ofAfrican Studies*, 29, 2,(1995), 434; Kwame Bediako, *Christianity in Africa* (Edinburgh: Edinbrugh University Press, 1995).

21. Timothy Paul Longman, "Christianity and Democratisation in Rwanda: Assessing Churches Responses to Political Crises in the 1990's", Gifford, *Christianity and Democratization*: 188-204; S. Van Hoyweghen, "The Disintegration of the Catholic Church of Rwanda: A Study of the Fragmentation of Politics and Religious Authority" *African Affairs* 95, 380 (July 1996): 379-401.

    Frank Chalk, "Genocide in the Twentieth Century", Symposium on 20th Century Genocides, McGill University, 2 April 1997; Gerald van ,t Spijer, "Are Missions and Churches Responsible for the Rwandese Genocide?", Yale-Endinburgh Seminar, New Haven, Yale Divinity School, 5 June 1997;Charles Deogratsias, "The Rwandan Tragedy and Future Prospects", Seminar on African Christianity, Wycliffe College, Unversity of Toronto, 6 March, 1998; Hugh McCullum, The *Angels Have Left Us: The Rwanda Tragedy and the Churches*. (Geneva: WCC, 1995); Ian Linden, *The Church and Revolution in Rwanda*. (Manchester: Manchester University Press,1977).

22. J. C. Chakanza, "The Pro-Democracy Movement in Malawi: The Catholic Church's Contribution, 1960-1992", *Religion in Malawi*, 4 (1994), 8 ff; K. R. Ross, *God, People and Power in Malawi* (Blantyre: Christian Literature Association in Malawi, 1996).

23. Sabar-Friedman,"Politics and Power," (1995), 432.

24. Paul Gifford, *The New Crusaders*. (London: Pluto Press, 1991).

25. Jeff Haynes, *Religion in Third World Politics* (Boulder, CO: Lynne Rienner Publishers, 1994), 27.

26. Lyn Graybill, *Religion and Resistance Politics in South Africa* (Westport, CT: Praeger, 1995), 87, 91.

27. Allan Boesak, *Black Theology, Black Power*. (London, 1978), 83.

28. Sara Diamond, *Spiritual Warfare: The Politics of the Christian Right* (Boston, MA: South End Press, 1989); J. Marishane," Prayer, Profit and Power: US Religious Right and Foreign Policy" Review of African Political Economy 52, (1991): 73-77; Paul Gifford, "Christian Fundamentalism and Development in Africa" Ibid., 9-20; The entire

November issue of *ROAPE*, 52 is devoted to the theme and contains Ian Linden's review of Gifford's *New Crusaders*.

29. Karla Poewe, *Charismatic Christianity as a Global Culture* (Columbia, SC: University of South Carolina Press, 1994).

30. R. Schreiter, *Reconciliation* (Maryknoll, NY: Orbis Books, 1992).

31. Donald Shriver, *An Ethic for Enemies* (Oxford: Oxford University Press, 1995).

32. A number of essays pursue this line of thought in Denise and John Carmody, *The Future of Prophetic Christianity* (Maryknoll, NY:Orbis Books, 1993), see part II.

Chapter Five
Beauty for Ashes: Pentecostalism, Power, and Poverty, 1970-1996

1. THE OLD WASTE PLACES: EXPLORING PROBLEMS AND PARADIGMS

The recent explosion of Pentecostalism in Africa has attracted some measure of scholarly attention as an aspect of the shift of the center of Christianity from the northern hemisphere to the southern. It has also been characterized as the new dimension of Christianity in Africa that is drastically reshaping the face of Christianity in that continent. Not everyone is applauding however: some concerns have been raised about sheep-stealing. This raises the question whether the growth of the movement indicates the absolute growth of Christianity or is it merely laundering among those who are already converted. Others allege that the movement puts a strain on the ecumenical understanding woven by the mainline churches, the inheritors of missionary traditions and respectability.

Some point to the impact of the aggressive resurgence on the prospect of the delicate pursuit of pluralism in the midst of the virulent pauperization and competition for scarce resources in African countries. As commentators note, the enlargement of the political space for religious actors has been followed by increased violence and assertion of orthodoxy. Above all, there has been some debate in the third world about the impact of this phenomenon on the current spate of the legitimacy crises, economic collapse, and the abuse of the environment or in the rebuilding of the old waste places. Pentecostals perceive themselves much differently and are fond of quoting a passage from the Old Testament, Isaiah 58:12, brimming with hope that one day God will fulfill His promise in Africa, using the born-again Christians in bringing a new dispensation to the continent:

> And they that shall be with thee shall build the old waste
> places; thou shalt raise up the foundations of many
> generations, and thou shalt be called the repairer of the
> breach

The first caveat is that while the phenomenon is acknowledged as the cutting edge of contemporary African church history, it has not been adequately studied. With the predominating interest of an avalanche of sociologists, theorization is running ahead of concrete data. There is much likelihood that the fate of the study of African independent churches (AIC) that ended with much romanticization will befall the new religious movement. The geographical spread of the field data is uneven; some countries have not been carefully studied. There are nagging questions about the African character of the movement, given its tendency toward eclecticism; there is a need for a proper typology, a proper understanding of the interior structures; of the vertical and horizontal expansion; the external linkages, and responses to the socioeconomic and political challenges.

Some of these are larger issues than can be adequately handled here; suffice it to say that until in-depth, multidisciplinary research could be mobilized, much of the conclusions so far are at best tentative. Indeed, the statistical base and demographic structure of the movement are uncertain for understanding the full nature of the phenomenon. The key concern of this chapter is limited to exploring the political theology and practice of the Pentecostals. Are they as apolitical as their detractors claim; a form of crossless Christianity, pandering an enervating, other-worldly placebo instead of an activist theology of engagement?

The approach here weaves together three paradigms: first, it is urged that charismatic movements had flourished at various times in Africa but that the modern Pentecostal movement gathered wind in its sails from the 1970s. It is not an off-shoot of the Azusa Street revival, which Seymour started in California in 1907, or an extension of American electronic church or a creation of tele-evangelists. It has a certain uniqueness that could best be understood from its fit in the African primal worldview. It is a strand in the element of continuity between African traditional religion and Christianity. Its problematics and idiom are sourced from the interior of African spirituality, and the resolutions are a reconstruction of that source from Christian and biblical perspectives. This gives the end-product its peculiarity. It should therefore be necessary to return to certain aspects of the African worldview and mine the resonances in the biblical tradition.

Second, Pentecostalism is postured as the *third* response by Africans to the missionary message. It has been argued earlier that Africans were not passive recipients of the gospel. The image of a tabula rasa, a clean slate on which the gospel-bearers wrote their script, was better buried in the hardware of the missionary than real-life experience would confirm. For some, the need to rewrite the script shocked them into early invalidation. The resourceful ones changed tack. This ability to revamp strategy explains why the missionary movement endured longer than its comrade the colonial regime. The tensile strength of the primal religion and culture, the exigencies of the mission field, and the initiative of the receptors created a new form of Christianity that sometimes appeared antistructural. The *first* response appeared quite early. As soon as the nineteenth century missionary enterprise got underway, a nationalist elite, dubbed as *Ethiopians*, wove a network of cultural protest against white domination in power and culture over the church. Some broke away to found African churches. Ardent ones, as Mojola Agbebi, for example went beyond rhetoric to invent a way that one could be both an African and a Christian without white tutelage. Their resourceful use of political space flowered into the quest for political independence.

The *second* response followed apace in the midst of the influenza and meningitis epidemic. Chapter One discusses the five types of this movement that is named differently in various regionsof Africa as *zionist* in southern and central Africa, *abaroho* in eastern Africa, and *aladura*/spiritual churches in western Africa: the zionists, messianic, revivalist, nativistic, and vitalistic. There are three reasons for this excursion: first, the tendency to see these groups as examples of African creativity in Christianity leaves the wrong impression. Second, the relationship between the AICs and Pentecostalism, the third form of African response, is crucial. Both constituted a pneumatic challenge to missionary message, but are AICs the first form of African Pentecostalism? If postured as a spectrum, both lie on the same side of the typology of Christian forms. Both drew from the issues raised in primal religion. A. F. Walls points out that both trace continuities in African maps of the universe by reordering the worldview and introducing new symbols and sources. He, however, notes the sharp conflict and explains that:

> Perhaps the core of the conflict, the element which makes relationships so tense, is the issue whether subor-

dinate spiritual beings, who represent the continuity of
the religious consciousness demonstrated in the divinity
element in older cosmologies, may be recognized as the
obedient agents of God, or must be anathematized as
evil entities opposed to him...They use the same maps of
the universe- even if they colour them differently.[1]

The Pentecostals see the matter differently; the mandate to test the
spirits in every manifestation, using the Bible as the litmus, may sound
like flatbook use of the Bible but is a major point of departure.

Third, to what extent are the AICs engaged with socioeconomic
and political issues?C. Oosthuizen has argued that the AICs are
neither otherworldly nor uninvolved with major modernizing forces.
Much to the contrary,

AICs are best seen as civil society mobilizations of the
poor which are addressing the issues of poverty and
underdevelopment through a holistic strategy combin-
ing social support with tangible development intervention. The AICs are thus a pro-active social movement
with a strong potential for involvement in wider social
and economic development issues.[2]

Naming the movement

Pentecostalism, as a *third* response, is a recovery of the diminished theology of the Holy Spirit, the Third Person of the Trinity in
the missionary message. Rationalism, race, and neo-orthodoxy in the
Protestant doctrine and theology may have accounted for that fact.
Yet Hegel interpreted the Enlightenment as the third age, that is, the
age of the spirit. But as rationalism and pietism of the period tangoed,
one strand colored European imagination so drastically that the contemporary resurgence of Pentecostalism is viewed as the Cinderella
of Western theology.[3] It was Bishop Lesslie Newbigin who placed
the significance of Pentecostalism on a solid theological basis in his
lectures at Trinity College, Glasgow, on the nature of the church.
Alongside the Protestant emphasis, what think you of Christ?, i.e.,
hearing the gospel with faith; and the Catholic emphasis, what think
you of the church?, i.e., the sacramental life of the historic church,
he placed the emphasis by Paul, did you receive the Holy Spirit when
you believed? Newbigin viewed the first two positions as tending
toward the static, while the third position provides dynamism.

Borrowing a phrase from Henry P. van Dusen, Newbigin termed
Pentecostalism, the third force in twentieth-century Christianity.[4] It

is said that Karl Barth's last words were that he dreamed of a new theology that would begin with the third article of the creed and would realize in a new way the real concern of his old opponent, Schleiermacher. Indeed, the current implosion of Pentecostalism in Africa has been perceived as the third evangelization of the continent after the Iberian and the Victorian enterprises. As Texeira said, following Christ implies a triple movement: exodus, commitment and closeness. These are metaphors for intensification and reconstruction of the religious experience or authentic conversion.[5] Indeed, the American Evangelicals who have closed rank with Pentecostals call themselves the Third Wave.[6] Thus we are witnessing the implosion of a third force, moved by the wind of the third person of the Trinity in the triple task of reevangelization, intensification and reconstruction of Christian experience in contemporary Africa.

A third reconstruction paradigm has been articulated by Ruth Marshall in what she dubs the setting to work of foreign doctrines and institutions. The focus is on the specific innovations and reinventions emerging in the creative process of appropriating the gospel and reconstruction of the social world, at individual and collective levels. The key concern is the extent to which Pentecostals, with their central theme of personal and social rebirth, have invented powerful metaphors for new types of practice, as well as symbolic and material resources for the

> elaboration of a conceptual challenge to the power monopolies, for the creation of autonomous spaces of practice which defy the oppressive logic of current monopolies and for the articulation of strategies to create, exercise and legitimate new power relations and new opportunities for survival.[7]

Do Pentecostals, in their emphasis on the spiritual dimension of reality, offer symbols of hope in the midst of the shadow that has covered Africa at noontide and bred Afro-pessimism? Do they offer beauty for the ashes that our leaders have poured on our faces?

Brueggemann argued that the prophetic imagination offers such symbols and performs two tasks: the first is to mine the memory of the people and educate them to use the tools of hope. The other is to recognize how singularly words, phrases, speech, and language shape consciousness and define reality.[8] Thus, by the use of these tools of hope, people are conscientized to contradict

> the presumed world of the kings showing both that presumed world does not square with the facts and that we

have been taught a lie and have believed it because the
people with the hardware and printing press told us it
was that way.

Conscientized people begin to know something different and become
prepared, out of their own anguish and amazement, to know that the
closed world of managed reality is false.

Brueggemann contends that this occurs when people are imbued
with a prophetic imagination that knows the real world is the one
that has its beginning and dynamic in the promising speech of God
and that this is true even in a world where kings have tried to banish
all speech but their own.Dykstra, in his *Vision and Character*, calls it
the imaginal transformation. By experiencing the holy, there is a creative reorganization of the imagination (the self) and the emergence
of a new Gestalt. This breeds social action directed by this altered
perception of the world.[9] As Lewis R. Rambo has argued:

> religious beliefs and myths can function as potent intel-
> lectual systems that enable people to make sense of the
> flux of history, their own place in history, and the nature
> of the world.

This is often achieved through rhetoric or the language of transformation, often betrayed in rich biographical testimonies.[10] For instance,
an African pastor who tells the congregation that SAP means *supreme
above problems* is not suggesting that the Structural Adjustment
Program is not real or biting, but that they should walk by faith in
God's promises for their lives and work to reject depression and to
triumph over all difficulties. The use of a language of transformation
becomes the first tool for perceiving the hopeless situation differently.

Brueggemann in *Texts Under Negotiation*, posits the reconstruction paradigm within the larger shift in postmodern theory of
knowledge. He begins with the formal premise that

> our knowing is essentially imaginative, that is, an act of
> organizing social reality around dominant, authoritative
> images.[11]

Thus, missionary evangelical theology emerged in a world imagined
through the privilege of white, male, Western, colonial hegemony,
with all its pluses and minuses. It was imbued with Cartesian flight
to objectivity, certitudes, and Enlightenment scienticism. It was an
imaginative construal. And, if it is a construal, then from any other
perspective, the world can yet be construed differently. To appro-

priate his words in another context, it is the claim of Pentecostal faith and the warrant of Pentecostal ministry to insist that the Bible provides the materials out of which an alternately construed world can be properly imagined. Pentecostalism is, therefore, a child of the demise of modernism, a product of a great shift in interpretive practice which asserts that in the post-Cartesian situation knowing consists not in settled certitudes but in the actual work of imagination. He defines imagination as:

> the human capacity to picture, portray, receive and practice the word in ways other than it appears to be at first glance when seen through a dominant, habitual, unexamined lens.

Finally, it would appear that the need for reconstruction is based on the low intensity and fatigue of missionary evangelical theology. This is a point that Ruth Marshall emphasizes with data from the Nigerian context, arguing that:

the Pentecostals or born agains are the most dynamic group of Christians in Nigeria today precisely because they engage with this contemporary situation and the history that has brought it into being. This movement gathers its force not in spite of the failures of the church in the past but precisely because of them. The history... is the failure to construct a redemptive and empowering theology, a Christian identity and practice which could have helped alleviate (pauperization)...This failure is indissolubly linked to the failure of the post-colonial state to redeem its promises of democracy and development while at the same time allowing a few to enjoy the facets of modernity to an obscene extent.[12]

The mainline churches, products of the evangelical revival and missionary enterprise, failed at that meeting point of liturgy and proclamation to provide people with new materials or old materials freshly voiced that would fund, feed, nurture, nourish, legitimate, and authorize a counterimagination of the world. Ethiopianism did not do so either. The Bantu Prophets achieved much as the literature has demonstrated to the point of romanticization.[13] The third response brings the full gospel into the task in a new way. J.I. Packer put it simply:

> The movement is forcing all Christendom to ask what it means to be a Christian and to be Spirit-filled. It is bringing into recognizably evangelical experience people whose ears were once closed to evangelical witness as such. As egghead radical theology invites the church

into the wilderness of a new Unitarianism, is not (dare I
say) just like God to have raised up against it not a new
Calvin but a scratch movement that proclaims the deity
and potency of the Son and Spirit not by great theological acumen or accuracy, but by the evidence of renewed
lives and a changed lifestyle? A movement which by its
very existence reminds both the world and the church
that Christianity in essence is not words only but also a
person and a power? Surely we see divine strategy here.

The one issue that can best illustrate the weakness of missionary theology and practice in Africa is the problem of evil and affliction; yet the resources for responding to this fills the pages of the
Scriptures. Affliction is a pivotal issue in the theology of the African
primal world. It can be caused by a contravention of the moral code.
For instance, the Earth deity supervises the moral order on the land.
Matters such as stealing, adultery, incest, other forms of wrong-doing
and breakdown in social relations are abomination to it. Failure to
propitiate the earth deity is visited with afflictions that take different forms such as illness or misfortune. The manifestation may be
individual or communal. Political instability, economic disaster,
an upsurge in the mortality rate, an increase in robbery and other
unwholesome social facts are regarded as disease, requiring divina-
tory diagnosis and spiritual cure. Disease could, therefore, be caused
by religious, social, and natural causes. To reestablish the security of
the moral order and to reconcile broken social relationships, medicine becomes important. A diviner diagnoses the problem and provides curative and protective spiritual powers-either through herbs
or by covenanting the individual or community to protective spirits.
Festivals, dances, masquerades, and commensality are employed to
reenergize ancestral and other covenants. The challenges of the ecosystem are core determinants for prioritizing their choices.

This is a religious worldview. Going through life is like spiritual
warfare, and religious ardor may appear very materialistic as people
strive to preserve their material sustenance in the midst of the machinations of pervasive evil forces. Behind it is a strong sense of the
moral and spiritual moorings of life. The challenge for Christianity
is how to witness the gospel in a highly spiritualized environment
where the recognition of the powers has not been banished in a Cartesian flight to objectivity and enlightenment. The power question is
ultimate and suffuses the African primal worldview, demanding an
answer from the new Christian change-agent. It points to the need
for continuity in change. Earlier missionary effort to sidestep with

charitable institutions and the Western worldview failed, leaving the field open for reevangelization. The born-agains have picked up the gauntlet. The argument here is that Pentecostalism in Africa derived its coloring from the texture of the African soil and from the interior her idiom, nurture and growth; its fruits serve more adequately the challenges and problems of the African ecosystem than the earlier missionary fruits.

2. THE BIRTH OF BORN-AGAINS: THE VERTICAL EXPANSION OF PENTECOSTALISM

The debate about globalization and the character of African Pentecostalism points to some of the streams that have fed into the vertical expansion of the movement. The qualifier here is to perceive the phenomenon; first, within the strand of continuity in primal religion; and second, as the fruit of missionary enterprise in Africa, bearing seeds of discontinuity. This enables the historian to place the contributions of outsiders in proper perspectives. To achieve this, attention should be given to periodization precisely because, in the twenty-five years under review (1970-1995), both the reasons and the pattern of vertical expansion changed. For instance, there was Pentecostal ferment prior to 1970, when the Wind of God began to blow like a gale. In the mid-1980s, it assumed a different character with the increase of the Faith Movement and the proliferation of prosperity preachers. A high growth pattern continued into the 1990s but with the sobering return to the holiness emphasis in many countries where the Intercessors for Africa became more visible in the paradigm shift to a theology of political engagement.

Three models characterize the historiography on the origins of Pentecostalism in Africa. The first is a *cultural-historical model.* This emphasizes two discourses: the African roots of Pentecostalism, and the ferment of revivalism that characterized African appropriation of the gospel. Scholars have traced the spirituality of Azusa Street phenomenon to West African spirituality. That is not quite the point here; rather, the rise of the movement is an aspect of African attempts to link the resources of a new religiosity with an ongoing effort to solve problems in the ecosystem. It is a continuation of African religiosity and emerges from the African worldview but critiquing the old solutions that lost efficacy as the old system fell apart. African Pentecostalism started with numerous manifestations of the Holy Spirit through various charismatic figures. Each suddenly appeared in the midst of urgent conditions in the community, almost like the judges of old. Adrian Hastings has traced the import of this through the careers of William Koyi, a Xhosa; Frank Zigubu of Shonaland; Molimele Molele, a Sotho;Samuel Kona, a Fingo; Eliachib Mandlakusasa, a Tsonga;Wade Harris of the Ivory Coast; Garrick Braide of the Niger Delta; Sampson Oppong an Ashanti; and such-like individuals whose charismatic ministries had no connection with Azusa Street but emerged in the pressure of primal religion and culture on the Christian message:

> What was happening in place after place was a spiritual
> revolution sparked off by native evangelists in conditions
> created by the unsettlement of early colonial rule.[14]

This fact points also in two directions: first, the relationship with the Aladura at the inception: the early Pentecostals emerged in the garb of Zionists. Later, some abandoned the use of instruments and became more fully Pentecostal. Second, the impact of the translation of the Bible and the Christian message and the manifestation of the Holy Spirit were evident in mission churches but the resistance was strong.

A good example could be taken from the origins of Assemblies of God in Nigeria. A certain Wogu who was a member of Faith Tabernacle found that he suddenly received baptism of the Holy Spirit and started to speak in tongues. Some friends joined him but all were excommunicated. They formed *Church of Jesus Christ* (CJC) in 1934; five years later, they invited the Assemblies of God from the United States to take over the CJC. Similarly, the Welsh Apostolic Church was invited to Ghana and to Nigeria by indigenous founders who wanted legitimacy under the hostile colonial environment. Reverend James McKeown's pioneering effort was supplementary to Babalola's charismatic ministry in Nigeria and Peter Anim's in Ghana, as the latter had received the Holy Ghost baptism four years before linking with the Welshman. The Garrick Braide Movement, 1914-1918, the Spirit Revival among the neighboring Ibibio, 1927-1928, the deliverance ministry of the Welsh Apostolic pastors Idris Vaughan and George Perfect, 1930-1933, on the Cross River, all these set the southeastern parts of Nigeria aflame with spiritual fire from 1914 through 1940. The reaction of the Qua Iboe Mission was typical. At first, they rejoiced at the Spirit Revival, saying that they had prayed fervently for it. But soon they feared the spiritual freedom of their black converts and sought to restrain the black's spiritual exuberance. Racism scorched the fruits of their prayer and message.[15] This is reminiscent of the reaction to the *Balokole* revival movement that swept from Rwanda of the 1930's through Uganda, Kenya, and most of East and Central Africa, where converts yelled, *tukutendereza Yezu*, We praises you, Jesus.

The largest Pentecostal church in Africa is, perhaps, the Deeper Life Bible Church, founded by William Kumuyi in Nigeria, with branches in most parts of Africa. As M.A. Ojo has shown, Kumuyi was a member of Apostolic Church and imbibed his holiness ethic from the discipline of that church. Pa S.G. Elton, a veteran missionary of that church would, later, become a key source of inspiration to the generation of Pentecostals of the 1970s in Nigeria. He linked Benson A. Idahosa to Reverend and Mrs. Gordon Lindsay of Dallas, Texas. The couple trained, ordained, and funded Idahosa's successful ministry in the West coast of Africa.[16]

This weaves into a second explanation model, namely, the *providential*. In situations where Classical Pentecostals came into Africa before 1970, there was little vertical growth to write home about until the gale blew all over the continent in that year. This inexplicable fact leads to a religious explanation along providential lines. It shifts attention away from Azusa Street to perceive the movement as universal in origin, a spontaneous global outpouring of the Holy Spirit. This is the argument that Paul A. Pomerville proffers in *The Third Force in Missions* and is the finger of God conceptual scheme in history.[17] Case studies from most parts of Africa agree on the explosion of the phenomenon from 1970. Quite typical of this is the inexplicable explosion of both Bethel and Transcea churches in Liberia. As the case of Liberia shows, the fatigue of mainline churches and their collusion with years of corruption and power monopoly elicited a pneumatic challenge that some have perceived as God's judgment and reclamation of His people. [18]

One key characteristic of the 1970s is the proliferation of young preachers called, *aliliki* in Malawi. Richard van Djik has done a good sociological analysis of the ages and backgrounds of the young preachers in Malawi.[19] The spiritual the radicalization of the students in both secondary schools and universities provided the midwives for the birth of born-agains. In Nigeria, for an example, the movement in the southwest was pioneered by university students of both the University of Ibadan and the University of Ife (renamed Obafemi Awolowo University). Graduates of tertiary institutions pioneered the evangelization of northern Nigerian cities. In the southeast, secondary school students, who had joined the Scripture Union (SU), were most prominent when suddenly the SU, which had been a sedate Bible study body, started exhibiting charismatic signs and wonders, including the raising of the dead at a rally in the sprawling, commercial city of Onitsha. Students from Nigeria, who went for French language study, evangelized their fellows in Ivory Coast, Benin, and Guinea.

In Kenya, the Fellowship of Christian Unions (FOCUS) facilitated the spread of beliefs throughout Eastern Africa. Ojo traced both the impact of a FOCUS training course held in 1974 and the role of Kenyan University students in promoting the movement in the rest of the region.However, charismatic ministry had been a feature of Christainity especially in western Kenya from about 1906. Similarly, the movement started in secondary schools and spread into tertiary cadres in Tanzania during the same period.[20] Political and ideological factors delayed the spread into Uganda, Ethiopia, Mozambique, Angola, and Zimbabwe till the 1980s. The youthful pattern, which could also be seen in Ghana and Sierra Leone, was not quite so in South Africa or in Zaire. In South Africa, as was the case in Zimbabwe, the role of American and European Pentecostal missionary groups was prominent, prompting Paul Gifford to perceive the insidiously gloved hands of anti-Communist American right-wing Christianity. When FRELIMO opened the doors to Christianity in the 1980s many Pentecostal churches from South Africa, Zimbabwe, and Malawi rushed along with mainline churches and hundreds of NGOs into Mozambique.[21]

These Pentecostals, such as the Rhema and the Faith Ministries from Johannesburgh and Harare had support from the USA. Other American groups defied the Mozambican government to aid RENAMO rebels in any obvious ideological manner. These groups included Open Doors Ministries, End-time Handmaidens, Don Normand Ministries of Florida, Jimmy Swaggart Ministries, World Missionary Assistance Plan of California, and Christ for the Nations of Dallas. Two conclusions emerge: first, that in spite of African initiatives, there was foreign influence in the proliferation of Pentecostalism in Africa. The size varied in different countries due to the resource base-manpower, finance, and population. The trend increased in the 1980s. The nature of the relationship is another matter precisely because the tendency was towards more independence among the Africans. Foreign contact was useful for prestige, legitimation, rapidly-acquired degrees the home universities would not grant to the pastor and funds for the infrastructure and media costs. It was not a south-north trend only; there was a south-south, lateral relationship in the ministerial formation of African pastors. Hackett has traced the influence of African connection to Pentecostal bodies in India, Singapore, Malaysia, Philippines, Hongkong, and

South Korea. The Haggai Institute in Singapore has trained many African pastors. The variety of relationships run from pulpit-sharing, loose contacts to missionary exchange programs. Some of these contacts supplement the tutelage by big American enterprises such as Morris Cerullo World Outreach programs. The Haggai Institute in Singapore has its headquarters in Atlanta.[22]

Second, the movement was not always a youthful affair; it isnot only that as it aged the character changed, but that the patronage soon engulfed adults. President Chiluba, who declared Zambia a Christian nation, was not engaging in political gymnastics; he was born again before his ascension into power. In the periodization, 1985 is a watershed. Reinhard Bonnke's Harare Fire Convention brought together four thousand African pastors from forty-one countries for over a week of training. The theme was a declaration; that *Africa shall be Saved*. The impact was enormous and created a band of enthusiastic evangelists, many of whom participated in organizing over eighteen Bonnke outreaches within the next five years. The 1980s witnessed the enlargement of scale including prosperity ministries, Intercessors for Africa, charismatic bands within the mainline churches (a survival strategy as women and youths dominated the charismatic movements) and the growth of groups such as Gideon Bible International, Full Gospel Businessmen's Fellowship International, and Women's Aglow. These last two provided born-again professionals with alternatives to humanistic sodalities such as Rotary Club and Lion's Club and saved them from the clutches of Rosicrucians and Freemasons.

The period from 1985-1995 also witnessed the enormous collapse of the economies of Africa, legitimacy crises, and environmental degradation. Civil wars, droughts, and a host of misfortunes touched off vast emigration and refugee trends. These untoward backdrops have given rise to a third explanation model, namely, the *functionalist model* which explains the rise of Pentecostalism in Africa by its appeal to materialist and instrumentalist factors. The context in which conversion takes place is crucial because religion is basically related to problem-solving. The only cautions are to avoid monocausal analysis and reductionist explanations that ignore the complexities in a multicausal explanation. Karla Poewe has shown that the functionalist model reflects a dilemma in the use of the social science method to study a religious phenomenon. In the case of South Africa, she debunked some of the so-called scientific findings that attributed the growth to the fears and paranoia of white charismatics.[23]

It should be noted that some growth occurred from a host of internal reasons, including splintering because of personality clashes, the immorality of a leader, the clash of vision, the faithful, the vigorous evangelistic program, and the cellular nature of the movement. Applying the functionalist model, the pre-1970 growth is explained with the backdrop of influenza, 1919-1925, on the western coast of Africa and the psychosocial pressures of colonialism. In the 1970 era, civil wars, upward mobility trends in the midst of buoyant economies, youthful rebellions against patriarchal authority patterns, and the monopoly of resources are adduced. In Southern Africa, the quest for belonging fueled the movement among blacks, while black political insurgence drove whites into a quest for security in the warm embrace of the Holy Spirit. The collapse of the state as an agent of modernization enlarged the political space for religious actors and gave fillip to the Pentecostal moral diagnosis for political and economic woes. Evangelicals became born-agains too, thereby blurring the lines of divide that appear more boldly in the West. Quite interesting is the patronage of dictators of this new form of populism. Paul Gifford illustrates it with the reception accorded Bonnke in Kenya, Togo, and the Ivory Coast.[24] As Marxist states collapsed, the field widened for Pentecostals and Evangelicals in the period dubbed the Second Liberation of Africa.

There is need for statistical study of the growth pattern. Commentators are not in doubt that the Pentecostal fire has continued to spread rapidly; this detracts from the African independent churches. By strategically opening to charismatic influences, the mainline churches did not only stem numerical loss but earned real growth. Meanwhile, an internal debate continues within the bastions of orthodoxy on the adequate response to the challenge that is brewing from the inside; demanding a more biblical Christianity.[25] The growth of the movement has been aided by a plurality of voices and typology with an African peculiarity. The born-agains are a broad movement consisting of :

- Interdenominational fellowships;
- Evangelistic ministries e.g. Deeper Life Bible Church (Nigeria);
- Deliverance ministries, specializing in exorcism;
- Prosperity or Faith ministries, sometimes promoting positive thinking, e.g. Zoe Ministry and Idahosa's Church of God Mission (Nigeria);
- Intercessors-members of Intercessors for Africa and Prayer for the Nation groups;

- Bible Distribution ministries , e.g. Gideon Bible International who insists that members must be born- again, and active in their churches;
- Missionary and Rural Evangelism, e.g. The Christian Evangelical Social Movement; Christian Missionary Foundation;
- Children Evangelism ministry whose branches mushroomed from the 1980s;
- Classical Pentecostals, e.g. Four Square Gospel, Assemblies of God.

The argument here is that a typology could be constructed based on ministry or specialized service emphasis. These types could be found all over Africa and have global contacts. Two organizations have arisen to mobilize born- agains across Africa: fellowships (para-churches) and churches.A major line of divide is bewteen holiness and word-faith groups. There has been a sustained attack on those who emphasize prosperity, word-faith, and health (those who privilege deliverance or exorcism).Some scholars like H. Terri Neuman, argued the cultic origins of the word-faith theology. He avers that it originated from the positive confession taught by the New Thought, Christian Science, and the Unity School of Christianity. E. W. Kenyon is supposed to have brought it into the fold, and Kenneth Hagin plagiarized extensively from Kenyon and thereby popularized it within the born-again camp.[26] However, Robert M.Bowman has rebutted many of the allegations. He discussed the historical context from which the Word of Faith movement was born and the biblical, extra-biblical foundations, exegetical weaknesses, and practical applications of this theological system.He insisted that the movement had orthodox roots in the Higher Life movement of the nineteenth century and in early Pentecostal/holiness tradition. He emphasized that it is not rooted in cultic, metaphysical tradition, and that Kenyon kept a wide distance from metaphysical New Thought teaching of Ralph Waldo Trine and others.He traced the origins to Keneth Hagin, Oral Roberts, And WilliAm BrAnhAm, pioneers in the post-World War II healing revivals.[27]A rapid spread of a wide range of ministries or para-churches enable large numbers of clients to move between the various charismatic groups and their mainline churches. Much clientele relationship exists.Ministers who exhibit charismatic power are dubbed as strong men of God, and attract large numbers to their retreats, outreaches, and power-ministrations.

The theological emphases are equally contextual.The first component is the doctrine of salvation by faith and the Holy Spirit baptism as a second birth--the born again experience. But doctrinal affirmations are eclectic, depending on whose influence is pervasive. The second component is sanctification as a process, requiring measures to ensure that the believer does not backslide but runs a good race so as to win a crown. Holiness ethic plays a major role with bible study, prayer, and fasting. The third component is victorious living. The key is the power for abundant life in the precarious socioeconomic and political environment. Thus, the holiness ethic is pursued as a prerequisite for harnessing the healing, signs, and wonders that follow belief in Christ. Prosperity and deliverance are signs of the presence of the Holy Spirit in one's life as well as equipping one for service. Tongues, as heavenly language, serve certain purposes: a sign of being born again, identity, aid for praying and a means of confusing Satan in the quest for victorious living, as these pilgrim people wait for the rapture. So, a familiar greeting is, Brother, be rapturable! This consciousness for the terror which shall be at the end constitutes a core evangelical message. Everyone wants to rapture before the great tribulation or even before the Second Coming! The *charismata*, computed to be up to twenty-seven, are coveted in a highly spiritualized Christianity. Victorious living is pursued through defense against the demons in the culture and offense against the principalities, powers, and their cohorts.

The broad character of African Pentecostalism is that it is very ecumenical not only bringing together Christians of various hues into a new bonding in Christ but being against ethnicity or tribalism. Aggressive evangelism is buttressed with strong encapsulation strategies; thus, there are clear lines drawn from a range of unbelievers including primal religionists, lukewarm Christians, Moslems, AICs and those who cannot profess with certainty that they are born again. This non-inclusive attitude causes rancor, allegations of sheep-stealing, and hubris. But it is the old Evangelicalism writ large with pneumatic salting, emphasizing biblicism, crucicentrism, social activism, and missionary zeal. There is a streak of anti-Catholicism because of Mariology, veneration of saints, use of candles, holy water and other ritual instruments. This factor causes immense strain between the Catholic charismatic movement and the official church. On the whole, in spite of the amorphous nature of the movement, there is a certain order to enable an irenic history.

3. REPAIRERS OF THE BREACH: RECONSTRUCTING THE PRIMAL WORLDVIEW

The character of Pentecostalism informs their activities: with the understanding that the mainline churches have practised powerless Christianity, leaving the spirits that govern the gates of communities unconquered, there is a process of reevangelization of the entire continent. Missionary fatigue has produced compromises of the gospel, allowing people to have their feet in both primal religion and biblical Christianity. The answer is to utilize charismatic or power evangelism as well as modern resources such as media and management techniques in promoting a personal faith commitment to Jesus Christ and Holy Spirit baptism. The extensive and creative use of the media by Pentecostals elicits a revisit to the view that they are antimodern. Much to the contrary, as some have argued that:

> charismatic churches have the distinct ability to explore innovative ways of bringing together various cultural backgrounds, from tradition and village to modernity and the global level.[28]

Other innovative strategies include new forms of polities that open opportunities for service to all; cell groups, prayer, fasting, Bible study retreats, tracting, newsletters, popular outreaches in stadia, new hymnody (choruses), preaching in buses, door evangelism, and mail prayer ministry. Some specialize in billboards and car stickers. The enlargement has turned the architecture into Warehouse Temples. Many cinema houses and public parks and schools have been taken over. The liturgy has benefited from the innovations of the AICs adding electronic and other instruments. The temper radiates with the indigenous African mode of joyful worship- with much dancing, clapping, and free movement. These innovative strategies bring the impact of the gospel into the daily lives of the people as a transformative experience.

The major contribution of the movement is how these religious groups address the continued reality of the forces expressed in African cultural forms especially in the second and third components of their endeavor. Contrary to the early missionary attitude that urged cultural rejection, Pentecostals take the African map of the universe seriously, acknowledging that culture is both a redemptive gift as well as capable of being highjacked. They perceive a kindred atmosphere and resonance in a biblical contrast between a Godly covenant and the snares of other covenants and, therefore, the need for testing the spirits. They appreciate the tensile strength of the spiritual ecology in

Africa and the clash of covenants in the effort to displace the spirits at the gates of individuals and communities with a legitimate spiritual authority. Salvation is posed in a conflict scenario. As the Garrick Braide people used to sing: *Jesus has come and Satan has run away!* Pentecostals, therefore, explore the lines of resonance that go beyond deconstruction to a new construction of reality.

First, at the structural level, scholars have noted the similarity in myths of creation, emphasizing the activity of a creator and the creation of the world from a chaotic, marshy base. This says much about the nature of humans and their relative powers in the universe. There is also a shared perception of a three-dimensional space by both biblical and African worldviews in spite of a cyclical concept of time. But there is a declaration that at the name of Jesus, every knee shall bow, whether it exists in the heavenlies, earth (land and water) or in the earth-beneath (ancestral world). Second, Africans affirm, just as the writer of Hebrews did in chapter eleven, verse three, that the things which are seen are made of things which are not seen, and that conflicts in the manifest world are first decided in the spirit world, therefore, the weapons of our warfare are not carnal but spiritual. This does not remove human agency but limits it with possibilities of situations that are beyond human control and are inexplicable. It regains a lost worldview where the inexplicable was taken for a valid aspect of reality. It must be added that this is the tendency of postmodernism.

Both the indigenous African and the Christian worldviews are spiritualized or charismatic worldviews. The rule of Yahweh, the Lordship of Christ and saints perform the same functions as many spirits do in the African religious ecology. Third, the biblical worldview is that life is just as precarious as the traditional African imagines; the enemy is ranged in military formations such as principalities, powers, rulers of darkness, and wickedness in high places. The Pentecostal goes through life as keenly aware of the presence of evil forces as the African does. The Western urban dweller substitutes with ESP, other psychic services, and the spirits of Eastern religions. As an aside: there is much controversy raging within the Evangelical camps, against the Third Wavers. Some argue that demons have been given more space than the gospel permits. There is the beautiful quip by the ancestor of Western theologians, Karl Barth, that:

> it has never been good for anyone to look too frequently
> or lengthily or seriously at demons. It does not make the
> slightest impression on the demons if we do so, and there

> is the imminent danger that in so doing we ourselves
> might become just a little more than a little demonic.
> (Dogmatics, 3, 3;51:3)

The perspective here gingerly hops over the minefields of Western theological debate so as to capture what the Africans are saying and doing, unaware of the great debates in the pages of *Pneuma*, the journal of the Society for Pentecostal Studies. Others are concerned about a dualistic view of reality in which God and Satan lock horns, and they wonder what happens to the natural and whether this scenario is biblical. Various exegetical and hermeneutical approaches answer the questions differently.

But in Africa, there is a certain ritual at New Yam Festival when the celebrant gives a piece of yam to a masquerader with the left hand, saying that he came to the world to meet the evil spirits fighting the good ones; he does not know the source of the quarrel but would prefer to be left out of it; so, he gives yam to God with the right hand and to evil spirits with the left. He buys his peace in a dualistic worldview buzzing with conflict.

The indigenous theology of the world is built on an alive universe where power is central; the world is suffused with powerful forces in competition; humans manipulate the services of the good gods against the machinations of the evil ones, in the quest for an abundant life. Fourth, there are human beings who are given false powers by evil forces to exercise control over individuals, families and communities. Satan even promised Jesus some of these powers if he complied. Thus, Pentecostals perceive dictatorial and corrupt rulers as being possessed. Fifth, the Pentecostal perceives witchcraft and sorcery as real, a soul-to-soul attack.

To explain these assertions, the Pentecostal does not ignore the fact that the word *kosmos* can refer to the material universe and to the inhabitants of the world; but they fasten onto the third usage, which refers to worldly affairs, ie., to worldly goods, endowments, riches, pleasures, and allurements (*kosmetikos*) that seduce one away from God. Thus, behind the classical idea of *kosmos* as an orderly arrangement is a mind behind the system, a world system established after the Fall by a *kosmokrator*, a world ruler, the prince of this world, in rebellion. Friendship with him is enmity with God. It is a short step from here to perceive territorial spirits allocated to various spaces for unGodly activities. This idea was, after all, very prominent in Judaism and in the early church. There is a confluence of the spiritual and material worlds denying the myth of materialism. In his trilogy on naming, engaging, and unmasking the powers, Walter Wink explored the concepts of power in the New Testament and concluded that:

> Every power has a visible and invisible pole, an outer and inner spirit or driving force that animates, legitimates and regulates its physical manifestation in the world. Principalities and powers are the inner and outer aspects of any given manifestation of power. As the inner aspects, they are the spirituality of institutions, the within of corporate structures and systems, the inner essence of outer organizations of power.[29]

Analyzing further, he argues that the language of power pervades the entire New Testament, and that while it could be liquid, imprecise, interchangeable, and unsystematic, a clear pattern of usage emerges. Powers could be used to refer to heavenly, divine, spiritual, invisible forces as well as to earthly, human, political and structural manifestations as long as we realize that:

> The world of the ancients was not a physical planet spinning in empty space in a rotation around a nuclear reactor, the sun; it was a single continuum of heaven and earth, in which spiritual beings were as much at home as humans.[30]

Paul used *dunamis*(power) to focus on the spiritual dimension of power in its capacity to determine terrestrial existence for weal or for woe. Later, it became the designation for God's enemies, engaged in a cosmic struggle to assert lordship over the earth.

Some have assumed that African Christians have manufactured demons and enlarged their space in theology. Others draw attention to a number of facts: how local Christianity emerges by reconceptualizing indigenous powers and the biblical powers. Birgit Meyer's *Translating the Devil* showed that local converts absorbed the missionary images and representation of evil. Devil, Satan, demons became missionary representationsof the evil power in human world.Soon, they were used to distinguish between the clean spirits in Christianity and the unclean spirits or the gods of the local communities. The complexity is that in some African communities, the word translated in the vernacular Bible as Satan might refer to an ancestral deity. She argued that born again Christians often complained that mainline Christianity encouraged nominal church members by failing to take seriously the powers of the Holy Spirit and the Devil.Imagination of the demons represented less of false consciousness than attempts

to make sense of reality, provide explanation and control of predica-
ments whether social, political, or economic. It enables charismatic
groups to articualte people's problems in terms that they understood.
A study of the concepts of Satan, Devil, and demons in Pentecostal
rhetoric would expose their attitude to the African past and its indigenous cultures and beliefs.[31]

Walter Wink provides another approach that examines the
naming of power in the cultural background to the New Testament.
Concepts of the demons abound in Jewish literature as defecting
angels, sired giants who were drowned in the flood, their spirits live
on as demons, evil spirits, or powers of *Mastema*. Their leaders were
variously called *Azazel, Mastema, Satan,* and *Beliar.* Early Christians
devised elaborate instructions on how to discern them. The ministry
of Jesus was very much a cosmic battle in which Jesus rescued humanity from evil powers. African Pentecostals have equated principalities, powers, and demons with the various categories of spirits in the
primal worldview and as enemies of man and God. They reinforce
the explanations of cause and effect in the primal worldview before
providing a solution beyond the purviews of indigenous cosmology.
They rework the Pauline structure with native ingredients:

1.Principalities
- Apollyon
- Abaddon
- Belial
- The Beast; symbol; the leopard
- Ariel

2. Powers
- Ashteroth (agricultural deities)
- Baal (shrines on the earth and other places of worship of the
  earth)
- Magog, eg., Ogun (Yoruba powers for medicine related to
  cutlass, gun, iron)
- Beelzebub (witchcraft, wizardry)
- Asmodee (sexual immorality)
- Mammon (powers related to love of money and to control by
  the allure of money)
- Paimon (celestial demons that empower occultists)
- Aritan (magic, satanic justice)

3. Rulers of Darkness

- Ogeaso (among the Bini), Ogbanje (among the Igbo) – (spirits of children who come with a pact to return early into the spirit world)
- Jezeebel (dark goddess of the loins, seductive spirit, harlotry)
- Moleck (promoter of nudist fashion and ponography)
- Leviathan (a spirit which attract people into unwholesome covenants)
- Jeptha (patron of thieves and robbers).[32]

By turning the Bible into a canon of tribal history and weaving it into African worldviews, Pentecostals directly address the problems of evil forces in four ways: (i) they mine the interior of the worldviews to establish that the same covenantal structure exists in both; therefore the solution to the problem of affliction and defeat in life is to exchange the covenant with the wicked spirits for the covenant with Christ;

(ii) they produce large quantities of literature as discourses that expose these forces, show individuals and communities how to overcome their dangerous and destructive influences;

(iii) they enable individuals and groups to constitute historical agents, empowered to do battle with these principalities and powers; and

(iv) incite public testimonies about the works and victory over the wicked forces. Former agents of the spirits describe in gory details their years of bondage serving the false spirits. Testimonies in public worship become ceremonies of degradation and bridge-burning. As Ruth Marshall argued, they do not reject the past wholesale but engage with it, refashioning the history and domesticating it; they combine a wide range of self-help discourses with exposures of spiritual machinations at groundlevel, at the occult and territorial spirit levels. With spiritual diagnosis of social malaise goes the raising of an army to recapture the land.[33] For instance, corruption is attributed to the operation of the hunter or Nimrod spirit among Africans rulers, descendants of Ham. The shedding of blood through fratricide (civil wars) brings curses reminiscent of the Cain/Abel saga in which the land withheld its increase. Africa's economic woes are caused by polluting the land with blood. Emigration follows ineluctably as the earth spews out its people.[34]

All of life is subjected to the authority of Christ and, while not denying personal responsibility, it recognizes that individuals and

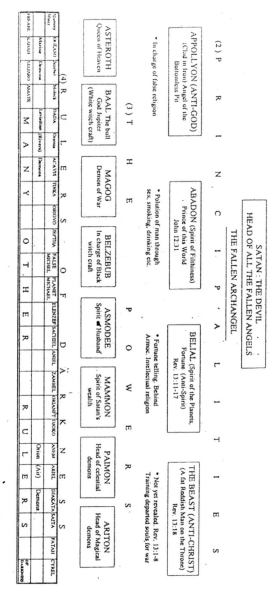

circumstances might be driven by forces beyond their control. Here, the Pentecostal explanation for witchcraft and sorcery by appeal to a biblical anthropology is fascinating. Arguing that God formed man and breathed Himself into the body and man became *nephesh*, a living soul, the fall is imaged as a house that collapsed, burying the spiritual resources. The soul (*psuche*), consisting of the intellect, will power, and emotions constitutes the strongest part of man, seeking to dominate both the spirit man (*pneuma*) and the body *(soma)*. Salvation comes by the spirit of God, taking over the pneuma and exuding the power into the psyche, redeeming the constituent parts and the recovering the soma which is driven by lusts of the flesh, the eye, and the pride of life. In this anthropology, witchcraft operates in the quest to tap the latent powers of the soul and use these to perform false miracles or to hurt other people with a soul-to-soul attack. Sorcery worsens matters by using things that provide contact with the victim. It could be the hair, clothes, food, or suchlike. Since incantations are used and curses pronounced, Christians are admonished to also speak the reversal using the name of Jesus, the blood, and the resources of the Holy Spirit. As Wink said, *onoma*, name is a metonymy, the part representing the whole. The name of Jesus designates his office, dignity and power of God in him. The text often cited is 1 John 5:8 and many others recounting the powers of Jesus and His position in the God-head. ThePentecostals avoid the use of instruments, limiting these to olive oil and anointed handkerchiefs and laying of hands.

The language of God in Pentecostal liturgy buttresses this fact. They explore the language that communities use in addressing their sustaining divinities, ancestors, and the Supreme Being and use these to describe God and Christ, demonstrating their superiority over all the powers available in the people's map of their universe. The reconstructed world is brought home to individual lives and circumstances by applying what could be termed, *bumper sticker hermeneutics*. Karla Poewe calls it experiential literalism and Cheryl B. Johns said that Pentecostal hermeneutics is praxis-oriented with experience and Scripture being maintained in a dialectical relationship. The Holy Spirit maintains the ongoing relationship. The truth must be fulfilled in life experiences. Lived faith is the result of a knowledge of the Scriptures.[35] The emphases are on oral faith, the experiential, relational, emotional, immediacy of the text, and on the freedom to interpret and appropriate the multiple meanings of the biblical texts. By a pneumatic illumination, it recognizes a spiritual kinship between the authors and readers and the ongoing continuity

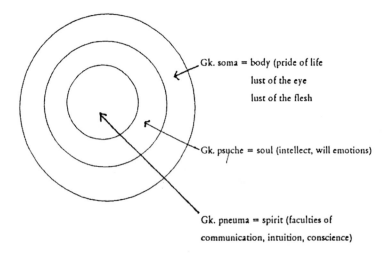

Gk. soma = body (pride of life
lust of the eye
lust of the flesh

Gk. psyche = soul (intellect, will emotions)

Gk. pneuma = spirit (faculties of
communication, intuition, conscience)

Christian View of the Human Person

with the New Testament church. Personal and corporate experiences weave into the hermeneutical task.

The literature on this matter has burgeoned; suffice it to point to the emphasis on the power of the Word in spiritual formation, resisting forces that could lead one to backslide; reversing curses, deliverance, and commanding the things that the Lord's hands have made. The brethren arrive for Bible studies and Sunday worship with notebooks to take down the message or revelations so as to apply these during the week for victory. Everyone is urged to be an overcomer and a demon destroyer. This is hermeneutics for conscientization, choreographed with a vigorous homiletic that mines the people's experiences, dramatizes these, props them up with real-life testimonies, and brings the promises in the Bible to respond to problems so that no one should leave bearing the burdens of yesterday. A pastor would tell the story of a woman who was carrying a heavy load on her head. A car stopped and offered to assist the woman; she accepted the offer, got into the car, but continued to carry the load on her head instead of setting it down. The congregation will indicate that it was a foolish thing to do. Often a sermon would be interrupted with choruses to bring home a point. Pentecostal homiletic is language crafted in a transformative manner and choreographed as a ritual of validation and commitment. As Rambo argues, the songs, dances, and yells elicit audience participation and aid believers to perform ritualistically before rationalizing the process. Such rituals

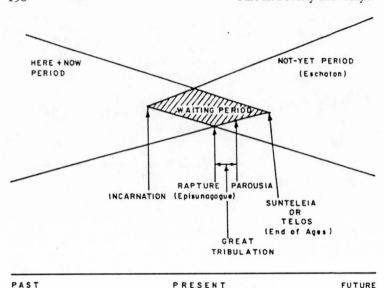

The New Testament Worldview

offer knowledge in a distinct form, enabling the believer to understand, experience and embody the new way of life.[36]

The Pentecostal approach to the African map of the universe
comes out most clearly in the response to the current legitimacy crises
and economic collapse. When there is drought or famine or social
distress, Africans look to the land, to their relationship with the Earth
deity, as economic and moral order are within its purview. The Pentecostals bring to the problem the importance of land among the Israel-
ites. As Brueggemann said, land referred to actual earthly turf and also
symbolically to express the wholeness of joy and well-being characterized by social coherence and personal ease in prosperity, security and
freedom.[37] Land as promise, as holy and symbolic of our covenant
relationship with God has tremendous resonance in the attitude to
land in African primal societies. The *brethren* plumb these resonances
and move to the impact of pollution caused by the actions of rulers
and the ruled. Shrines, festivals to Baal and Ashteroths, witchcraft,
and corruption are all listed as sources of the woes. The IMF and
World Bank are evangelists of the Beast who is equally behind the
European Union and the divinity of the market economy that is
sapping African countries with debt repayment. SAP is the Structural
Adjustment Program and comes with conditionalities.

Certain literature on the end time prophecies from the West provide the armory for this application of the Bible to both contemporary events and to the African primal map of the universe. Both the internal and external forces are brought under the gospel anvil in a manner that is understandable to the unlettered, because behind the macroeconomics of the global market is the divine will. Pentecostals urge members not to judge by sight but by revelation as to which spirits are operating behind manifest events. Land deliverance is only one of the strategies employed. It is subtle and avoids overt iconoclasm: believers can walk around hostile ground or polluted ground and command the spirits to leave; sometimes, at emotional crusades, those with authority over the land and the affairs of the community will be asked to confess the iniquities of the fathers that are being visited upon their progenies and to hand over the land to the authority of Jesus. This will ensure prosperity for all the people. In these ways, the born-again brethren in Africa bring a spiritual solution to the great issues of the day, taking the context, the world-view, and the ecology seriously but within the gospel mandate.

A major dimension that requires comment is that critics do not perceive a rigorous and critical response to social, political and economic realities of contemporary Africa in Pentecostal teaching and practice. This is the main contention in Paul Gifford, *Ghana's New Christianity.*He images Pentecostal teaching and practice as lacking in social and political activism he alleges that Penyecostals spiritualize politics by claiming that only God can change human socities for better, not governments; that they divert attention from practical effectiveness by moralising about institutional issues as if moral education could curb corruption.[38] In this *instrumentalist discourse*, it is argued that people use religion to achieve certain non-religious ends; and that the growth of Christianity in the southern hemisphere, and especially the explosion of Pentecostal/charismatic spirituality are related to the collapse of economies and legitimacy crises in those regions. Rebuttals abound.Crises and conversion are always connected; revivals have occurred in the midst of plenty and among affluent nations;the growth of Pentecostalism arises from a combination of its message, answers to life situations, aggressive evangelism, and the religious mood that it creates. Its political theology must be examined within its spiritual interpretation of Africa's political stagnation because Pentecostal theology links the profane and sacred worlds, and rejects the dichotomy and secularist theory of enlightenment worldview. Moreover, the degree of the political of engagement of the public space among Pentecostals vary from one African nation to the other.

4. PRACTICING THE VICTORIOUS LIFE: PENTECOSTAL POLITICAL PRACTICE

The key question is whether a spiritual perception of reality and diagnosis of Africa's political stagnation, the acknowledgment of the ultimacy of God's act in history or "spiritualizing politics", denies the data from social sciences and rejects social activism? Pentecostal political practice runs in four interlocking grooves: (i) rebuilding the individual, thus bestowing the power to be truly human; (ii) the call to social activism, attacking sociopolitical structures; (iii) the rule of saints and the politics of engagement; and (iv)building the new Israel, empowerment, and foretaste of new order. It thus breaks the dichotomy of individual/society, private/public, weaving a multifaceted and wholistic response to human predicament in the African ecosystem, using the resources of the gospel.

The pauperization of communities often manifests through physical (health), psychological (emotional), and material ways as people struggle to eke out a living while inflation reduces their purchasing powers. Political instability and the militarization of the society combine to create vulnerability, insecurity, and hopelessness. The first task of Christianity in such situations is to save people from hopelessness by creating new tools of empowerment and new sources of security, not by repeating the old excuses about suffering as a sign of being like Christ. Victims of predatory states are often great cynics; they see the gap, the shadow between the promises of the rulers and the harsh reality of their conditions. The Pentecostal message of God's promises of prosperity has been an empowerment and tool of hope, contradicting the rulers. Prosperity goes beyond material wealth to cover such matters as spiritual renewal of the relationship with God in Christ through the power of the Holy Spirit to provide health, reversal of economic desolation and political and social well-being of individuals and communities.

Psalm 24:1-2 says that when the land is returned to its owner, peace will reign and prosperity return. Prosperity could be a function of repentance and renewal of a relationship which had been broken by sin and pollution; it is also a sign that healing has occurred. The process involves both repentance and claiming of promises in the Bible. Objectors to the faith-word movement point to insufficient recognition of the sovereignty and freedom of God. He is not a coin box. Others point to the danger of pursuing material things as the

Gentiles do: their ignorance of the spirit behind things and the allure of the material world. In certain African conditions, the argument is academic because of the degree of lack.

Pentecostals conscientize the individual to fight back, to refuse to accept defeat, want, failure, pessimism or negativity. This would make the person in the image of the rulers and the controllers of the wealth. In the Bible, Jabez, among others, strove to reverse the verdict of poverty, refused to accept defeat, and cried out to the Lord. The contours of the prosperity gospel do not bear much repetition; suffice it to say that it does not teach the individual not apply managerial techniques or not to work hard; much to the contrary these self-help aids are taught at special seminars during outreach. Pentecostal students' fellowships provide extra lessons for members in various subject areas to avoid the shame of seeing born -again students who fail their courses. It is not a crossless Christianity, but it refuses to idolize suffering. Quite often the discussion on why certain prayers are not answered leads back to sin and the patience taught by suffering. However, as the movement broadened, some preachers, in the heat of competition, have moved into positive thinking, urging members to repeat certain laws or principles and to claim material things and health!

As said earlier, the movement is usually an ecumenical bonding, creating a new family, the brethren, a caring, supportive group providing solidarity in the midst of the breakdown of old moorings. Those of the household of faith constitute a new identity, serving in ways that missionary denominations could not and buffering many in the midst of stagnation and economic collapse. This new community nurtures and builds a corps of human agency to work with the divine in the process of restoration. Within its ambits and spirituality, people receive the call to foray into the wider political arena. This is important because participation in the public space must be rooted in the conviction that God actually sent, therefore, He will sustain and fund the participation. This the root of an ethic of metanoia, accountability and transparency. The values that the World Bank mouthed could not be achieved through secularist ethics.Pentecostals quote with seriousness, the passage in Ecclesiastics 10:7:

> I have seen servants upon horses and princes walking as
> servants upon the earth.

This is an unnatural trend. As Jesus did with the woman who had a spinal problem, healing her and restoring her sense of worth as the daughter of Abraham, so do Pentecostals urge their members to know who they are in God's scheme of affairs; that they are sons, daughters, princes, and citizens of the heavenly kingdom. They are to be heads not tails, to ride on horses rather than walk as servants. They foray to recover their lost position, described as taking the chair back from Satan, through deliverance and intercessory ministries. Deliverance includes expelling hindering spirits from individuals, places, offices and from the affairs of people, families, and communities. It is more than exorcism but includes replenishment with new power for coping victoriously. Some believe that as soon as one is born again, one person would start to gain victories in life-situations. Others argue that until old covenants have been deliberately broken such covenants would still be operative, because Satan is very legalistic and has legal authority to make demands on the individual.

It is believed that both individual and communal problems are as results of such pollution, disobedience, and iniquities of the fathers. Land deliverance becomes a restoration of the covenant relationship between God, man, and nature. As the deliverance of the land is done and handed back to its owner, the political, economic, and social affairs of the community will begin to improve. The hindrances or devourers have been driven away and their authority withdrawn. The relation of deliverance to politics sometimes arises from the diagnosis that some rulers hold the community in fearful sway by witchcraft or bewitchment. They tap unwholesome powers from marine spirits or other evil sources to secure themselves and their political offices. Brethren counter such powers through intercession and deliverance rituals.

The import of this is that affairs of the earth can be changed through prayers. Political dissent and action can be pursued on the knees instead of carrying placards; that the worn knee approach is more effective and salutary because it seeks the will of God on the earth and the battle is the Lord's. Human agency and divine activity is the surest means of gaining true victory. Humanistic projects are often tainted and may not always be vicarious. This explains why revolutions derail and become more totalitarian than the system they replaced. To deal with the spirits of wickedness that possess rulers, Pentecostals apply fasting, prayer retreats, researches on the dominant spirits possessing the gates of the communities and prayer actions. These may involve traveling through the boundaries of the community, speaking and calling into being the good of the community. Everyone does not have the gift of intercession; so the first activity is a Gideon method of selecting and training participants. Holy living, deliverance, the sense of call, and the gift of prayer are the prerequisites. In recent times, Urban Prayer projects are proliferating in Africa. They are attempts to deal with the rising level of frustration, unemployment, and crimes in urban settings. The police cannot be trusted, since they are likely to be participants in the crime waves. Intercessors, reassure themselves that God loves the city and has plans for the good of the city; Satan has hijacked the cities through evil rulers and wicked people; their sins have produced the famine in the land. The counter is to delegate prayer warriors to key areas of the city such as the markets, city hall, major industrial sites, banks, and so on. The group will denounce the evil spirits, order them to leave their strongholds, confess all the evils that have been perpetrated since the founding of the city, hand over those areas to God, and anoint the walls or ground with olive oil, signifying sanctification and the presence of the Holy Spirit.

From cities the battle is carried to the whole country. The Intercessors for Africa have National Prayer Houses in each country; that for Nigeria is, for instance, made up by young professionals who acquired university education in the 1970s and have gradually gone into full-time intercessory ministry. Emeka Nwankpa is a barrister-at-law; he studied at the University of Ife and is coordinator for the Eastern zone. Steve Okitika, an electrical engineer, studied at the University of Ife and is responsible for the entire house. Kola Akinboboye is a medical doctor in charge of the western zone. Uduak Udofia is a medical doctor and responsible for the southeastern zone. Ntiensen Inyang, a computer engineer trained in the USA, is in charge of Lagos. The Nigerian body is linked to other national houses in Africa such as Nandjui Dogbo Simon of the AD 2000 and Beyond Movement, Cote d'Ivoire, Sam Otu-Boateng, coordinator for Ghana; and Violet Ntegha for Abidjan. As the brochure says:

> The Ministry is nondenominational but complements and supplements the Church as a service arm. Intercessors for Nigeria has a network of cells in many cities of the country and each day of the week a number of cells uphold the country in prayers according to Is.62:6-7. Between God's prophetic abundance for Nigeria and its realization stands the intercessor to pray it into being.

The Ghana Intercessors publish a teaching magazine, *Obrapa*.[39] Affirming the relationship between divine initiative and human agency, they apply prayer as a tool to combat power and poverty. They do not ignore economic analyses but use these as knowing what to pray for when they refer the situation to God, who is the court of first instance.

Pentecostals affirm the rule of the saints as essential for the recovery of the nation. This implies getting entangled in soap-box hustling. ‚Praying brethren into offices' is now a familiar endeavor because when a ruler is just, the people rejoice. The first aspect is the trenchant criticism of the state not only in words but in action. City projects, prayer tours, retreats at crucial moments in the life of the nation (so as to confess the sins of the leaders that brought God's anger on the land, the rulers and the people) all constitute strategies of political dissent, an exercise of infrapolitics. For instance, during the Constitutional Conference of 1995 in Abuja, Nigeria, some Muslims proposed changing the Nigerian flag by adding a red star. The committee was led by a powerful Muslim traditional ruler. Adoption seemed imminent. The National Prayer House summoned about a hundred of its members to camp at the Sheraton Hotel, Abuja, for three days before the plenary session would vote. They prayed to God, telling Him that they realized this change was a ploy to impose and to display the Islamic symbol, that they were opposed to it. They implored God to intervene in spite of the high position of the chair of the committee. On the fourth day, the matter was tabled for voting. Suddenly someone stood up, declaring tinkering with the flag and the national anthem to be diversionary. The conferees yelled in support, and the motion was rejected- to the confusion of the big man. The jubilant prayer warriors thanked God and packed for home. This episode presentedis a new form of Christian political activism in the country. Without denying that Nigeria is a secular state, they act with the vision of a theocracy, where Yahweh rules. Pentecostals are, therefore, heavily involved in the Christian Association of Nigeria, designed to promote the interest of Christianity in a hostile environment in which the Muslims seek dominance and the use of Nigerian state to prosper the interests of Islam.

I.M.Enwerem calls this a dangerous awakening, because it threatens the pluralistic ideology of the modern state and it demonizes Islam as the spirit of the bondwoman.[40]Coming at the same time as the rise of Islamic fundamentalism, it has contributed to the surge of religious violence as frustrated Muslims watch resurgent Christianity in the preserved zone that colonialism carved. This explains the Moslem protest that led to the cancellation of Reinhardt Bonkee's program in Kano, 1994. The literature on the implosion of religion into the public space in Africa has burgeoned. The rise of Pentecostal theology of engagement is a crucial aspect to these developments as the 1997 Chalcedon Reports, concluded with the example of Zambia. The irony, however, is that sometimes the Pentecostals use the image of Cyrus to move beyond sectarian lines when praying for a leader who will be guided by the fingers of God. This radical politics has enabled Pentecostals to work with interfaith groups in the political arena in such places as Malawi, Kenya, Benin and Guinea. Here, the relationship between evangelism and political mobilization must be emphasized. There is a conscious use of evangelism to build up potential voters for Godly candidates.

Beyond running for office and encouraging the brethren in top political posts to be Modercais, their political theology has a very strong eschatological emphasis. The not-yet has intruded into the here-and-now. The foretaste of the not-yet should be increasingly experienced as the dynamic waiting period draws towards a close. Admittedly, Satan's reaction would increase but the fruits of a victorious life must be experienced. Human agency works with the divine in charitable institutions, refugee programs, financial investment institutions, and various forms of aid to those of the household of faith. Pentecostals run not only Bible schools but also nurseries. the Total Child Program is built around the Jesus model: he grew in body, spirit, and knowledge. A program of Christian education for children which combines learning with Christian formation is carried out by the Children Evangelism Ministry. It is nationwide in spread. This encapsulation program attaches great care to bringing up the children of brethren in Godly environment devoid of the foul spirits found among unbelievers. Family studies, clinics, marriage counseling are instruments of building up the Godly band.

The Intercessors and other ministries have spent much in the Liberian refugees problem and in assisting Liberian churches in their recovery projects. Many born again Christians have volunteered to serve as nurses, teachers, and doctors in Liberia, without remuneration. In Nigeria, for instance a call went out at the Onitsha Prayer Conference in January 1996 for those to whom the spirit ministered to take leaves of absence and to serve for God's approved time in Liberia. Some ministries have opened financial investment houses to assist members, provide jobs and funding for projects. But every ministry emphasizes charity as a virtue that God rewards. One's prosperity depends on how much one is willing to give back into the storehouse of the Lord and to aid the brethren. Every member is encouraged to assist another member instead of encouraging the person to ‚be warm' without providing the wherewithal. Such aid brings the foretaste and communalism of the future to the present.

Thus mobilized, Pentecostals could move into the political space that is widening in the wake of legitimacy crisis. From this perspective, the rise of Pentecostalism in Nigeria has more political import than has been realized by a narrow purview of what constitutes the political. This fact is not lost on Nigeria's Muslim-dominated military government. They have imposed tight immigration control on the entry of any person or persons with Christian motive for entering Nigeria. And so a new prayer point has been created for the band of prayer warriors who are using a variety of churchly means for radical politics.

For Pentecostalism, the political consists of discourse and activity on extraction and allocation of resources and services, providing the individual and community with spiritual and material benefits which the state promised but failed to provide. By creating a social order in that one can live a wholesome life with regulated, disciplined conduct, it mobilizes the multiple identities. By inventing and redefining a transnational identity, it brings the wider world into the village. Rooting in the primal world villagizes the urban context. It challenges the doctrine of the *l'etat theologique* by revisiting the state's modes of organizing power, its institutionalized domination, its general principles of state and norms of behavior. This is an enormous shift from a pietistic view of social activism as a means of restraining evil to politics as a means of advancing the kingdom. Pentecostals reconceptualize the moral order, claiming for it a redemptive vision of citizenship; and by reinstilling values in the family, they empower the vulnerable. Paul Gifford said that in Ghana,

> the appeal of these new churches is not only that they constitute new communities providing support no longer provided by dissolving traditional structures;or that they perform socail functions(like arranging marriages) that traditional procedures no longer accomplish;or that they give opportunity to the youth to exercise authority in gerontocratic society; or that they redress gender imbalance, or provide material assistance, employment, identity or opportunity, or bring colour (through their exuberant worship) to otherwise drab lives. They do not flourish primarily because they are a place to feel at home, or a homefor the homeless, or because they meet the quest for belonging.Undoubtedly many do these things in various ways and to various degrees, but they flourish mainly because they claim to have the answers to Ghanaians'existential problems and especially to their most pressing existentail problem, economic survival.[41]

He is partially right because he missed the most important aspect, namely, the religious revival that is blowing theough Africa as the wind of God.

Notes

1. A. F. Walls, "African Christianity in the History of Religious" *Christianity in Africa in the 1990's* eds. C. Fyfe and A. F. Walls (Edinburgh, Center for African Studies, 1996), 8-9; Ogbu U Kalu, "Estranged Bedfellows?: The Demonization of the Aladura in African Pentecostal Rhetoric" *Missionalia 28, 2/3* (August/November, 2000):121-142.

2. G. Oosthuizen, "African Environment: An Empirical Analysis", *African Insight,* 26, 4 (1996): 308-324, See, p. 309

3. J. Moltmann, *The Spirit of Life: A Universal Affirmation.* (London: SCM Press, 1992).

4. E. Sullivan, "Can Pentecostal Movement Renew the Churches?" *Study Encounter,* 8, 4 (1972): 1-16, esp. 4.

5. In J. Moltmann, *Pentecostalism as an Ecumenical Challenge* (London: SCM Press, 1996).

6. C. Peter Wagner, *Healing Ministry* (Ventura, CA: Regal Books, 1988).

7. Ruth Marshall, " Power in the Name of Jesus" *Review of African Political Economy* 52, (November 1991): 21-37.

8. W. Brueggemann, *The Prophetic Imagination.* (Philadelphia, PA: Fortress Press, 1978), 66-67.

9. C. Dykstra, *Vision and Character.* (New York: Paulist Press, 1981), 81.

10. Lewis R. Rambo, *Understanding Religious Conversion* (New Haven, CT: Yale University Press, 1993), 82, 137.

11. Walter Brueggemann, *Texts Under Negotiation: The Bible and Post-Modern Imagination* (Philadelphia, Fortress Press, 1993), 13-18.

12. Ruth Marshall, "God is not a Democrat: Pentecostalism and Democratization in Nigeria" ed. P. Gifford, *The Christian Churches and the Democratization of Africa,* :239-260, esp. 245.

13. J. I. Packer, *Knowing God* (Wheaton, IL: Harold Shaw Publishers, 1995), 178.

14. Adrian Hasting, The *Church in Africa, 1450-1950.* (Oxford: Clarendon Press, 1994), 453.

15. O. U. Kalu, *Embattled Gods,* chap. 10.

16. M. A. Ojo, "Deeper Life Bible Church of Nigeria" *New Dimensions of African Christianity ed.Paul Gifford (Nairobi,* AACC Publications, 1992): 161-185.

17. P. A. Pommerville, *The Third Force in Mission.* (Peabody, MA: Hendrickson Publishers, 1985), 41-62.

18. Paul Gifford, ed., *New Dimensions of African Christianity,* chap. 2; ibid., *Christianity in Doe's Liberia.* (Cambridge: Cambridge University Press, 1993).

19. R. Van Djik, "Young Born Again Preachers in Post-Independent Malawi" In Gifford, *New Dimensions*: 66-96.

20. M. A. Ojo, "Charismatic Movements in Africa" *Christianity Africa in the 1990's* eds. Fyfe and Walls: 92-110.

21. C. Omenyo, "The Charismatic Renewal Movement in Ghana" *Pneuma,* 16, 2 (1994):169-185;D. R. M. Smith, "A Survey and Theological Analysis of Spiritual and Evangelist Churches in Freetown, Sierra-Leone", (University of Edinburgh, Ph.D Dissertation, 1994); P. Gifford, *The New Crusaders.* (London: Pluto Press, 1991).

22. Rosalind Hackett, "New Directions and Connections for African and Asian Charismatics", *Pneuma,* 18, 1 (Spring, 1996): 69-77.

23. Karla Poewe, *Charismatic Christianity as a Global Culture* (Columbia, SC, University of South Carolina Press, 1994), chap. 2.

24. Gifford, *New Dimensions,* 186-214.

25. O. U. Kalu, "Who Is Afraid of the Holy Spirit?: Pentecostal-Charismatic Debate in the Presbyterian Church of Nigeria, 1970-1996", Commencement Lecture, Presbyterian College, McGill University, May, 1997.

26. H. Terris Neuman, "Cultic Origins of Word-Faith Theology within the Charismatic Movement", *Pneuma,* 12, 1 (Spring 1990), 32-55.

27. Robert M.Bowman, *The Word-Faith Controversy: Understanding the Health and Wealth Gospel* (Grand Rapids, MI:Baker Books, 2001).

28. Ruth Marshall-Fratani, "Mediating the Global and the Local in Nigerian Pentecostalism" JRA, 28, 3 (1998): 278-315.

29. Walter Wink, *Naming the Powers: The Language of Power in the New Testament* (Philadelphia, PA: Fortress Press, 1984), 5.

30. Ibid., 15.

31. Birgit Meyer, *Translating the Devil:Religion and Modernity Among the Ewe in Ghana* (Trenton, NJ:Africa World Press, 1999).

32. O. U. Kalu, "Unconquered Spiritual Gates: Inculturation Theology in Africa Revisisted" *Journal of Inculturation Theology,* 1, 1 (1994), 25-37.

33. Ruth Marshall-Fratani, "Mediating the Global and the Local in Nigerian Pentecostalism" *Journal of Religion in Africa,* 28, 3 (1998): 278-315;Birgit Meyer, "Delivered from the Powers of Darkness:Confessions of Satanic Riches in Christian Ghana", *Africa* 65, (1995): 236-55; ibid., "Make a Complete Break with the Past:Memory and Postcolonial Modernity in Ghanaian Pentecostal Discourse" *Journal of Religion in Africa, 28(1998): 316-49.*

34. Stephen Ellis and G.ter Haar, "Religion and Politics in SubSaharan Africa" *Journal of Modern African Studies 36 (1998):175-201.*

35. Ogbu U. Kalu, "The Third Response: Pentecostalism and the Reconstruction of Christian Experience in Africa, 1970-1996" *Journal of African Christian Thought*, 1, 2 (1998): 1-21; Karla Poewe, *Charismatic Christianity;*Cheryl Bridges Johns, *Pentecostal Formation.* (Shelfield: Academic Press, 1993), 86.

36. Rambo, *Understanding Religious Conversion*, 113-116.

37. W. Brueggemann, *The Land* (Philadelphia, Fortress Press, 1977), 2.

38. Paul Gifford, *Ghana's New Christianity: Pentecostalism in a Globalizing African Economy* (Bloomington, IN: Indiana University Press, 2004).

39. Kwame Bediako, *Christianity in Africa; The Renewal of a Non-Western Religion* (Maryknoll, NY: Orbis Books, 1995), 84.

40. I. M. Enwerem, A *Dangerous Awakening : The Politicization of Religion in Nigeria.* (Ibadan: IFRA, 1995).

41. Gifford, *Ghana's New Christianity,* ix

Chapter Six
Violent Faces of Religion:
The Dilemma of Pluralism in Nigeria

1. THE CHALLENGE OF PLURALISM: CONCEPT AND CONTEXT

The pressures of world security and the unabated insurgence of the global market economy have fueled the quest for world peace and the capacity for states to absorb and nurture racial and religious diversity. It used to be discussed under the rubric of secularism. Recently, this has been made obsolete by:

> the very dynamics of globalization which have posed anew the fundamental questions of the meaning, destiny, purpose and positioning of human existence within an increasingly complex order. [1]

With the end of the cold war, certain trends that were already in the air have assumed more prominence, such as the concept of the global village driven by innovations in communication and in new forms of modernization theory. Meanwhile, some themes that were expected to disappear have waxed stronger such as religion and ethnic identity. Some explain the new trend with the shift in the theory of knowledge from the predominance of the enlightenment worldview to a postmodernist paradigm. For Africa, the globalization trend poses the danger of recolonization or becoming a satellite of those nations that control the means of production. Some have suggested that Africa delink from the unequal global capitalist system, over which they have no control and concentrate on the logic of domestic developmental priorities. This death wish begs many questions. But the ideology of multiculturalism, that postures nations as cultural mosaics, growing from the deliberate exploitation of the rich cultural heritages within national boundaries, holds many prospects against the virulent ethnicity that power adventures exploited to commit genocide in Rwanda, and that has fueled numerous civil wars throughout the continent.

Unhappily, the choice is not so simple, because pluralism has many dimensions: at the sociological level, the cultural values of the constituent parts of the nation-state may have competing visions about life and the goals of the nation. Analysts have paid attention on the impact of tribes and tongues in inchoate nation-state boundaries on the stability of states. This raises the political dilemma about the distribution of political power and the specific institutional arrangements for sharing governmental power. [2] Sometimes these are entangled at the religious level with the coexistence of groups that hold divergent and incompatible views with regard to religious questions-those ultimate questions that concern the nature and destiny of man within a universe that stands under the reign of God. Their attitudes toward the state may be determined by the religious lens. This point is core in Samuel P. Huntington's *The Clash of Civilizations,* that has elicited much scholarly discussion. The return to the sacred, he said, is occurring in many parts of the world and most notably in the cultural resurgence in Asian and Islamic countries generated in large part by their economic and demographic dynamism. [3]Such Islamic countries have woven a wide international network that is spreading with much fervor into Africa. This fusion between religion, ethnicity, nationalism (both cultural and political), and civilization will constitute the determinant factors in world order rather than in ideology. With demands to know which side one might belong, this new force demands that one should affirm who one is.

For African, national politics is quite often perceived through these religious lenses, crafted in foreign cultures and bearing the cultural signatures of the craftsmen. Though Huntington notes the force of resurgent Islam his worst fears may be the Confucian civilization of China. Some scholars, such as P. P. Ekeh, have focused on sociocultural pluralism. The determinant external change-agent is colonialism, which is crucial for appreciating the challenging dilemma of pluralism. For one:

> The moral and social order which formally encased the pre-colonial indigenous institutions is burst by the social forces of colonialism and they seek new anchors in the changed milieux of colonialism.

Therefore, the task becomes:

> How to define a new cultural identity linked to the dimensions of the polity's populace, while eschewing identification of the state with any one of the cultural segments within it, which would immediately threaten the identity of other collectives. [4]

The ambiguities of authoritarian states in Africa only made the dilemma worse as they destroyed competing indigenous power nodes without building viable alternatives. Meanwhile, the states have failed to understand the force of religion as an attack on sociopolitical pluralism or to devise adequate measures that would to motivate the various religious groups to develop common principles that would allow each to function in a pluralistic context of community while maintaining differing identities.

Pluralism, therefore, poses enormous problems for Christianity in Africa. At the political level some perceive it as one of the sources of national instability. The argument is that the nation-state sets out to mobilize tribes and tongues within its boundaries for development, but that religious allegiances are manipulated by power-seekers for dysfunctional purposes. For Christianity, its record of collusion during the colonial era is a further liability. This plays into the socialist despair about the irridentism of religion; and from here the hegemonic state derives the excuse to become a competitor for the religious space. A new dilemma emerges as religious groups essay to deal with the problem of power and piety. Christianity comes under pressure to live with non-Christian religions, to maintain a certain ascendancy won during the past, era and to proselytize among primal religionists. As said in an earlier chapter, the biggest problem for Christian missionaries was how to deal with primal religions and cultures of Africa.

In non-Islamic states, Christianity faced the challenge of Islam from at least three angles: as the political space widened, the mounting pressures of the modern state created a virulent competition in variant political theologies and practices; then fundamentalists appeared vocally on the wings, installing orthodoxy in the midst of lost certitudes. Meanwhile, women escaped from purdah and enforced silence challenging patriarchy in the church, mosque and state. Fundamentalists, argue Marty and Appleby, have five characteristics: antisecularism, protection of identity and way of life, with weapons selected out of tradition, and against those seen as enemies to their cause, under God. [5]

The challenge of pluralism to Christianity is, however, fraught with irony. Pluralism is embedded in the core of the gospel and, in many ways, is a child of the missionary movement: it created the religious underpinning to democratic liberalism, it pandered the notion that religion is a matter of personal faith, based on personal persuasion and choice; and it succoured the ideology of the autonomous secular state. As Lamin Sanneh intoned, Christianity while strengthening Muslim territoriality, reinforced the privatization of Christianity. He traced the long journey in which the church confidently entered:

> Uncritically upon the heritage of its secular captors, gave up its autonomy as the price for being included in the affairs of the state. This created a peculiar situation as the church appropriated the national cultural enterprise as a devout vocation. [6]

Thus, the notion of religion as a social ornament predominated. While Christianity wriggled in secular captivity and intellectual reasonableness, Islamic political thought agonized through five positions with the challenges of pluralism: (i) a rejection of the rigid separation of religion and politics. Here the everydayness and grassroot use of the shariat radicates religion in a community and the political expression of the community perforce must be in religious terms; (ii) notional separation of religion and politics; (iii) affirmation that the religious sphere is non-identical though connected with the political sphere; (iv) the notion that coercion is worthy of religious integrity. This raises the question about the equal treatment of nonMuslims in an Islamic state; and (v) the fundamentalist head-on attack on modern confidence in political ultimacy and in the state as a finality.

The irony continues unabated precisely because Christianity is neither as open as the liberals project; nor does it embody a secularist worldview. The claim of uniqueness and normativeness arising from the doctrine of Christology led to exclusiveness. The relativism that ran like a thread from Kant through Schleiemacher to Troeltsch was decisively countered by Karl Barth until recently. Modern apologists for relativism take the theocentric highroad of Tillich, Wilfred Smith, and John Hick. This opens the way to other theocentric or Abrahamic religions such as Judaism and Islam. It does not adequately accommodate Buddhists who reject God as the ultimate reality. [7] Moreover, Tillich, like modern Judaistic theologians, emphasized the depth-dimension of faith as

> the idea that the inner religious essence, the Holy Spirit,
> is the dynamic and creative breading out through secu-
> larism and demonism to new forms of religious tran-
> scendence. [8]

By mining the creation saga and the covenant idea, the prophetic tradition in the Christian arsenal do not yield to a secularist dream. The
focus here is, therefore, how both Christians and Muslims worked
through the dilemma of pluralism in a modern African context,
fraught as it could be with all manners of political dangers. The patterns of the church's responses to the challenges of primal African
culture and religion, the theological pretensions of the state, the
resurgence of Islam, and the pluralism created by modernization and
the global market economy, are essential indicators of its capacity to
respond to the other challenges of power and poverty. These are the
stuff of modern African church history.

The effort here isolates a single issue with a case study of a
context where Christians and Muslims square off on equal numerical
strength and where their attitudes determine the fate of a nation
whose economy is in free fall. This is the story of the religious factor
in modern Nigeria. This West African nation has a population of
over a hundred million people, an enormous land size and mineral
resources that include oil. Nigeria became independent from British
rule in 1960. Instead of sourcing a polity from within, the country
adopted the Westminster political structure. Within half a decade,
the military smashed the system, caused a civil war and have been
in power for twenty-seven of the last thirty-two years. The unitary
command of the army has vitiated the federal structure of the polity,
and the militarization of the society, praetorian dictatorship and
unbridled corruption have stunned the populace into apathy and
cynicism. Every effort towards the return to democracy has met with
impasse. As R. Fatton argued, African military bear little resemblance
to a complex organization capable to providing an efficient, nation-
ally oriented and stable administration. Rather, the military makes
up armed camps owing primary clientellist allegiance to a handful of
mutually competitive officers of different ranks and seething with a
variety of corporate, ethnic, and personal grievances. [9] Even the Com-
monwealth heads of state have been forced to intervene on behalf of
the many political prisoners and against the execution of social activ-
ists. Economic collapse forced huge emigration of educated people
as the infrastructure rot. The Structural Adjustment Program has, as
usual, taken immense toll among the poorer sector of the popula-

tion This is because the crisis is not only at the macroeconomic level (where the debt stands at twenty- seven billion dollars in 1998) but in the agricultural sector, for the industrial and baking sectors have given way. Income per capita is now less than three hundred dollars.

The demise of the state has terrible implications: the public space is monologic and morally empty as the military constitutes itself into a theological state, monopolizing every discourse about the national interest and essaying to intrude into every aspect of the individual's life. In Nigeria, the politicization of the military dovetails into the militarization of the society and politics. The military is virtually a party comprising those who serve, retired officers, and their friends. The wealth of the nation is concentrated in their hands, and they can buy the political process at will. Civil society is emasculated, and the political class compromised in a certain intimacy of power as the government controls all the access to resources, utilizing patronage networks to web local elites in a powerful state. The spoils are called settlements, denoting the practice of buying potential opposition with money and brutalizing any who refuses to cooperate.

In such a highly pluralistic and segmented society this method is very effective. Indeed, the local constituency expects their representative to bring home their own share from the government, which is the only surviving industry. Ironically, as the state's resources diminish, the competition in this *politics of the belly* will grow more virulent. The centralization of power and resources has fueled more violent forms of ethnic and religious competition. Commentators use the technical terms *moral ethnicity* and *political tribalism* in describing the deliberate construction of new identities and communities and the clawing among such groups to appropriate the state's power for their own in a struggle for a piece of the national cake.

Meanwhile, politics has turned into the only arena for wealth as other means have dried up in the harmattan of military rule, and causing havoc on political culture and morality. Perhaps, it should be mentioned that what made the economic collapse traumatic was that the new nation state started life with a buoyant coffer based on agricultural cash crops. Oil created a boom in the 1970s, distorting the trend towards a single-product foreign exchange earner. The boom assisted the healing of the wounds of the civil war of 1967-1970, but the aftereffect was moral ruin. Corruption and indiscipline of the ruling class spawned strategies that soon wiped out all the assets and created debts in itswake within decades. Hosting the African Festival of Arts (1977) further opened the flood gates of squandermania.

Multinational corporations teamed with indigenous thieves or chiefs. It was as if a society that worshipped success deliberately blocked all the legitimate routes, leaving the entrepreneurs to invent illegal ones. In order to survive low wages and state predation, the bureaucracy fended for itself by erecting virulent forms of pen-robbery. Smuggling, fraud, and other forms of deviance become lucrative business among the majority.

A number of implications follow: the stability of the nation, especially the pursuit of pluralism, is threatened. First, Nigeria was carved out of many tribes and tongues as the old national anthem declared but with the hope that in brotherhood, we stand to hail the motherland. But soon, the hope became forlorn as the calabash of blood broke on our heads. Second, the religious divide between Islam and Christianity has a geographical consolidation; most of the north is Muslim, while the south is Christian; many of the northern ethnic groups came under Arab influence as early as the tenth century long before Christians came from the Atlantic ocean in the south in the nineteenth century (since earlier contact in the seventeenth century failed). The interweave of ethnicity, religion, and ecology redefines pluralism in the Nigerian context. As Ruth Marshall-Fratani put the matter:

> Pluralism in Nigeria means not, as theorists of liberal democracy explain it, plurality of interests meeting in a public sphere whose underlying cohesion is determined by a principle of citizenship captured by the ideology of juridical equality and symbolic force of the nation. Rather, it means a plurality of citizenship, each with its own moral vision, invented history, symbolic forms, models of power and authority, and institutional expressions, all interacting in the context of an authoritarian power whose control over public goods and accumulation is constantly under the pressure of their claims, and whose legitimacy is challenged by their alternate vision.
> 10

The problem of multiple identities, pauperization and collapse of social infrastructure combined to bring religion into the public square; the enlarged field brought out all the frustrations of the past. The quest for new moorings caused anger and violence. Religious violence in Nigeria has bedevilled the Nigerian political culture since the early 1980s.

Commentators have noted the resurgence of international Islamic fundamentalism from the 1980s. Nigeria has been pivotal precisely because of the invented histories of the Sokoto Caliphate and the Bornu-Kanem Empire. Oil became crucial in the OPEC efforts to counter Western dominance through oil politics. Islamic politics had two other dimensions: first, the process of decolonization built in a safety valve for the Muslim north by leaving it in control of the political rein. The background is embedded in the innards of colonialism in Nigeria, which we cannot indulge here. Second, in the interior of Islam is the concept of state power as necessary for the promotion of religion. The call for a rotational presidency and power-sharing in the Constitutional Conference of 1996 became a struggle that combined religion, economics, politics, and ethnicity. The Muslim north perceived a threat to rob them of their hold on power. Equally important is that the top military echelon in Nigeria has been dominated by the northerners, giving a certain coloring to the political culture and the tone and major issues in Christian political theology and practice in the last two decades. The Christian response to Islamic insurgence in Nigeria, therefore, raises all the crucial aspects of the role of religion and the dilemma of pluralism when religion essays to be a power node in contemporary Africa.

2. RELIGION AND THE CALABASH OF BLOOD, 1960-1970

The high profile of religion in the politics of independence harks back to the sunset of colonialism when various efforts were made to put the independent new state in constitutional order. The catalogue of constitutional experiments need not delay us; the journey is still long. Suffice it to say that the Nigerian Constitution (1960) is a modification of the 1954 Constitution that declared self-government for Nigeria under the British Crown. But the fears of minority ethnic groups loomed large in the last days of colonial rule. The new constitutions, therefore, entrenched a section of fundamental human rights. Most of the clauses were lifted from the European Convention for Protection of Human Rights and Fundamental Freedoms.

On specifically religious matters, the 1960 Constitution was silent on such issues as state religion. It neither prohibited the establishment of any state religion nor directly encouraged it. There was no wall separating church and state, even religious plurality was assumed based on, Section 23, which, *inter alia*, provided that:

> Every person shall be entitled to freedom of thought, conscience and religion, including freedom to change religion or belief and freedom either alone or in community with others, and in public or private to manifest

> and propagate his religion or belief in worship, teaching,
> practice and observance. (1960 Constitution)

Here, freedom of religion, as a juridical principle, deals with the external relations of individuals and groups. It endeavors to define in a vague manner the freedom to believe and to act by an individual, religious group, or the state.

One emphasis ensures that no individual could be forced to believe any set of religious doctrines. The second part of Section 23, which forbids religious instruction in other than one's affirmed religion reinforces this. Another emphasis on the freedom to propagate one's religion has had a long history from Lugard's protection of the Hausa/Fulani North from Christian missionaries to the gradual opening of the way to free evangelism. The tantalizing suggestion was that the way was now fully clear for unhindered evangelization and school openings so that parents could have the choice of selecting a school for their children. Was the sociopolitical context conducive to such an interpretation of the constitution?

As the nationalist euphoria rose in crescendo, the church suspected an attack from the state. The battle ground was education, because the missions used this as a tool for evangelization. Colman M. Cooke has examined the issue in eastern Nigeria, from 1950-1967, focusing on the Roman Catholic perspective while A. E. Afigbo continued the study to 1971 complementing Cooke's with a wider viewpoint. In that year, the federal and state (regional) governments took over the control of schools, ousting the churches. [11]Behind the debate on Universal Primary Education Program (1957), the common religious syllabus controversy (1963) and the state take-over of schools (1971) were deep-seated ideological cleavages. Matters were complicated by the Roman Catholic-Protestant rivalry, which spilled over into the political life of the new self-governing state. As Cooke states, the Roman Catholic ideology was hooked to the papal encyclical, *Divinus Illius*(Pius XI, December 1929). The basic contention is that man is both spiritual and physical; only religious values can supply the integrating principle that unifies these diverse but inseparable elements. In education, the rights of the family and the church are prior to those of the state made by natural and divine law.

Down from this high horse is the fact that Roman Catholics dominated primary school education in Eastern Nigeria though not secondary grammar schools. Moreover, the new political dispensation installed men in governance who did not consult adequately with the church; these men were coincidentally Protestants as only one Roman

Catholic was found in the first Azikiwe cabinet in eastern Nigeria, and the first minister of education, R. J. Uzoma, was an Anglican. Poor planning and inadequate consultation led to the failure of the UPE program, while the Roman Catholic awakening to the value of politics changed their numerical status in the 1957 cabinet. It is also clear that fear of loss of control of this vital agency for evangelization led to the rejection of the new uniform curriculum as well as the rise of Local Authority schools. As independence approached the erstwhile cordial relationship between Roman Catholics and the state broke down. Why?

The undergirding ideological source of the collapse was well studied by panels led by eminent Nigerian educationists such as Kenneth Dike and Alvan Ikoku. The nationalists condemned:

- the low level of science education and inadequate technological preparation,
- lack of emphasis on agriculture,
- neglect of traditional culture and civic education, and
- the predominantly Western, alien-based educational ideology.

Missionary education was alleged to have miseducated the people and laid the roots of underdevelopment. Obviously too, local people felt burdened by the cost of mission education and mistook increased government intervention as prospective relief. Even the Adefarasin Commission of 1965 on Teachers' Salaries indicated that many teachers in mission schools preferred to come under government employ in the hope of better conditions. Yet the church planned confrontations with the state. Though they were not united (as the Protestants were more receptive to state intervention), Christianity started life in the newly independent nation on a sour note.

While this titanic struggle was going on in eastern Nigeria, western Nigeria under the rulership of Obafemi Awolowo took a socialist posture that drew much inspiration from Kwame Nkrumah and other apostles of African socialism. The churches in western Nigeria were diplomatic and dared not confront him. Meanwhile, a contrary wind blew in the north as the seeds of Islamic fundamentalism were being sowed. This veritable religious and political challenge to Christianity was nursed in the early days of independence. The conflict between Christianity and Islam was, at first, an aspect of regional rivalry and development. The horrid face appeared later.

The figure of Sir Ahmadu Bello, the Sarduana of Sokoto, looms large in the religious politics of these years. He represented the ambition of the Sokoto Caliphate in the new dispensation. In the past, the British had smashed the caliphate, reduced the power of its leader from being *al-mir-mununi* with wide political powers to that a sultan (spiritual leader). But the British turned around to use the Fulani rulers and their traditional *sarauta* political system, coalesced in the hands of Emirs. Two consequences followed: first, while the Fulani rulers were endeared to the British, a significant section of the populace felt a religious affront which manifested the Mahdist revolts in the villages of Satiru, Bromi, and Dumbulwa. Second, quite a significant section of the north that was not conquered by the jihadists were imposed with Hausa/Fulani chieftains. But the image of a united north remained a mirage.

To mobilize and unite the north, the sardauna used religion and embarked on an extensive, evangelistic campaign of Islamization. He wanted to restore the glory of the caliphate. His conversion tours constituted a new form of jihad using political clout. He distributed free copies of the Quran and Islamic literature, rewarded those who converted with civil service posts and rulership over communities, and encouraged Muslim settlers to combine economic and political power. There was massive renaming of villages with Muslim names, acquiscent village heads were rewarded with cash amounting to five pounds sterling. The sardauna claimed that he converted over 60, 000 persons to islam in five months. Realizing the prerequisites of modernity, he nurtured the *madarasa* or Western education in an Islamic setting. He bred a new class of intellectuals to replace outmoded ulama. He mobilized funds for these by linking the north to international Islam. Thus, Saudi Arabia, Egypt, Pakistan, Iran, Turkey contributed cash and other forms of aid. It was this intrepid man who dusted up and hoisted the sharia. He assiduously implemented the recommendations of Justice Muhammed Abu Ranner Panel on the place of Islam in the new nation state.

In 1962, the sardauna formed the *Jama'tu Nasril Islam* (Victory for Islam) as a central body to coordinate the resurgence. The Supreme Head was the Sultan of Sokoto, his deputy was the Shehu of Borno. All Muslim traditional rulers served as patrons while a central council was chaired by Sheikh Mahumud Gumi, the Grand Khadi of the northern region. The goals were to establish and run schools, hospitals, dispensaries, public enlightenment programs, through seminars lectures and conferences. [12] The intense politicization of religion reached great heights in the party, the Northern Peoples' Congress (NPC). The sardauna used state apparati, funds, and conversion tours to campaign for the party and to discipline the opposition. Reactions followed: the Hausa city of Kano revolted and formed the Northern Elements' Progressive Union (NEPU). Thus, party politics was fought along an intramural religious divide. Furthermore, the Tivs resented their subjugation and enforced Islamization. State clout was used to rout the Tiv revolt between 1960-1964. The Tivs countered by forming the United Middle Belt Congress (UMBC), a political party allied to the Yoruba party, Action Group (AG). Non-Muslims who lived in the northern region resented the policy of One people One North as being tantamount to religious bondage. K. W. Post (1963), B. J. Dudley (1968), J. I. Tseayo (1975), R. Anifowose (1984), Bala Usman (1987), P. A. Williams (1988), A. E. Ekoko and L. O. Amadi (1989) have all drawn attention to the use of religion as an instrument of sociopolitical oppression. This laid the eggs which hatched into ethnoreligious conflicts of 1980s-1990s. However, John Paden's biography of Sir Ahmadu Bello (1986) tried to paint over these foundations of political instability. He proved unconvincing in the shadow of cloud of witnesses. [13]

Indeed, the sardauna's activities touched off an intra-mural warfare within Islam which reverberated into the political scene. Over 90% of the Muslims in the north belong to *sufi* brotherhoods (*tariqas*). Sir Ahmadu Bello, as well as many other prominent politicians within the ruling party (who then had bureaucratic, economic, and political powers) were all members of the *Qadiriyya*. This gave brotherhood an edge over the *Tiyaniyya* in the region. The NPC politicians used the state apparatus to suppress the latter. The Northern Elements Progressive Union (NEPU) became the platform for anti-Qadiriyya and Emirate protests. Malam Aminu Kano a *Tiyaniyya* scholar and a populist politician equated the Qadiriyya and the *sarauta* system of the ruling class as the subjugators of the poor (*talakawa*). Religion and class allied to question the erastian conception of power among the Fulani, caliphate elite. The NEPU position was bolstered by the arrival of the saintly Sheikh Ibrahim Niass from Senegal. Whatever this holy man lacked in political power, he made up with *barka* (spiritual power). He turned the *Tiyaniyya* into a formidable power. Even the sardauna sought his legitimizing nod. Soon this spirituality created a reformist inner group within the sufi orders further exacerbating the forms of intra-Muslim religious conflict. The attack of the *sufi* orders on the *Ahmadiyya* is a larger issue.

Then, the civil war broke a calabash of blood on the head of the nation in 1967. Explanations are rife and there is substantial effort to disengage religion from the cause and consign it to Biafran propaganda. The trouble in western Nigeria that triggered the political chaos had no explicit religious cleavage and the killing of Igbo people (Ndigbo) could be given a political rationale. Such explanation fails to understand the psychological impact of the death of the sardauna on the Islamic resurgent force that he revved up. It simply disorganized matters and the ,pogrom' was the unleashing of pent-up frustration. Later, in 1984, the Gamji Memorial Club was formed in Zaria in an effort to turn Ahmadu Bello into a patron saint and a rallying symbol for aggressive Islam. Religion was important in the politics of the civil war because starvation was used as a weapon of war and this attracted relief organizations, most of whom were from Christian groups. The World Council of Churches and the Roman Catholic Caritas, the CanAir relief (inspired by the Presbyterians of Canada) spent millions of dollars to succour victims on both sides of the great divide. Religion was an instrument of diplomacy, as both sides sent prominent clerics as emissaries to Europe to seek support. Christians divided as those in the West turned against those in Biafra. Typical was Bola Ige's diatribe at the WCC Assembly in Uppsala (1968) against those who aided the rebels through what he termed as misguided relief.

The force of this division is best grasped by recalling the character of pre-civil war Christianity. Political nationalism seeped into the churches and inspired the debates on indigenization and moratorium. The goal was to make Christianity more relevant to the African context. Inculturation was a form of cultural nationalism. Its strident form, moratorium, wanted the Europeans to stop sending material and human resources for a period so that the African churches could achieve a measure of authenticity. It was a heady, optimistic period as missions turned into local churches claiming maturity. Soon the Protestants planned a church union called Church of Nigeria by collapsing denominational differences imported from Europe in the guises of Anglicans, Methodists, and Presbyterians. Admittedly, the union was programmed as a united Protestant face against Roman Catholics. [14]

The political aspect of this rivalry has not received adequate scholarly attention. There was more than mere rivalry for turf; each religious group became a political pressure group, struggling to field candidates in the polls and to capture the regional houses of assembly. [15] This quest for political power was a means of protecting enormous investments in education and healthcare delivery. Nationalists breathed secularist ideology, forcing Christians into the political affray in self-defense. At first Christians sought to maintain the dalliance of an earlier period; then they declared the political zone to be neutral and irreligious, not to be occupied by any religious group. Lately, Christian insurgents have sought to fight for every privilege given to Muslims and to capture the command-controls of the state. Before this last posture, the civil war destroyed the united front towards cultural and political nationalism. Religion was used to legitimize the rebellion of Biafra as well as the revengeful insensitivity of other Nigerians, which the Aburi Accord could not stop.

As Chris Okigbo lamented in his poem *Path of the Thunder* both the winners and the losers in the civil war paid dearly. Besides, the civil war spurred anti-Christian forces: for one, traditional religion was heavily patronized in the wave of cultural revival. Second, the *Ahiara Declaration* (1968) signaled the incursion of socialist ideology into political discourse in Biafra and this planted the roots for the growth of state power signaled by thestate-take over of the churches' social welfare apparatus in the immediate aftermath of the civil war. The federal government moved to restrict the movement of European and American Christian leaders who were connected with relief to Biafra. For instance, Dr. E. H. Johnston, the secretary of the Board of World Mission of the Presbyterian Church in Canada, was denied a visa for mounting the CanAir Relief Program. The decline in the number of missionaries to Nigeria started from this point. Many Irish Holy Ghost priests were repatriated from eastern Nigeria.

3. RELIGIOUS RIVALRY AND OIL BOOM, 1971-1979.

Certain healing balms aided Nigeria to recover from the social wounds of the war: at the religious level, there was a wind of spiritual revival; at the administrative level were the breakdown of the old regions into twelve states, the oil boom, and Christian ethics that informed General Gowon's policies. At the economic level, the indigenization decree paid huge dividends to those who won the war and ensured the marginalization of those returning from the rebellious enclave. The oil boom, equally bred intensive competition for the national cake inducing social policies to ensure social justice and equity: universal primary education, quota system, catchment areas, federal character, and the insertion of the secularity of the state into the constitution. The creation of more states from twelve (1967) to nineteen (1976), twenty-one (1987), and thirty (1991)mandated in the 1979 constitution provided for broad-based criteria for political parties and electoral success, designed to mellow ethnic conflicts and recognize the voice of minority ethnic groups. However, as the regions became increasing unviable economic units, the power fulcrum concentrated in the center and intensified rivalry for resources of the center. Along with these was the centralization of education through the National Universities Commission, the Committee of Vice-Chancellors, the Joint Admission and Matriculation Board, and civil service reforms.

However, certain issues remained intractable – revenue sharing, allocation of industries and infrastructure, utilization of external debts and suchlike. In this welter of policies, the central government grew by leaps and bounds, monopolized extensive power and purse, and drastically encroached upon the legislative powers formerly left to the regions. The cost to maintain the government escalated. The states were economically dependent on the center. As said earlier, military rule with its unified command virtually ran a unitary rather than a federal structure. Rivalry intensified as the character of federalism was skewed.

More than this, the rabid pursuit of petro-naira enticed people away from agriculture and other productive sectors into brief-case contracting. It debased moral values and the political culture. It raised to the fore the issue of ethics of power – the value system that undergirds the perception and exercise of power. Croynism, clientelism, and unbridled corruption ate deeply into the moral fabric of Nigerian society. Recovery has proved difficult. The Constitutional Conference and Constitution of 1979 sought to deal with many of these problems while Operation Feed the Nation and belt-tightening regulations of the economy sought to cool the squandermania characterized by the international festival of arts and culture (FESTAC 7 hosted by Nigeria at a great expense. As usual, rivalry in the socio-economic and political spheres was played out in the religious space. Let us focus on three facets: religion in the 1979 Constitution, the rise of religious fundamentalism, and proliferation of para-religious cults. All had immense political overtones.

The Constitutional Conference, 1978-79 provided politicians with an opportunity to indulge in religious politics and open old wounds. The provisions on fundamental human rights are indubitable. Sections 23, 26, and 27 dealt with three issues: to define the status of religion, the posture of the state in religious matters, the freedoms and the status of the sharia laws in the midst of inherited Western judiciary system. An effort was made to curb the force of religion in national politics by a weak form of separation of religion and state. It enshrined a secularist ideology that struck at the theocratic conception of power and drew a boundary between the sacred and profane which ran contrary to prevalent worldviews. Besides, ambiguities pervaded this claim for neutrality which did not spell indifference. Would the state no longer aid pilgrims, donate to religious organizations, use the state apparatus or functionaries to assist the observation of religious holidays and occasions or use religious symbols? The constitution avoided specifics as if the problem would disappear in silence. Yet the constitution declared several freedoms – to practice and change religion, manifest, propagate one's belief privately, and worship and teach publicly. There was protection from coercion, and citizens could receive religious instructions in any place of education maintained wholly by one's religious community. It shielded state schools from religious controversy.

The constitution further webbed itself into the dilemma of pluralism by dovetailing an English judiciary system to an Islamic one:

- A Sharia court of appeal for each state consisting of a Grand Quadi and such numbers of Quadi as may be prescribed by the legislature of each state;
- The Sharia court shall operate where there is one in existence on the date when this section (of the Constitution) comes into force;
- After the date when this section comes into force, Sharia courts could be established if the House of Assembly passes a resolution bringing the subsection into force and the governor of the state by order confirms that resolution.

Muslims sought to use the sharia controversy to urge for an Islamic state. They used symposia in schools to urge the Islamic position. The Christians countered by forming Christian Association of Nigeria (CAN). It was presumed that the JNI could sustain their attack because of centralized structures. The CAN publicity unit produced a series entitled *Leadership in Nigeria* to argue (i) Christian responsibility in politics, (ii) the dominance of Muslims in the governance of northern minorities, and jointly-owned institutions such as the Bank of the North, and (iii) Muslim dominance of the political leadership of Nigeria. Monsignor H. A. Adigwe examined the portentous event in a bestseller, entitled, *Nigeria Joins the Organization of Islamic Conference (OIC): The implications for Nigeria*. It sold 24, 000 copies in one year, indicating that all forms of media were utilized to make religion a political keg of gun powder.

The *Report of the Political Bureau, Federal Government of Nigeria*, March 1997 has adequately pointed to the dysfunctional role of organized religion in Nigerian politics but does not explore the roots. It argued that it is endemic in the nature of organized religion to create competing social orders, to direct how social life and society in general should be organized; that religion allies with the political power structure in society and could be used by the moneyed class for their own ends. Since religion claims to be a basic community that submerges and transcends the ethnic community, it tends to periodically challenge national community; it delays national integration and fails to remedy the fate of the poor. Organized religion by its competing loyalty, interference with economic processes, and foreign linkages constitutes a danger to national development. In the element of mysticism lies buried the roots of volcanic violence, warned the report. Some Muslims quickly attacked the implications of this leftist sociological analysis informing the report. There is no indication that the federal government gave it any attention precisely because the leaders were Muslims.

The rise of religion into prominence in national politics threatening the fragile structure, conjuring confederation and breathing disintegration has roots in the changing faces of religions in the aftermath of the civil war. A revivalist spiritual wind blew throughout the world. In Nigeria, for instance, Pentecostal-charismatic spirituality challenged the evangelical ardor and political theology of mainline churches. The new political theology of engagement countered Islamic insurgence and its monopoly of the public space. The Christian presence in the Muslim North became loud and uncomfortable. The moral and social order created by colonialism was shattered as attacks were mounted on the historic protection of the north by the colonial masters. The new Christian religiosity provided new hope for un-Islamized northern communities, a veritable religion of the oppressed. Of great importance in this period was the rise of youthful charismatism that flowed like a molten lava from the south to the north. The new evangelical force caused an intra mural conflict within the Christian camp. Fervent young preachers ignored the accomodationist culture that the mainline churches had established with the Islamic rulers of the north. The born-agains confronted the older missions as bench-warmers and carnal Christians, and renewed the old evangelical crusade to convert Muslims. Their rhetoric demonized Islam as the religion of the bondservant. Such confrontation was bound to elicit violent response.

It must be stressed that religious revival in Nigeria was not only among Christians and Muslims. Beyond the Christian pale, parareligious or theosophic movements flowered: Eckankar, the Grail Message, AMORC/Rosicrucians, Freemasonry, the Aetherius Society, and Odd Fellows. Their internal histories, that have so far eluded scholarly inquiry indicate rapid vertical expansion. An interviewed (Grail) crossbearer argued that the suffering during the civil war was a spiritual cleansing that opened people up to new religious ardor. It was as if the nation indulged in an extensive religious quest. A sharpened spiritual consciousness has immense sociopolitical implications. For instance, there was a renaissance of indigenous religious rites and symbols during the civil war as people resortd to the old spiritual forms that served effectively in the past. In the new dispensation, it became easy for people to use indigenous cults as powerful support as they forayed into competition for the resources of the modern public space. Stephen Ellis and Gerrie Ter Haar have been attentive to the importance of indigenous cults in modern Africa's political dynamics. [16]

Similarly, in Islam several things were happening:

- a perceived gap widened between Muslim realities and Islamic ideals;
- an intellectual renaissance within Islam exposed the unIslamic character of a community (*umma*) suffering from the sideeffects of oil boom, moral decadence, and spiritual bankruptcy;
- a social movement grew, urging political action, a form of jihad, to recapture political power in order to change the realities, and to bring the community to an Islamic ideal;
- unemployment created a demographic bulge among the *almajiri*, youths who function as students of mallams, and survive through begging.

The challenge for Muslims was how to respond to the pluralistic modern state, the new economic order, and the new morality. The plurality of voices within Islam further challenged the possibility of a concerted response. Lamin Sanneh explains the matter aptly:

> as committed Muslims see it, the state as it has operated
> in the Africa or elsewhere is hard to ignore: Its predomi-
> nance brings it four square into Islam's comprehensive
> sphere, thus causing Muslims to bristle at the autonomy
> the modern Western claims for state jurisdiction. Such
> a claim turns the state into an explicit rival religion bol-
> stered by an impregnable system of rewards and induce-
> ments, as well sanctions and penalties. It specifically
> excludes faith of the religious kind. [17]

Worldwide Islamic trends stimulated by the Iranian Revolution further inspired this trend while the game of religious arithmetic (the claim that Nigeria was 70% Muslim) underpropped this facet.

Islamic political theology rejected the claim for the primacy of the secular state that was enshrined in the constitution. Meanwhile, the reform of Islam through antisufism gained momentum, ensuring that intramural conflicts increased as shiites and sunnites won patronage from Iran and Saudi Arabia to propagate varieties of Islam.

The columns of Ibrahim Sulaiman and the goal of *Radiance* magazine, the activities of the Moslem Students Society (MSS) and the Council of Ulama betray the intellectual streak. The *izalatu* associated with Sheik Gumi carried the other burdens assisted in the political sphere by MSS. Alhaji Gumi, scholar and Islamic judge was a close associate of Sir Ahmadu Bello and used his polemic articles in *Gaskya ta fi Kwabo* (Truth is worth more than a penny) to good effect. His *tafsir* (Quaranic exegesis) sessions on Federal Radio, Kaduna, were used to relate the doctrines and practices of the Islamic faith and to attack the beliefs and practices of the *sufi* brotherhoods.

This intramural warfare explains his controversy with al-Ilori a Muslim clerical leader from Ilorin, southwestern Nigeria. Gumi trained many young scholars whom he posted to secular schools to prevent loss of faith. In July 1978, some of these young people formed an organization whose goal was the prevention of innovation – *Jama's Izalat al Bidt's a wa Iqamat as Sunnah* (Izalatu for short). It was led by an ex-soldier, Ismaila Idris. Through rallies, public preaching, recorded audio cassettes, building of mosques, and an aggressive use of the media, they spread like harmattan fire. The *Izalatu* was different from MSS which was founded in 1977 and operated from Ahmadu Bello University, Zaria. By scrawling *Islam Only* on walls, the MSS sought to imprint Islam on tertiary institutions of the north at the expense of non-Islamic inhabitants of the ivory tower. The Council of Ulama, an adult version of MSS, was composed of prominent Muslims, trained in Western education, seeking to guide Islam in the face of modernization. The council served as the voice of the educated Muslim elite, and as the pool from which Muslim control of the federal government's key bureaucratic and parastatal positions were filled.

The proliferation of radical groups within Islam needs careful delineation; for instance, the Muslim Students' Society, which actually initiated with Yoruba students in Lagos, was turned into more radical confrontational force by the Ahmadu Bello University students. But it soon divided into factions lured by foreign money – an *anti Darika*, pro-Saudi group called *Dawah* was led by a certain Aminu deen Abubakar. *Umma*, a pro-Iranian group, also came into being, often cooperating with the Izalatu. Meanwhile, some students in the Movement for Progressive Nigeria sought to deal with the crisis of identity within a nation state that was increasingly secularized and suffused with material temptations they perceived as a threat to the Muslim faith. [18]

Thus, by the end of the 1970s Nigeria was witnessing intra-religious conflicts, interreligious conflicts, and interethnic conflicts, many of which had religious dimensions. This last feature was an attempt by non-Islamized northern ethnic groups to throw off Islamic rule imposed on them at an earlier period. However, it must be stressed that the turmoil had both religious and theological reasons as well as socioeconomic context.

4. VIOLENT FACES OF RELIGIOUS POLITICS: 1980-1996

From 1980, violent religious-related clashes became predominant as to the number of incidences, the macabre level of brutality, and the geographical spread. It mostly occurred in the North and for the larger part during military rule. The connection with the military, says Hassan, is that:

> by its nature, military rule denies access to all other channels of organized opposition;. . . for many fundamentalists, military rule imposes all kinds of limitations on their ability to negotiate with the state; discontent finds expression in religions violence in speech and action. [19]

The phenomenon of the violent face of religion is attested by the following data:

TABLE 6.1 – Kano Riots, 30 October, 1982; Churches Attacked

Name	Type	Location/Road
Christ Redemption Church	Aladura	Burma Road
The Church of the Lord	Aladura	Burma
Cherubim & Seraphim Movement	Aladura	Freeman
Pentecostal Church of Christ	Pentecostal	Festing
Cherubim and Seraphim	Aladura	Sani Giwa
Cherubim & Seraphim Church	Aladura	Sanusi
Igbala Apostolic Church	Pentecostal	Whetherhead
Church of Light	Aladura	Hughes

TABLE 6.2 – Ethnoreligious Religious Clashes: Northern Nigeria, 1980-1992

Date	Location
1980	Kusuwan Magani
1984	Zangon-Kataf, Gure-Kahugu
1987	Kafachan, Lere
1989	Ilorin, Lere
1991	Tafawa Balewa
1992	Zangon-Kataf

TABLE 6.3 – Maitatsine Uprising, 1980-1985

Location	Ward State	Date	Death	Arrest
Awaki	Kano	18-20/12/80	1, 171	1, 673
Bulumkutu, Maiduguri	Borno	26-29/10/82	118	411
Rigassa/Tundun Wada	Kaduna	29/9-3/10/82	53	116
Dobeli, Jimeta, Yola	Gongola	27/2-5/3.84	568	980
Pantami, Gombe	Bauchi	26-28/4/85	105	295

*Compiled from Official sources.

Within a two year period, 1987-1988 three religious clashes occurred in educational institutions of various levels ranging from secondary through teachers' college to the university. Just as the Kano riot was masterminded by students, so did they trigger off the riots in Kafancan and Zaria in 1987. In the first instance, Kafanchan town had a majority of Christians ruled by Muslim chiefs. The cause celebre was an outreach by the Joint Christian Fellowshipin March 1987. Protest over their propaganda soon spilled into an alleged misinterpretation of the Quran. The MSS attacked but the fight extended into the town and ended with decimation of Islamic forces. The news created reprisals in Funtua, Zaira, Kankia, Daura and Kaduna – where the Federal Government Radio was used in mobilizing the Islamic faithful. Two months later, it was the turn of Queen Amina College, Kaduna. The girls insisted that they want to wear Islamic uniform. The most extensive religious clash in a tertiary educational institution occurred in the Ahmadu Bello University, Zaria when the MSS clashed with Christian students from the south in the electoral contest over the leadership of the students' union on 13 June 1988. The Muslim students used the Gamji Memorial Club (in honor of the late sardauna) as their instrument. They fielded Lawal Usman. The Movement for Progressive Nigeria fielded Salihu Lukman Mohammed, and the Christians offered Steve Awobi, a Yoruba. When it appeared that the Christians won, the Muslim students rampaged into the hall where the ballots were being counted. The election was canceled. Mayhem ensued.

The three tables indicate that beginning in 1980 Islamic revivalism took a violent turn as a welter of brutal religious outbursts occurred in a consistent and unrelenting fashion through a decade. Some were at educational institutions. For instance, the Queen Amina Secondary School incident showed that the mood had seeped into youthful environments. Others have focused on antiChristian targets, while the Maitatsine have proven to be the most complex. Still others mixed ethnic with religious factors, betraying the bitterness of yesteryears. All carried immense political overtones.

Incidentally, some scholars ignore the religious politics of the period because the political parties were a hybrid of ethnic and religious components and the cabinets in military regimes bore various religious colorings. Indeed, a survey of socioeconomic policies of the period 1975-1993 indicate a massive effort by the federal government of Nigeria to improve the economy, extend the range of the social infrastructure, revitalize agriculture, bring government to the grassroots, detribalize the culture; pander to religious groups, and create more states. The irony is that the number of states further vitiated their viability. The government endeavoured to salvage the morals of the nation and to clean the environment. Indeed, the transition program of the1990's was the most elaborate effort to sanitize the political culture. The war against fraudsters, drug traffickers, and hired assassins were complemented with more elaborate information-sharing (MAMSER), mobilization of the womenfolk (Better Life Program) and provision for a rural infrastructure (DFRRI). Attention on these matters of great moment may ignore the fact that the religious factor continued to mirror the instability of the nation and they legitimacy crises.

But the period witnessed enduring debates on education – nomadic and otherwise, Nigeria's membership in Organization of Islamic Conference (OIC), Sharia Courts – both at state level where they do not exist and at Appeal and Supreme Court levels. The government responded by creating an Advisory Council on Religious Affairs, and by reestablishing diplomatic ties with Israel – to please the Christians who protested over the surreptitious registering of Nigeria as a member of Organization of Islamic Countries. [20]

The violent language and brinkmanship in these debates, especially those led by newspapers such as the Islamic-sponsored *New Nigeria* and Alhaji M. K. O. Abiola's *Concord*, touched on raw religious nerves. Various explanations have been proffered the for these outbursts. The religious explanation, the conspiratorial, and the socioeconomic signified by the Lubeck model. The religious explanation argues that trends in both Islam and Christianity produced the horrendous situations. Muhammad Sani Umar has pointed out that there was a loss of confidence in the Islamic elite by fellow Muslims. The creation of more states, which dismantled the regional system, weakened political Islam at the national level, and the national leaders of the old northern region, who would have liked to pass as protectors of Islam, woefully failed to demonstrate the Islamic imprint on their public lives:

- deeply engrossed in material acquisition, they rode rough-shod of ribah prohibitions in their economic live;
- the legal manifestation of Islam was destroyed because they could not enforce the tenets of sharia. The damage was so extensive that even Moslems opted out of sharia in protest of corrupt practices;
- religious piety was vitiated by formalism, leaving little spiritual observance despite the proliferation of mosques;
- educational/intellectual manifestation appeared so helpless and impotent, that it could not control deviations;
- despite of the formation of the Supreme Council for Islamic Affairs, richly endowed by the Pakistani, Yusuf Farde, it failed to be effective and to muster sufficient authority and influence.

These explain why the baton passed to the students, the unemployed and the exploitative mallams to protect Islam in the way they knew best. As mentioned earlier, the rise of Charismatic/Pentecostals who dared into the old North with greater confidence and garnered votaries exacerbated matters. A description of the preparation, advertisement, and royal arrival of the German tele-evangelist Reinhard Bonkee into Kano (1991) captures much of the Muslim disgust. They rose in violent protest. This was similar to the Kano riot of 1982 over the extension of an Anglican church in the Feggae ward. Inexplicably, the attack (as shown in Table 7: 1) focused on Aladura/Pentecostals – those whose pneumatic theology produced proactive political theology and practice.

Similarly, the rise of the Christian Association of Nigeria (CAN) achieved strange results: It brought Christians in the north and south together. Efforts of yesteryears had failed to do so because many of the Evangelical missionaries who served in northern Nigeria were nondenominational and apolitical. Political awareness bred a new social ecumenism – cooperation on the sociopolitical interface. Even old diatribes against Catholics vanished. This block/ecumenical pattern has immense political importance. The argument here is that the conflict had some religious roots even when religious passion was being manipulated for political ends.

The conspiratorial model emphasizes that these students had a hidden political agenda; that history tends to impress it upon Muslims that true Islamic religion cannot be established without political supremacy. Therefore, there is a need to rebel against injustice and oppression (seen as the predominance of Christian symbols and orientation in modern Nigerian structures); to essay to establish an Islamic state at an opportune time, and to replace or purify a corrupt Muslim leadership. External funding and inspiration from international bodies and foreign Arab countries accentuate this political agenda. As Ruth Marshall-Fratani says of new Islamic movements:

> although rooted in local contexts and engaged directly
> with local and national issues, have the particular-
> ity of being part of trans national movement. This participa-
> tion has important consequences not only in terms of the
> ways in which identity is constructed and community
> imagined, but the terms upon which these movements
> engage with the state. [21]

It breeds the tendency to use religion as a cultural signifier and as a marker in dealing with the non-Muslims ansd southerners. The conspiratorial model weaves into the manipulation theory that avers that the northern political elite harnessed the activities of the young revivalists mostly for the advancement of their political needs.

This explains some of the contradictory aspects in the Maitatsine. For instance, Marwa Maitatsine vituperated endlessly against rich Muslims. His followers postured as jihadists, a revolutionary enterprise to restore orthodoxy and to establish an Islamic state. The governemnt of Kano state appeared frightened to stamp out the charismatic religious leader, and even pandered him with so much freedom that he reigned in a section of the city. Some faceless politicians exploited this antiChristian rhetoric in the heady competition for political power, and the resources of the federal government.

Fundamentalist patronized the Maitatsine because of a shared dream of a new reformed Islamic *umma* with a new set of leadership abandoning the old brigade who discredited the *darika* philosophy and disengaged from the grassroots. B. J. Takya has argued that northern Nigeria was a good soil for Maitatsine because of a relatively high rate of unemployment. The young unemployed cadre variously known as *almajirai, gardawa, yan-dako,* and *yan amalanke* were victims of a poor income distribution structure, wide income differentials, and poor Western education. [22] Yet the Maitatsine was an affront to orthodox Islam because of his unorthodox modes of prayers and observances, antiauthoritarianism, derogatory doctrines, condemnation of modern social and material objects of culture, and display of eccentricities such as drinking human blood and tattooing.

The Lubeck model focuses on these socioeconomic roots and sees violent fundamentalism as a reaction of precapitalist institutions to developments in modern setting. He argued that the *gardawa* system or mass attachment of unemployed youths to mallams for the purposes of acquiring Islamic education also has a socioeconomic role. It produced rural-urban linkages, and contributed to political and cultural integration. The *gardawa* system created important interrelationship between ecology, economy and ideology. It fostered the growth of a moral economy. The oil- boom years transformed Kano and Islam and undermined the system. [23] Droughts and the collapse of both rural economy and the economy of the rentier state produced astronomic sideeffects. Elizabeth Isichei and M. Hiskett, following the Aniagolu Report on the riot, have emphasized this model. [24] The ghetto locations of the Maitatsine revolts (see Table 6: 3) lend weight to this aspect to the aspect disaster. There is a certain irony that Islamic revolutionaries respond to the scourge of poverty by using violence against the pluralistic ideology of the state as if that was the cause. Underneath is a moral judgment on rulers, and lacking are projects to empower the poor.

Finally, the violent face of religion and the brinkmanship in religious politics have failed to provide an alternative moral political economy or to address the political issues in such a manner as to rid Nigeria of military dictators. Various leaders, civilian and military, have therefore reacted by crying more than the bereaved: Gowon made hortatory speeches on the collapse of morality; then Shagari proclaimed an Ethical Revolution drive, Buhari and Idiagbon renamed the program War Against Indiscipline (WAI) and Abacha added corruption to the WAI. The question remained in its classic version: Quis Custodiet Custodes? Who controls the rulers? Are these not sterile utilitarian ethics? The lack of salient political values among the elite is matched by an unrestrained level of moral turpitude by the generality. The image of Nigeria at home and abroad has darkened. Nigerian womanhood was debased in new methods of drug trafficking. Behind these daring, primitive feats was a basic national ideology, namely, that everything is possible by any means available. Thus the irony that religious politics rose in crescendo amidst decline in religious piety.

In summary, the churches in Nigeria have responded to the challenge of ethnic pluralism by widely expanding the range of their evangelical activities, especially when the colonial government opened access to evangelizing the North. The counter measures by the Sardauna of Sokoto did not daunt that spread because many parts of the North had escaped the onslaught of the jihad. Besides, many southerners were trading and working in government bureaucracy in the north and formed Christian congregations. Unlike Islam, Christianity has a larger pluralistic ethnic base and has, through vernacular translation of the Bible served to preserve many indigenous cultures and languages. In response to indigenous cultures and religions, Christianity for a long time agonized over the ambiguities embedded in the relationship between the gospel mandate to mission cultures and the inbuilt pluralistic tradition in Christian history. The tensile strength of cultures ensured that conversion did not mean the total abandonment of traditions. Indeed, current church historiography in Africa has sought to write histories of religions that bridge indigenous values and the African Christianity. Yet the mandate to baptize all nations or mission-to culture has remained a guiding light. As Emil Brunner said, mission belongs to the church as burning belongs to fire. The gospel, said Emilio Castro, is the movement of God in Christ, searching, looking, incarnating in order to call all humankind. [25] The church in Africa has made significant efforts to reshape its culture policy. Perhaps, it needs to learn the pluralism of indigenous Africa which is elastic, tolerant, and does not separate the state and religion and thereby provided for a moral assessment of the ethics of power.

The greatest challenge of pluralism for Christianity has been posed by resurgent Islam. In the Nigerian context, this has been worsened by the activities of a corrupt state. For instance, the violence that has become endemic is a reflection of the growing violence in the larger society. Quite often, the law enforcement personnel cooperates with the underworld to predate the populace. It has escalated as a result of the pauperization of the masses. The centralization of power, which the praetorian state has induced, is one of the reasons for the outbreak of violence. The use of the state apparatus by northern Islamic military personnel to protect Islamic interests and tohug power in northern Islamic ambits cannot solve the legitimacy crises and will hurt everyone in the long run. Violence begets violence; thus, the Christian groups have learnt to arm themselves to counter any Islamic attack. As one preacher said, the Bible advises that when someone slaps you, you should turn the other cheek. When he slaps you for the second time, the Bible goes silent; so you should now do everything possible to ensure that your cheek is intact for preaching the gospel of the kingdom. A day will come when the fly has to checkmate the big cow. Since Islam contends for the control of the government, Christians have adopted a wide range of rhetoric and measures to use evangelism as a mode of mobilizing voters. The obvious weakness of this posture is that both parties ignore the power that hurts them and, like rats in a cage, eat themselves. The examples from many African countries show that any viable opposition to the predatory state must be multifaith, joint action. Democracy cannot be consolidated on a partisan basis. Thus, a dialogical approach is inescapable.

5. DIALOGUE AS ANTIDOTE

Dialogue here does not mean debate. Indeed, dialogue conjures a number of postures such as reflection, study, interaction, discussion, debate, and sharing. Civic virtue and loyalty have not been strong in Nigeria. In most of Africa, the struggle to domesticate the foreign institution of the state has remained a problem. But the constraints of modernity require deliberate efforts to invent bonding strands of unity, economically and ideologically. Somehow, many Nigerians leaders perceive the task as one of coining slogans and creating inane projects. At the core is the need for a wholesome ethic of power. Both Christians and Muslims harp on the moral debauchery of leaders. Indeed, their canons contain salient political values that could be harnessed; for instance, both believe that political practice should be a service to God and community, and is open to God's judgment. They share such political values as equity, honesty, and love for the neighbor. There is a large prescription of sensitivity for the poor and for response to the needs of the vulnerable. These affirmations are the bases for new political ethics of power and dialogue.

As Lesslie Newbigin put it,

> We participate in dialogue with men of other faiths believing that we and they share a common nature as those who have been created by one God who is the

Father of all, that we live by his kindness, that we are both
responsible to him and that he purposes the same bless-
ing for us all. We meet as children of one Father, whether
or not our partners have accepted their sonship.[26]

This does not allow for the relativist, the complacent pluralism
that sees no differences in religions. This is in fact a product of privatization and retreat from religion. It rejects the jellyfish approach
or the humane anonymous Christian concept usually associated
with Karl Rahner. It certainly rejects the demonization of Islam by
Evangelical-Charismatic and Pentecostal bands. Dialogue requires
being rooted in one's traditions and open to the other's tradition. It
is interfaith tolerance, a risky venture involving listening, sharing,
affirming the otherness of the other, recognizing the aspirations of
non-Christian faiths, and risking the possibilities of change.

In Islamic scholarship, it has been shown that:

> The standard classicist prescription advocated by many
> Muslims that because of its fundamentally theocratic
> nature, the fullest realization of Islam can only be found
> in the seizing of political power and the establishment
> of the theocratic politics are in the light of historical evi-
> dence not the only political positions allowed in Islam.
> Many social and political options were available within
> the context of Muslim discourse.[27]

Ilesanmi traces the creative pacifist contours through the careers of
the marabouts lineage structures in Mauritania and Senegal River
valley, the Jakhanke who urged a moral critique of political rule; the
pedagogical network of sufi brotherhoods as models of reformed
social organization, and the religious education policy of the
madrassa movement in Mali and El Kanemi's query to Dan Fodio,
which raised prominently the problem of using force to propagate
the message. As Lamin Sanneh commented about this confrontation, El Kanemi showed that since no age or nation is without its
share of heresy and sin:

> any immutable division of the world between *dar al-
> Islam* and *dar al-harb* would fly in the face of this reality
> and reduce to ashes all sincere but inadequate attempts
> at truth and obedience. We could not find revealed truth
> in the blinding flames of fanaticism fed by the short-
> fused *fatwas*.[28]

Ilesanmi further examined the teaching of Ibn Khaldun, one of the foremost Islamic political theorists. Admittedly, Khaldun accepted the ideal of khilafa, a state whose nature and purpose was the combination of religious conviction and political power since the Prophet Muhammed had established a tradition in which territoriality served as the handmaid of religious faith. Khaldun did not fail to see that ideological secularism is riddled with compromise, but he acknowledged that human civilization has reached a new level, dictating otherwise than the ideal. Nation-states, he argued, had their origin in human reason and in the will to power and domination; they are to provide security, general welfare, and comforts of life. Therefore, he rejects any direct and explicit ideological mixing of religion and politics. An imam should distance himself from the malik lest he wreaks havoc on the moral foundations of religion. Khaldun insists on the inevitable gap between the ideal demands of the ideal sharia and the political reality. Religion supports the state by sublimating humanity's base nature through the explication of the values that encourage public decorum without inviting doctrinal indifference.[29]

Lamin Sanneh has, therefore, demonstrated the immense voluntarist impetus in Islam and how it fits with democratic liberalism, leaving it detheocratized without being disenfranchised. To hew liberal democracy from this prideful rock of orthodoxy is based on the imperative of separating religion and state so as to protect human rights, foster pluralism, and safeguard the conscience. In spite of the dilemma posed by secularity:

> Political realism and religious integrity have a common purpose in distinguishing between a Caesar crowned and a Caesar turbaned, and, that purpose is to prevent constituted government from meddling with religion.[30]

In Nigeria, as in the rest of Africa, there is much room for both Christians and Muslims to mine the ethical principles in their teachings as a source of a moral critique on the political culture, on leaders, and the nations. Interfaith dialogue does not mean consensus; rather, it means living together in pursuit of salient values that would make humans truly human. Dialogue is an antidote to the violent faces of religion in Africa.

Notes

1.   M. Hutchinson and O. U. Kalu, eds., *A Global Faith: Essays on Evan-gelicalism and Globalization* (Sydney: Center for the Study of Austra-lian Christianity, 1998), 33

2.   Simeon O. Ilesanmi, *Religious Pluralism and the Nigerian State* (Athens OH: Ohio University Center for International Studies, 1997), 5.

3.   See, a discussion of Samuel P. Huntington's concept in Chee Pang Choong, "Samuel Huntington's Clash of Civilizations and the Implica-tions for Christian Identity in Asia" *A Global Faith*, eds., Hutchinson and Kalu, chap. 11

4.   P. P. Ekeh, *Colonialism and Social Structure*. (Ibadan: Ibadan University Press, 1983), 28-29.

5.   M. E. Marty and R. S. Appleby, (eds., *Fundamentalism Observed*. (Chicago: Chicago University Press, 1991).

6.   Lamin Sanneh, *Piety and Power: Muslims and Christians in West Africa*. (Maryknoll, NY: Orbis Books, 1996), 133, 135.

7.   This matter is pursued in greater detail by Harold Coward, *Pluralism: Challenge to World Religions*. (Maryknoll, NY: Orbis Books, 1985), chaps. 1 and 2.

8.   Ibid., 10.

9.   R. Fatton, "Africa in the Age of Democratization: The Civic Limita-tions of Civil Society", *African Studies Review*, 38, 2 (1995), 67-99.

10. Ruth Marshall-Fratani, "Winning Nigeria for Jesus", *Journal of Religion in Africa*, 28, 3 (1995): 278-315

11. C. M Cooke, "Church, State and Education: The Eastern Nigeria Experience, 1950-1967" *Christianity in Independent Africa* eds., E. Fashole-Luke et als (London: Rex Collings, 1989): 193-206;A. E. Afigbo, "The Missions, the State and Education in South-Eastern Nigeria, 1956-1971", *ibid*.: 176-192.

12. M. H. Kukah, *Religion, Politics and Power in Northern Nigeria* (Ibadan: Spectrum Publishers Ltd., 1994)

13. K. W. Post, *The Nigerian Federal Election of 1958* (London: Oxford University Press, 1963);B. J. Dudley, *Parties and Politics in Northern Nigeria* (London: Frank Cass, 1968);J. I. Iseayo, *Conflict and Incorpo-ration in Nigeria* (Zaria: Gaskiya Corporation, 1975); R. Anifowose, *Violence and Politics in Northern Nigeria: The Tiv and Yoruba Experience* (New York: Nok Publishers, 1984); Y. B. Usman, *The Manipulation of Religion in Nigeria, 1977-1987* (Kaduna: Vanguard Press, 1987);Pat A. Williams, "The State, Religion and Politics in Nigeria", Ph. D Dis-sertation, University of Ibadan, 1988; A. E. Ekoko and L. O. Amadi,

"Religion and Stability in Nigeria" *Nigeria Since Independence*, Vol. IX – Religion eds., I G. Ashiwaju and Y. Abubakar (Ibadan: Heinemann, 1989); John Paden, *Religion and Political Culture in Kano.* (Berkeley, CA: University of California Press, 1973); ibid., *Ahmadu Bello* (London: Halter and Stoughton, 1986).

14. Ogbu U. Kalu, *Divided People of God: Church Union Movement in Nigeria, 1867-1966* (New York: Nok Publishers Ltd, 1978).

15. Felix Ekechi, *Missionary Enterprise and Rivalry in Igboland, 1985-1914* (London: Frank Cass, 1971).

16. On the rise of youthful charismatism see Richard H. Burgess, "The Civil War Revival and Its Pentecostal Progeny" PhD dissertation, University of Birmingham, June 2004. On the intrusion of primal religion on the modern public space, see Stephen Ellis and Gerrie Ter Haar, *Worlds of Power: Religious Thought and Political Practice in Africa* (New York: Oxford University Press, 2004).

17. Lamin Sanneh, *The Turban and The Crown,* 180-181.

18. Jibrin Ibrahim, "Religion and Political Turbulence in Nigeria", *Journal of African Studies*, 29 (1991): 116-36.

19. M. Hassan Kukah, *Religion, Politics, and Power in Northern Nigeria* (Ibadan: Spectrum Books Ltd., 1994), 199-200.

20. H. A. Adigwe, *OIC: The Implications for Nigeria.* (Onitsha: Catholic Archidiocese Publications, 1986); M. S. Umar, "Islam in Nigeria: Its Concept, Manifestation and Role in Nation-Building", *Nigeria Since Independence*, vol ix eds. Ashiwaju and Abubakr (1989).

21. Ruth Marshall-Fratani, "Winning Nigeria for Jesus", 4.

22. B. J. Takya, "The Foundations of Religious Intolerance in Nigeria: Background for Understanding the Maitatsine Phenomenon", *Bulletin of Ecumenical Theology*, 2, 2 (1989): 31-41;Jibrin Ibrahim, "The Politics of Religion in Nigeria: The Parameters of the 1987 Crisis in Kaduna State", *Review of African Political Economy, 45/6, (1989): 65-82.*

23. Ekoko and Amadi, "Religion and Stability in Nigeria", op cit.

24. E. Isichei, "The Maitatsine Rising in Nigeria, 1908-1985: A Revolt of The Disinherited", *Journal of Religion in Africa*, 17, 3 (Oct. 1987): 194-208; M. Hiskett, "The Maitatsine Riots Kano, 1980: An Assessment", *Journal of Religion in Africa*, 17, 3 (1987): 209-223; Allan Christelow, "Religious Protests and Dissent in Northern Nigeria, from Madhism to Quaranic Integralism", *Journal of the Institute of Muslim Minority Affairs*, 6, 2 (July, 1985); P. M. I. Lubeck "Islamic Protest Under Semi Industrial Capitalism: Yan Yatsine Explained", *Africa*, 55, (1985): 369-398.

25. Emilio Castro, *Mission and Evangelization in a Pluralistic Society*, Occasional Paper no. 6, Center for Christian Studies, Toronto, 1985.

26. Lesslie Newbigin, "The Basis, Purpose and Manner of Inter-faith Dialogue", *Scottish Journal of Theology*, 30: 253-280. esp. 266.

27. S. O. Ilesanmi, *Religious Pluralism and the Nigerian State*, 34.

28. Lamin Sanneh, *The Crown and Turban*, 213.

29. Ilesanmi, *Religious Pluralism*, 37-38.

30. Lamin Sanneh, *Piety and Power*, 137.

Chapter Seven
Daughters of Ethiopia: Gender, Power, and Poverty in African Christianity

1. INTRODUCTION: HISTORICAL DISCOURSE AND LITERARY REVIEW

In the midst of the legitimacy crises, pauperization, and degradation of the environment, the voices of women in Africa have become strident both as victims and as potential healers. As Jesus restored the self-image of the unnamed woman, who was suffering from a spinal disease by calling her the daughter of Abraham, thus rooting her in an everlasting covenant with God, so are African women ,daughters of Ethiopia, inheritors and participants in the prophecy that Ethiopia shall hasten to stretch out its hands to God (Psalms 68:31).The posture here is that Christian feminism is a breed apart and rooted in the New Testament vision of the liberation of both men and women to enable both to serve fully, to their God-given capacity, in bringing the fruits of the kingdom into the lives of communities. A key demographic character of the African church is the preponderance of women in all types of churches, whether mission-founded, African indigenous, or Pentecostal. What is the impact of this fact on the response of the church to the challenges of poverty and pluralism? Are there constraints in mobilizing the full resources of the churches for the Godly cause? Can the failure of the church in Africa in responding to the issues of power and poverty be explained from the dominant gender ideology?

Admittedly, there is a plurality of voices, conflicting prescriptions, and a rich history in the mobilization of African women towards a common goal. It is not an isolated journey; white women, African-American women, and third world women with varied experiences are on the freedom road. Much effort is spent on distinguishing each posture, and yet there is a cross-fertilizing power. These factors are reflected in the pattern of the literature on African feminism. In the colonial era, the concern was to garner data for governance; therefore, anthropologists were recruited to understudy the roles of women in various settings. Incidents of women's rebellion against the colonial change agents surprised the assumptions of docile, suppressed wom-enfolk. An example comes from Lord Lugard's foreword to Sylvia Leith Ross, *African Women*. In the background of an image of invis-ible women, Lord Lugard emphasized the opposite tendencies:

> She is ambitious, courageous, self-reliant, hard-working and independent...she claims full equality with the opposite sex and would seem indeed to be the dominant partner. The Women's councils (approved and trusted by men) enact laws for the protection of the crops and enforce them by suitable penalties-including ridicule.[1]

Lugard was perhaps still reeling under the shock of the Aba Women's Revolt that caught the colonial rulers off-guard. But this profile set the trend for descriptive anthropological studies on the curious breed of African women: what were their roles in traditional societies? Were they as suppressed as they appeared? Did they exer-cise any powers in the religions of the people? This trend continued until the politics of modernization raised new vistas. The dominant mobilization theory urged the role of the state in mobilizing all power blocs in the society toward a single-minded pursuit of devel-opment. The rise of urbanization as well as the problem of assessing the aggregative contributions of women occupied the literature. In the 1980s, a further shift occurred, inspired by a certain awareness of women issues in the international scene. Urged by United Nations agencies, the scene was dominated by social scientists concerned with women, liberation, and development. Innumerable conferences by world organizations and by the Economic Commission for Africa, Addis Ababa, and others pondered over the roles of women in the changing socioeconomic landscape of Africa.[2] There was a significant shift from the descriptive anthropological studies of women to the gender dimension of the collapse of the African state. Declaring that the male-dominated state warps women's ability to make history on their own terms, a number of commentators described how ruling classes use gender as they seek hegemony. Women serve as cannon fodder for the males in the pursuit of votes. This was not a Marxist feast; much to the contrary, some revealed the silence of Marxism to gender issues.[3] The declared goal was to highlight gender in state formation, political participation, and resource allocation. It was frequently declared that women have virtually no power in the state structures in Africa and do not benefit from the patrimonial administrative structures that float over a variety of regime types.

Until the Beijing Women's Conference in 1995, secular feminism in Africa appeared weak at the ideological level. Even those who mobilized were anxious to show that they were not women libbers, obviously a perjuative label. Commentators have made much of the growth of female professionals, a few politicians and some powerful market women.[4] There is no doubt that the increase in female enrollment in tertiary educational institutions in some countries yielded a bulge in the demography of female-educated workforce, especially when the rate of male drop-outs in secondary schools became alarming in places such as Nigeria:

TABLE 7.1 – Enrollment of New Female Students in Nigerian Universities: 1980-1992.

Year	Number	%
1980	6,854	20.2
1981	7,161	19.6
1982	8,774	23.2
1983	10,327	23.7
1984	10,852	23.5
1985	11,862	24.5
1986	13,925	25.8
1987	15,858	27.1
1988	17,999	28.4
1989	17,384	27.8
1990	17,423	27.8
1991	20,411	27.1
1992	27,800	31.8

Sources: Federal Government of Nigeria, *Statistics on Education, 1990*; *Statistical Digest on Nigerian Universities, 1980-1992* (National Universities Commission, Abuja, 1995).

Modernization opened the marketplace for women but assessments of cooperatives have cast doubts about the real potentials of these for redressing the economic imbalance. In many countries of Africa, the data on women's economic activities appear thin.

Of interest is D.U.Iyam's analysis of gender among the Biase of southeastern Nigeria. He shows that in the rural communities, women are the primary entrepreneurs,although they are constrained by cultural factors from maximizing market opportunities.[5] Strangely however, the impact of patriarchy has been more severe on men; it diminished the role of men in production and reproduction and has led to a loss of respect and power in their families; this, in turn, affects the capacity of the political system. Thus, the weakening of traditional systems engendered by development failure has actually enlarged the real power of womenfolk. Thus, much complexity bedevils the matter. It can be safely concluded that beyond descriptions of women in traditional society and the burst of developmental analyses, which soon shriveled under the heat of the post-Beijing search for models of empowerment, the literature on secular feminism that has emerged from Africa is disparate because of the depth of the research. This does not mean that studies on women do not abound; but there is little ideologically based material from African women such as the works of Ifi Amadiume, Christine Obbo, Nina Mba, and C. Hoehler-Fatton.[6] Many NGOs have proliferated for the female cause: some focus on rights in the domestic and public spheres; others deal with the issue of violence; while still others delve into the forbidden religiocultural zone such as purdah. There is a brand of feminism, femocracy,that concentrates on assisting women to access the power structures of the state. Particularly crucial in generating secular feminist literature and activities in Africa is the United Nations Development Fund for Women. The involvement of the regional offices ranges from rural women to female university students. This is the rub: the NGOs and the UNIFEM are activity-oriented rather than devoted to academic research. They focus on public enlightenment programs and pilot projects to solve identified problems. Obviously, all these secular forces aided the rise of Christian feminism, which is acquiring a rich history.

Significant is that 1989 served as the beginning of the Circle of Concerned African Women Theologians (hereafter referred to as the Circle). As Teresia Hinga observed, the seventy women who gathered in Accra, Ghana, created a turning point.[7] Under the banner *The Will to Arise*, they sought to give the African voice an identifiable character, a handle to the matter from the pages of their publications. As the introduction put it:

> *The Will to Arise* is the voice of African women theolo-
> gians. It is grounded in the challenges of the scripture
> and the results from a new wave of change.
> African women reading the scriptures have begun to
> see that God's call is not passive. It is compelling and
> compulsory. It is a call to action and wholeness that chal-
> lenges the will and intellect.[8]

A few pages later, Oduyoye continued that:

> as long as men and Western strangers continue to write
> exclusively about Africa, African women will continue to
> be represented as if they were dead.

Talitha Qumi (1990) contains the proceedings of the 1989 Circle
conference. However, two points should be noted:first, that these are
educated women endeavoring to give voice to the pains and concerns
of innumerable but weaker vessels-a curious biblical image for those
trying to show that they are not as weak as may be presumed. They
set out to achieve this through research and apologetics, fitting into
the niche that feminist literature would dub organic intellectuals. The
obvious risk is that if they do not stand where the unlettered women
stand, they would merely give vent to the frustrations of people of
their own class. Second, their voice emerged from the ambits of the
Ecumenical Association of Third World Theologians (EATWOT)
and, therefore harking back to the implosion of theological consciousness among Third World peoples in the 1970's.[9] Fondly called
EATWOT, this association belongs to Christians of various hues
from the parts of the world where the most cogent question is, eat
what? Their understanding and practice of Christianity arise from a
soil with the same color as Jesus walked upon. The religious ferment
among them re-appropriated the understanding of theology as Jesus's
concern for the poor.

This consciousness produced several theological articulations.
Some have tried to distinguish between liberation theology, black
theology, African theology, and theology of liberation, the latter
being prevalent in South Africa.[10] These theologies shared much
in common. Chung Hyun Kyung describes the shifts in theological emphases within EATWOT, especially the formation of the
Women's Forum in 1981.[11] In what Oduyoye termed,the irruption
within irruption of the poor in the third world, the women withdrew
to their own discussion and made the males in EATWOT severely
aware that sexism is part of the intricate web of oppression and not
an indulgence by disgruntled women. At the sixth EATWOT Con-

ference in Geneva, 1983, the conferees drew the conclusion that sexism must not be addressed in isolation but within the context of the total struggle for the liberation in various countries. They created the Women's Commission, whose agenda shall be discussed later. In 1986, African women theologians met at Yaounde for the French-speakers and in Port Harcourt for the Anglophone. Together they drew up an agenda.[12] The Ecumenical Decade in Solidarity With Women also gave a fillip to women's advocacy.[13] In September1992, after years of discussion, the World Alliance of Reformed Churches created a commission on women with a full-time staff and designed to motivate member churches to utilize the special gifts of women and, above all, to listen to their voice in decision-making processes.[14] The Circle did not appear as deus ex machina, rather it was a culmination of years of efforts to consolidate a focus.

But the grand hope of an easy access to the literature of the Circle did not occur because the next publication emerged only in 1996. Meanwhile, members of the Circle contributed richly in various anthologies. For instance, in Ursula King's anthology Feminist Theology from the Third World (1994), Schussler-Fiorenza's Feminist Theology in Different Strokes (1996), Thistlethwaite and Engel's Lift Every Voice (1990), Stuart and Thatcher's Sexuality and Gender (1996), Mananzan and others' Women Resisting Violence (1996), Sugirtharajah's Voices from the Margin (1995), Gibellini's Paths of African Theology (1995), and journals such as the Reformed World, they all contain the stirrings of African feminist theology.[15] Members of the Circle have made invaluable contributions to the contemporary conversation on ecotheology.Prominent is the connection made between the degradation of the environment with the male attitudes towards women and children. The argument is that the roots of the crises are largely religious and, therefore, the solution must be religious, based on recovering a sacred attitude to the earth as a nurturer. Eleanor Rae even argues that a matricentric ideology preceded the patriarchal and its transcendent sky god.[16] Such speculation exists in the study of theIgbo religion, as some have surmised that the oracular title, Igwe ka Ala (the sky is mightier than the earth), the jubilation by the devotees of the sky deity in their new-fangled victory over the Earth deity, who had enjoyed ascendancy.[17] Thus, the ecofeminist arsenal has been acquired for the grand cause by a number of Africans including Isabel Phiri, Teresia Hinga, Sara Mvududu, Tumani Nyajeka, Denise Ackermann, and Tahira Joyner.[18] It remains to be seen whether they will go the full hog as their Western sisters. The last two women are from South Africa and provide a missing link:

where are white African women in the charmed Circle? [19]Another missing aspect has been a monograph with a wholesome articulation of the female contribution. This is the gap filled by Oduyoye's *Daughters of Anowa*.[20] On the whole, the literature is burgeoning in size and diversity, with some males in full-throated support.

2. MATTERS OF CONCERN :AGENDA OF THE CHARMED CIRCLE

Anderson and Clarke conducted a survey across Canada in 1990 on women in the ministry and were constantly confronted by bewildered men who asked, what do these women want in the church?[21] In Africa, the reception would have been more hostile. An Anglican bishop returning from a Lambeth Conference was interviewed about the decision to ordain women in the Anglican communion. He dismissed the matter as a concern for white people who have lost control of their homes. It was not a matter of concern, he said, for Africans. This cavalier and patronizing attitude is the point of departure. The first concern for women is beautifully put in a poem by a Japanese woman, who moans that:

> Originally, woman was Sun
> She was an authentic person
> But now, woman is the moon.
> She lives by depending on another
> And she shines by reflecting another's light
> Her face has a sickly pallor
> We must regain our hidden sun!
> Reveal our hidden sun
> Rediscover our natural gifts
> This is the ceaseless cry.[22]

African women who have been mobilizing for this task in recent years, are anxious to pursue the cause from an Africanist posture. They do not make the distinction between secular feminism and Christian feminism as Anderson and Clarke do. Rather, they are forced to move from the church to the society and back to the church because the snake whose tail is seen in the sanctuary has a head hidden in the bush outside. The plight of African women Christians is rooted in the social structure.

It is further complicated by the deep interweaving African sufferings during the idolatrous slave trade, humiliations, and exploitations of colonialism, and the sexism of modernity. White feminists have said enough about the connections between the Cartesian certitude and dialectic that undergirded the Enlightenment worldview and sexist ideology. The irony is that the African woman became the butt of all the pressures that the systems put on the African man. Her experience is like a stack pile of jeopardies. From primal structures through the colonial, the modern to the incursion of religious change agents such as Christianity and Islam, patriarchal ideology predominates. She is caged. Schussler-Fiorenza defines patriarchalism as a sociopolitical system and a social structure of graded subjugation and oppression. Patriarchy is the power of the fathers; it defines women as the other of men, as subordinated to men in power.[23] Male force subsumes the female and determines what part women shall or shall not play. It is a socioideological system that conceives of society as analogous to the patriarchal household, sustained by slave labor. It is a pyramidical power structure in which women's oppression is based on gender, class, race, and marital status. It is encrusted in a hierarchical worldview and in the legitimating canons. However, a patriarchal structure is not based solely on gender differentiation; it governs the relationship between the rest of the family members as well. It is a certain understanding of the power of, as it legitimates gerontocracy, the power of the old over the young, older clans or villages over those younger; undergirds social hierarchies and caste systems, and determines the control of resources, especially land.

The women's agenda includes going beyond the conventional discussion about the servile African woman who walks behind on the farm road, carrying a basket, while the male struts in front, wielding a machete. Sexism, which is the engine moving feminism in the Western world, appears rather mild in describing the experiences and the hopes of the African woman. Some African-American female academics made this point earlier and moved towards what they termed *womanist* theology. Linda Moody has clarified this in a nonpolemic manner.First of all, Womanist theology is directed against black males who, in the development of black theology:

> treat black women as if they were invisible creatures who
> are on the outside looking into the black experience, the
> black church and black theological enterprise.[24]

The concern is that women must be integral parts of the enterprise. Similarly, African women want to develop a niche in African theology which reflects on the multilayered jeopardies that characterize their lives. Some allege that African theology is a part of the conspiracy to oppress women. Second, like all conscientized minorities in North America, womanists link sexism with class and racism directed against them as well as against all black peoples. As Mercy Oduyoye has argued:

> The interwoven issues of racism and classism (having taken on demonic proportions in apartheid) are unquestionably the African oppression par excellence; indeed, given the human misery in Africa, they make sexism look like a pet peeve. [25]

This acknowledges the reality of sexism in women's daily lives but with a determination to combat it from a broader perspective, which begins by choosing life, discovering the true self, and then reaching out to the community, thereby reminding them of the bedrock of justice that enjoys powerful symbols in the cultural arsenal. There are four nuances that might easily be missed in this determination: the first urges women to seek the freedom to serve in the church and society; the second quests for an alternative mode of discourse in response to acts of oppression; and the third nurtures a spirituality that feeds acts of transformation and works for justice and human liberation. Letty Russell, in her Human liberation in a feminist perspective-theology (1974), made this point on which Ursula King elaborated in 1994 and to which Mercy Oduyoye applied cogently in response to the problem of violence against women.[26]

As Delores Williams said of *Sisters in the Wilderness*, the goal is to help black women see, affirm, and have confidence in the importance of their experience and their faith.[27] There is a proactive posture to assist them to live more productive and wholesome lives. Third, womanist theology acknowledges that the pains of women are rooted in the cultural history of the black community. Therefore, their theology must be rooted in the folk participating and anchored in the folk community both to recover and to critique it. The worldview, the socialization process that engenders so much violence, the impact of the economic structure and political power on the community all become the fabric for developing a theology that liberates from life-denying forces in state and church. This explains the discomfort by some African women with the tendency in African theology towards cultural theologizing. Sacralizing culture is risky because it could be deployed to sacralize patriarchy.

Chung, therefore, calls women to remembrance as a tool of liberation. This is an act of rediscovering the history of primal societies and resurrecting their women leaders, heroines, and saints; using their particular traditions as sources of cooperation and strength in the struggle. It calls for study and reconstruction of myths, proverbs, folktales, and cultures of African peoples as sources of empower-ment. But these are the bastions of patriarchal ideology; so the task is to revisit and purge them of the anti-woman didactic. The first and second cycles of *Daughters of Anowa* built on these premises before the third cycle, which dreamt of a new church in Africa. An element in Chung's method is to drink from the vitality of creation represented by the ancestral spirits. This so-called radical syncretism contrasts primal spirituality with that of the Christian, which focuses on fall and redemption. It ignores theological or religious boundar-ies as if a woman whose house is on fire does not dwell on nice-ties. It should be interesting to explore the use of this method by African women because there is some creative theological ferment in contemporary Africa akin to the conditions of the early church that Kwame Bediako describes in *Theology and Identity* (1992). Fourth, there is a call for women to bond, primarily among themselves but also in cooperation with women globally. Linda Moody uses two biblical images to show that across boundaries the issues are the same though the specific details may vary. Dialogue and covenanting will become instruments of mutual support; iron sharpens iron. She uses the ambivalent Biblical story of Ruth and Naomi as illustra-tion. Some feminists are uncomfortable with Ruth for abandoning her roots. In spite of the objections that have been raised about this story, from a hermeneutic of suspicion, Moody insists that Ruth and Naomi's relatedness in friendship across the boundary of difference is the embodiment of God's covenanting, which Letty Russell calls solidarity of groaning. That was in 1974; twenty years later she used the imagery of a round table to urge a new solidarity for a Church in the Round.[28] The Women's Forum in 1981 (within the ambit of the AETWOT) insisted that the struggle requires awareness, organiza-tion, unity, courage, and hope; it requires building small circles but linked together. There was a certain caution that third world women should develop theologies from the underside of history, and that would critique the theologies from the first world. They must not be sucked into a struggle fought over issues which are not relevant to their ecotheater. As Oduyoye put it:

> the solidarity we seek from the global sisterhood is that
> we get our rightful space to say our word....The cleav-
> age that has been observed between women of the South
> and those of the North is a real one, and I wish to say
> this applies in all issues and especially on the method of
> seeking reconstruction. Above all it is very exasperating
> to have impatient liberators on one's back.[29]

Members of the Circle may object to the style here, which employs the womanist lens in reconstructing African women's agenda. It is deliberate. There is an unmistakable resonance in the agenda of African, African-American, and other third world women. There is the same concern about the patriarchal ideology buried in the womb of myths, proverbs, and social customs. The theme of men as the victimizers, captured by the dictum, your comfort is my death, informs responses to domination in marriage and the church. Dorothy Ramodibe compares the possibility of women working with men in the church to whites working with blacks in the heat of apartheid.[30] Admittedly, some of the Circle members are not as polemic in attacking men. Nyambura J. Njoroge, for instance, advocates partnership with men as the aim of Christian women. As she said,

> This gender-based approach focuses on both women and men, rather than considering women in isolation. It attempts to change ideas, attitudes, beliefs and practices that hinder partnership of women and men in accordance to the gospel.[31]

Judy Mbugua's Our Time Has Come underscores the point, understandable for the group of evangelical Christian constituency that she represents and for the ideological cleavage that will become palpable later.[32] Oduyoye merely shrugs off the matter as a moot point:

> reconstruction demands a community of women and men making a concerted effort towards building up an empowering society that upholds and promotes the full humanity of every individual.[33]

The real issue is whether the men will be ready to recognize the fact. Her views on the matter are more subtle: arguing that neither patriarchy nor matriarchy alone determines the man-woman relationship, each system has the potential for diminishing the true nature of either gender, denying each the ability to live fully.[34] Adela Y. Collins put it aptly: Biblical anthropology on the man-woman relationship is pivoted on (i) men and women as originally created--the ontological view; (ii) as fallen and saved-the religious view; (iii) as ministers to God's people-the ecclesiastical view; and (iv) as husbands and wives and in relation to other humans-the social view.[35] Polemic tends to run roughshod over subtlety, a function of the imperatives of the struggle. Ursula King, therefore, cautioned that women should avoid

violent, militaristic language; women should say, no more violence
and, do no more violence. To which Oduyoye replies:

> on a theoretical level, I am in entire agreement with her,
> but in practice struggle requires strong language so as to
> shame men, which is like disarming the strongman who
> is guarding the gates to his strong hold.[36]

Crucial in the emergence of the new woman is a revisitation of the
canonical base of domination as well as the church's willingness to
source its gender ethics from the societal norms. The agenda of the
EATWOT Women's Commission emphasized biblical interpretation,
as Teresa Okure would say, to illustrate how God worked with women
as co-partners and to contrast this with the sinful human gendered
construct.[37] The commission set out a full theological schema that
would move from analysis of the oppressed experiences of women to
socioeconomic and political profiles of the various countries, which
would be then, followed by reflections on identified themes such as
hermeneutical analysis of primary oral sources , biblical canon, and
indigenous religions. Specific topics would include God-talk and
women, Christology and women, Mariology and women, pneuma-
tology and emerging forms of spirituality. While this is not ironclad,
it explains the dominant themes coursing through feminist literature
in Africa.

In the end, willy-nilly, men and women must join to respond to
the pauperization of the continent. The marginalization of Africa is
not new. Indeed, at the height of the missionary enterprise, Europe
was more intrigued with Asia. This fact led Robinson and Gallagher,
out of hubris, to argue that as far as the official mind was concerned,
Britain acquired African colonies in a fit of absent-mindedness. No
one could blame them because, as one proverb says, a woman whose
daughter gets pregnant outside marriage cannot have the voice to
reply to those who insult her.

The agenda of African women, therefore, moves in four
sequences: first, to recover their true selves in the midst of a living
death,which is called the birth of the new woman. Second, to destroy
the instruments of their oppression embedded in the many-layered
forms of patriarchy, which requires taking a radical and critical attitude toward culture and traditions, declaring that the ancient resting
place does not have to be ours. Third, to bond and tobuild part-
nerships among themselves and with men. Fourth, to engage the
socioeconomic and political arenas so as to create new opportunities.
Some argue that the sufferings of Africa arise from spiritual sources

and require a mobilization of our spiritual energies in going back to God. The great matter of concern should be whether the church in Africa, after independence, has woken up to the realities and the enormity of the challenge or whether the years of complicity with the state have crippled it. To recover its missional vocation to the society, the church must mobilize all its human resources.

3. PURALITY OF VOICES: FOUR-FOLD PRESCRIPTIONS AND REMEDIES

The character of the problem is generally agreed upon; so is the villain's identity easily paraded in the market square. How to remove the fly from the eye of the cow without blinding it, and in a concerted effort, is the task. In all forms of feminism, gender comprises a central focus; it is viewed as a problem because in virtually all social relations, institutions, or processes, social inequities, strains. and contradictions abound. Gendered relations are not viewed as either natural or immutable but rather as products of sociocultural and historical forces that are created and are constantly recreated by humans; therefore, it can be changed by human agency. But a gender discourse is not about women but about the sociallyconstructed relationship between men and women. Therefore location is important.

This may explain why battle strategies differ among feminists and across cultural boundaries. Of course, the first distinction would be between those who are secular and are pursuing the feminist cause without any concern for the women's role in the Ccurch. They are now mired in the defense of lesbianism as the logical conclusion of the advocacy of freedom. The Christian feminists have the added problem of seeking for an enhanced or uninhibited female participation in church matters. Among the latter, there are possibly four positions that could be labeled as (i) rejectionist, (ii) loyalist,(iii) liberationist, and (iv) reconstructionist. Like all labels, inaccuracy and overlap are part of the staple diets. Differences occur both because some are doing theology manque, while others are engaged in biblical scholarship, and there are different ways of engaging the gospel in the hermeneutical task. For instance, in the latter task, certain functions are required of the practioners : reading the text carefully (or the descriptive task), placing the text in a canonical context (the synthetic task), relating the text to our situation through a certain mode of appropriation and through appeal to other authorities, and finally, embracing the pragmatic task of living the text. Many theological enterprises tend to differ at the appropriation level, and some tend to put the foot heavily on the pragmatic task. It is as if

the experience of pain in one's social condition is too excruciating
to indulge in involuted exegesis. An oppressed or hungry person
may find the philosophical niceties in systematic theology to be an
avoidable luxury. In all cases, the lens used betrays the individual's
attitude toward the Bible as canon, the place of tradition, the Trinity,
and other sources for reconstructing reality. H.G.Wells divides the
spectrum of feminist theologies into Trinitarian, and non-Trinitarian
with the hope that the former holds the promise of the successful
integration of feminist insight into the regular preaching and teaching of the churches.[38]

The concern here is on explicit contextuality; to show the peculiarity of African articulation and yet to place it within the larger
context of what others are saying, both for the sake of interpreting
Africa to the world and for the sake of linking the church in Africa
with the global church. All Christians drink from the same well.
However, there is nothing among Africans of a *rejectionist* posture
that could be found in the works of some white feminists such as
Joanne Carlson Brown and Rebecca Parker.[39] Arguing that women
are acculturated to accept abuse, they scream in frustration against
the silence and blindness of women. They agree with Mary Daly's
Beyond God the Father that the qualities that Christianity idealizes,
especially those for women, are also those of a victim. Their solution
is quite trenchant:

> In order for us to become whole we must reject the
> culture that shapes our abuse and disassociate ourselves
> from the institutions that glorify our suffering. This leads
> to the conclusion that in order to be liberated we must
> leave the church, make our exodus from the halls of the
> oppressor.[40]

At first it sounds as if they are the patron parishioners, occupying the
front pew in Schussler-Fiorenza's women-church; but their position
might be just as unclarified but far-reaching:

> Feminist theologians who attempt to rework the tradi-
> tion by finding feminist undercurrents and counter-
> cultures, doing new quests for the historical feminist
> Jesus, and writing women back into the Bible and the
> tradition(the Inclusive Language Lectionary is a good
> example)are trying valiantly to fix the institution so that
> they can remain in it.[41]

They accept Daly's characterization of sisterhood as the bonding
of those who have escaped from the patriarchal space and the terri-

tory of nonbeing and compare those who do not exit as suffering a similar complex as battered women who do not divorce the brutish partners. Behind their rage is a rejection of Christ along with requisite concepts such as the Fall, the sacrifice, and the satisfactory theory of atonement. Rejectionists tend to be non-Trinitarian, post-Christians feminists who perceive the Bible as irretrievable.

Moreover, the exodus concept is beyond metaphor, as many women have taken the de-institutionalizing route in their faith journeys. Some rejectionists, in their exile in the wilderness, find ethereal comfort in nature religions or in mysticism based on woman's consciousness. They are attracted to the role of the Earth deity in primal religions. As mentioned earlier, the quest for a viable developmental strategy must perforce lead back to utilizing the salient ingredients of the primal worldview as a channel for domesticating change-agents. The contributions of African women in ecotheology have been in this vein. In the exilic character of contemporary life in Africa, it is suggested that solutions may lie in pursuing elements of continuities so that modernity will be ecosensitive. This is a far cry from propagating nature worship or romanticizing tradition. Isabel Phiri's study of the role of women in the *chisumphi* cult in Malawi provides a caution to the fascination for native religions among white feminists.[42]

Many African women theologians are *liberationists* because their posture is to be in continuity with Christian tradition as much as possible, indeed, to search to the fullest possible extent for the liberating elements within the Christian tradition. They exhibit all the nine characteristics of a Christian feminist culled from the literature: (i) sharp critique of patriarchy in the church and in society, (ii) rejection of exclusively male metaphors for God-language (though language concerns are mooted because of the innate structures), (iii) opposition to the legitimization of male dominance based on the maleness of Jesus, the disciples, and Pauline theology, (iv) concern for the emancipation of women and for all the marginalized, (v) explicit contextuality, (vi) large place for the category of experience, (vii) hermeneutical suspicion of long-standing interpretations of Bible, and (viii) doctrine, and (ix) intention to bring social analysis into contact with Scripture and tradition. A reformist-liberationist engages in reinterpretation and a reclaiming of the center and yet stays in continuity with Christian tradition. Elizabeth Johnson, in her seminal work *She Who Is*, calls it braiding:

> a footbridge between the ledges of classical and feminist Christian wisdom. Throwing hermeneutical span

> from side to side may enable some to cross over to the
> paradigm of women's coequal humanity without leaving
> behind all the riches of the tradition that has been their
> intellectual and spiritual home.[43]

With Letty Russell, this Trinitarian feminist theology is used as a
form of feminine contribution to liberation theology:

> an attempt to reflect upon the experience of oppression
> and our actions for the new creation of a more humane
> society.[44]

In the pursuit of this goal, some have reconstructed the social roles of
women in the Bible or used the results of such researches as Phyllis
Trible's recovery of maternal God-language in the Old Testament,
Schussler-Fiorenza's study of women apostleship in the early Christian movement, and Bernadette Brooten's work on the leadership
of women in the ancient synagogues. Others have focused on social
history, describing the fate of women in particular times and in social
relations, exposing the ideational issues of a text or time period. Some
have examined ancient androcentric and kyriocentric structures of
women's roles and status, particularly where these seem to be against
the domination system. Some of these reconstructions are based on
imaginal leaps to the extent of arousing worries about reliability. This
style is more prevalent among the reconstructionist genre, some of
whom use social science models. They argue that a knowledge of the
social world enables the scholar to recognize how the places and the
manner of women's presence may have been deleted or overlooked in
texts, to challenge limited analysis and androcentric interpretations,
and to rediscover women's roles in all aspects of Biblical analysis. The
viewpoints of those who were not writing or whose writings were not
preserved are recovered by mining the texts. It is a form of taking power.
But Schussler-Fiorenza does not think that this goes far enough. She
lashed out against Russell, Ruether, and Trible who argue:

> that the Bible is not totally androcentric but also con-
> tains some absolute ethical principles and feminist liber-
> ating traditions. In order to do so, they adopt a feminist
> neo-orthodox method that is in danger of reducing the
> ambiguity of historical struggle to theological essences
> and abstract timeless principles.[45]

In her famous dictum, Schussler-Fiorenza warned:

> a Christian feminist theology must cease its attempt
> to rescue the Bible from its feminist critics and assert

that the source of our power is also the source of our
oppression.[46]

This sets the stage for the reconstructionist view, which is characterized by a suspicious reading of the Bible as a document produced by
men, for men, and preserved and used by men for their androcentric
and sinful purposes. As Schussler-Fiorenza put it:

> all New Testament texts are androcentric codifications of
> patriarchal power and ideology that cannot claim to be
> the revelatory Word of God.[47]

This means that no single New Testament author or book can function as a canon within the canon. The real locus of authority, therefore, is not the canonical New Testament but the present-day experience and struggle of women for liberation. Unlike the rejectionists
who would run into the wilderness, the reconstructionist stands to
fight back and to recover what the men have robbed from them.
Schussler-Fiorenza, as the scholar who has made the most sustained
apology for this position, carries her fight from the vantage point
of her training as a biblical scholar. She posits women's struggle for
liberation and women's experiences as the only valid lenses for interpreting the Bible. She does this by interrogating the ancient texts,
searching them for hints and traces of evidence on women's equal
roles in the past. She uses imaginative exercise to recover these tips
of the iceberg precisely because she believes that the ministry of Jesus
was a reform movement within Judaism, a community; operating by
the spirit, where men and women served with freedom and equality.
Feminist spirituality is a quest to recover and resuscitate this form
of community where women enjoyed power,freedom, and independence. The biblical canon must be seen as a prototype not as an
archetype.[48] The latter is unchanging, fixed, and timeless; while the
former is open to the possibilities of transformation. The Bible, then,
cannot be trusted as divine revelation. Schussler-Fiorenza's method
is the historical-critical method, which she lauds in *Bread not Stone*
because it

(i)   asserts the meaning of the original witness;
(ii) restricts the assimilation of the text to parochial pietism and to
      church interest;
(iii) challenges our assumptions, worldviews, and practice; and
(iv) limits the number of interpretations that can be given to a
      text.[49]

She compares the enterprise to the method by the colonized and suppressed blacks in the recovery of their histories as a step toward liberation. But her method is often highly selective of the data, utilizing only those that suggest a community she believes once existed. Schussler-Fiorenza's rigorous method and contribution in recovering the role of women in the ancient texts are without question, and many have accepted her recommendation on using experience, including women's experience, as the lens for biblical interpretation.

R. B. Hays has, however, pointed out that the danger of her dissolution of the canon is to

> undermine the authority of the New Testament so thoroughly that its liberating power would be also lost, as the church finds her identity increasingly shaped by the ideals of liberal democracy and the apparent dictates of contemporary experience.[50]

Where are African women in these categories? African feminist theology tends to borrow the rhetoric of the reconstructionists without going the full hog. There are predominantly three voices in African Christian feminism, two of which are variations of the liberationist model, and one which is in the *loyalist* band. As said earlier, there are no discernible bands of rejectionists. We could hear Dorothy Ramodibe yelling:

> No, there can be no cooperation between women and men as long as the oppressive and exploitative structures of the church remain intact. There can be no cooperation as long as men retain their dominant position in the church.[51]

But by the end of her argument, she balked from the position of a radical feminist but took a liberationist position delivered with a combative rhetoric. In Africa, women theologians are very ardent believers who have committed most of their lives serving their various churches in many capacities. They still believe in the church as a vehicle for mediating Christ's glory to the disheveled continent. Indeed, the legitimacy crisis is increasing attention on the church. All churches are growing in numbers; so the post-Christian option does not attract. In terms of strategy, it might disable the women from being heard by the churchly masses. Quite poignant, therefore, is the paper by Therese Souga, who started with her statement of faith:

> Jesus Christ means everything to me...Christ is the true human, the one who makes it possible for all persons

to reach fulfillment and overcome the historic alienation
weighing them down.[52]

She perceives a deep bond, even complicity, between African women
and Jesus Christ. Louise Tappa, representing those who mine the
ancient texts for signals of feminine transcendence, picks up from
Souga to examine the attitude of Jesus toward Mary Magdalene.
Using sources such as the Gospel of Thomas, she builds an empowering case which is followed by contrasting the Levitical laws against
women with the manner in which Jesus responded to the unnamed
woman who came for help at the same time as Jairus (who was
named). It was the unnamed woman who subtly touched the hem
of His garment. In a similar vein, Teresa Okure, who is a biblical
scholar, reexamines the Genesis creation story, which is central to
the antifeminine practices in the church. She acknowledges the
method advocated by Fiorenza in her seminal work, In Memory of
Her (1983). Using the same critical tool, Okure argued that the two
Genesis accounts do not provide any basis for the denigration of
the womenfolk; rather, certain elements in the story have been both
misinterpreted and ignored because of the predominant patriarchal
ideology. She calls for a spirit of discernment in the use of the Bible
so as to differentiate between the divine and the human elements,
between the timeless truths and the culturallyconditioned.

Rereading the Bible demands the emphasis on the vocation
of women as mothers; so, Okure portrays Mary as the epitome of
women's vocation in the divine economy.[53] It should be pointed out
that her use of Schussler-Fiorenza's method is in the mode of reform-
ist-liberationists, rooted in the canon and seeking ways of reinter-
preting the texts so as to remove the patriarchal slurs. The Bible is her
starting point, her normative and theological resource in determining
that women's voice would be prophetic in the midst of our desolation
caused by male domination in decision-making processes. Her liturgical intent is to shape the biblical narrative into the feminist agenda.
Hers is a hermeneutic of trust rather than of consent and affirmation.
Being a Roman Catholic,ecclesial tradition is one leg of the tripod in
doing theology. Of great interest in the development of third world
feminism is the return of Mariology into the center of doing theology. It signifies the ecumenical dimension of the sisterhood.[54] It does
even more by providing a link between feminist theology and the
issue of poverty. Mary is portrayed as the patron saint of the poor.
One dire index of poverty in Africa is the health and fate of children
within the changing patterns of the family.

Biblical scholarship has not been strong among African women theologians. One excuse is the pattern of ministerial formation: there is both a lack of priority to training female theologians and no provision for gender issues in the curriculum. Another reason is the youthfulness of the movement. As John Mbiti has reminded the critics of African theology, cattle are born with ears, they grow horns later. Drawing from varied theological traditions, it has been difficult to develop a systematic theology. So we find that many African women theologians have tended to utilize Western resources on the roles of women in the Bible as a means of dealing with fear, violence, and the marginalization perpetrated by men in church and in society as a whole.

Jesus looms large in their theology precisely because they perceive in his attitude the restoration of women to their full humanity; in partnership with men as integral to the coming of God's egalitarian order.[55]Cheryl Bridges Johns says that Jesus

> reconciled women unto himself, and in order to do this marvelous action he dared to enter their world of alienation and pain, and critiqued the numbness of his society.[56]

Hisako Kinukawa has explored many of the familiar themes in her focus on *Women and Jesus in Mark* (1994): the hemorrhaging woman is perceived as a challenge to the cultural norms on pollution and ostracism; the Syrophoenician woman raises the issue of cultic purity; the poor widow becomes the occasion to reproach the scribes while the woman who anointed the head of Jesus is the most fascinating because of her bold intrusion into a male gathering and the significance of her action. The irony that it was a woman who anointed the head of a man is not lost on feminist theology. It was a prophetic action. The double irony is that although a woman performed the act, it was a man who was anointed. Kinukawa also dealt with the cases of women disciples as well as the reconstructive attitude of Jesus toward marriage, divorce, adultery, and prostitution. Collectively, these cases bring into question four crucial issues: were the twelve the only disciples? Were the twelve disciples priets? Why did God exclude the male factor in the birth of Jesus? And why did Jesus accept patriarchy? [57]

In spite of the use of these references in African feminine theology, there is little ideological theorization in the application of the texts. Indeed, Mosala has warned, from a Marxist paradigm, that the women's recourse to a figure such as Esther is misplaced, because she operated within the domination system that the more revolutionary Queen Vashti had challenged

This does not mean that African women have not criticized the way in which the Bible is used within the African churches. For instance, Oduyoye berates the tendency to absolutize the Bible, reading it uncritically, with out-dated exegesis and biblical interpretations that entrenched and nurtured the marginalization of women.[58] She traces the roots of this tendency to Victorian Christianity. Philip Turner made this point many years ago in his study of traditionalism in African churches. He quipped that the novelist Anthony Trollope (1815-1882) would find himself more at home in many Anglican churches in Africa than he would in contemporary England.[59]

Amba Mercy Oduyoye represents a peculiar voice among the liberationist band and deserves a special attention. She has provided leadership in mobilizing the women theologians, having participated in the beginnings of the theological ferment in Africa and the third world. She used her position as a deputy general secretary of the WCC most effectively to entrench the women's cause in the agenda of that body. The wide range of her publications, spanning a few decades of vibrant academic endeavor, has left an imprint on the articulation of women empowerment in Africa.

Her work, *Daughters of Anowa: African Women and Patriarchy* is the most sustained narrative on African Christian feminism thus far. It brings together much of her writings scattered in books and journals. Oduyoye sets out to practice what many have advocated in proposals. Quite often, African scholars spend much time saying what African theology should do without daring to do it. Since patriarchy in the church has its roots in the culture outside the church, she moves to reexamine the language and culture that encrust antifeminine ideology. Scholars have noted the ambiguities, complexities, and changing perceptions of women in African societies.[60] For instance, in traditional Igbo setting, the centrality of the female in production, reproduction, property, and status inheritance were often given cultural expression in strong matrifocal ideology, but the tendency to marginalize the womenfolk was equally strong. Igbo myths and proverbs betray this hidden ambiguity. Oduyoye does something intriguing by revisiting such myths, proverbs, and folktales in Ghanaian language and culture to show that they can be read with new eyes in such a manner that they enhance the image of the woman. The ambiguity lies in the eyes of the reader. She urges that:

> If we re-read and retell these myths to bring parity and
> justice to human relations, we should look for the human
> traits that are desirable for building up and maintaining
> personal (not just male/female) skills in this communal
> task. Our search should be focussed on what it means to
> be human, not to be feminine or masculine.[61]

She builds her reappraisal around the mythical ancestor among
the Akan who sustained, protected, and led her people through
adversities and founded a community. In spite of such figures in folk
memory, Oduyoye systematically shows, in her first cycle, how the
folktales still express a variety of negative images of women. Even
their function as a source of nourishment is bedevilled by a culture
that extends:

> her breast-feeding of helpless infants to a life-long role of
> self-effacing service in the home and a nearly complete
> absence from the pages of national histories.[62]

She exhorts women that, like the witches in the tales, they should
assert, dare, and recover God's story about them. Oduyoye used
materials from many African groups to validate her probing, but the
Akan and Yoruba cultures that she has experienced by birth and marriage served as controlling poles.

Turning to a second cycle, culture, she analyses the same ambiguity as patriarchy holds sway, buttressed by the colonial experience.
However, as to matters of politics:

> It becomes clear that these male-dominated structures
> made provisions for women to be heard, and even more
> important, women exerted leadership in their own orga-
> nizations. Women were able to form pressure groups so
> that a totally silenced West African woman is not a politi-
> cal reality today, nor was she in the past. Women's rep-
> resentation, as it was structured in traditional decision-
> making, guarded against women's complete bondage to
> culture as perceived by men.[63]

The overall picture is bleak with the feminization of poverty in Africa
evident in the new economic trends characterized by systematic
attempts to push women out of the land, the detrimental effects
of Westernization, the cultural maze in marriage, violence against
women, the customs regarding property ownership, and the political
stagnation in the continent.

Finally, Oduyoye begins to dream about the type of church she would like to see in Africa. This is the third cycle of the book. Taking a swipe at the dangerous feminine ideology of right-wing Christians, she now challenges the credibility of the church, calling it to account and to deal justly with women. God could not have created some to be inferior, and the second Genesis account could not be a lie. A church that preaches the equality of all races must perforce be justice- sensitive. This is to put her arguments rather tersely. Indeed, she argues the feminist cause vigorously, revisiting the theological discussions on the use of the Scriptures, worship, God and gender and the male attitude to matters of the Holy Spirit when women are concerned. Of interest is the explanation of the African woman's attitude to the issue of the fatherhood of God:

> For African Christians, African religio-cultural presup-
> positions have meant that the fatherhood of God in the
> bible does not confer any special priority on human
> fathers; in the tradition the father's role is carefully bal-
> anced by a mother's counterpart. So, calling God, father,
> or using a masculine pronoun in relation to God does
> not unsettle women in Africa. One could say the same
> is true for Christ, whose historical maleness in Jesus of
> Nazareth has yet to be interpreted in Africa as excluding
> women from associating with Christ's role or from being
> children of God.[64]

She rejects the maleness of Christ as a great concern in African feminist theology and as the basis for denying women ordination in a context where women are sometimes named after male fathers; she places such denial on the same chauvinist pedestal as the alleged pollution of menstruation. Her Christology is given a wider expression in an article co-authored with Elizabeth Amoah. They searched for images of Christ in African myths and found many male and female deliverers; mostly female scapegoats, but rare instances of expected ones and and nothing of the concept of eschatological completion. This absence in the African imagination is compounded by the use of the Christ figure to encrust domination and exclusivism. They, then, examined the Christologies of Mbiti, Dickson, Milingo, Pobee, Carr, and Setiloane, all of them male and representatives of the early practice of African theology. These are compared to Afua Kuma, a female member of the Church of the Pentecost. It would appear that Oduyoye's Christology is enamored to the *Christus Victor* motif and to victory over demonic forces such as that exhibited in the career of Archbishop Milingo and in Carr's pursuit of the political implica-

tions of redemptive violence as secretary of AACC and in the prophetess Afua's celebration of the faithfulness and victories of Christ in
her life.[65] In another article, she confirms this view:

> Bernadette Mbuya-Beya, writing on charismatic and
> feminist trends in Zaire, cites instances of women
> whose resistance to the crises of survival in Africa led
> them to create spiritual homes where the power of Jesus
> and the Gospel could be experienced in a more vivid
> and dynamic way than the official church provides. The
> charismatic movement and the rise of African Instituted
> Churches are the most organized forms of spirituality for
> the resistance of anonymity and the sense of having been
> abandoned by God.[66]

Two aspects are crucial. First, she recognizes that the exploding
charismatic spirituality, within and outside the mainline churches,
holds much prospect for turning the church in Africa to the reclamation of the glorious face of God. Second, Efua Kuma, who is a
Pentecostal and not a leader in the AIC, as claimed earlier, represents
an untapped resource in the study of new liturgical trends in Africa,
utilizing indigenous idioms. Evidence abounds among women's
groups in the Pentecostal and charismatic movements. Unfortunately,
Oduyoye disdains charismatic and Pentecostal movements and pays
scant attention to the typology of African indigenous churches. This
runs the risk of romanticizing the group, some of whom are not
Christian.[67]

Feminist scholarship is attentive to the lack of motivation among
the womenfolk shown by the detrimental effect of the silence of
female victims of violence, and by the high incidence of women-on
women violence in Africa.[68] Oduyoye rightly spends the last part of
the book in showing the consequences of disunity, class distinctions,
and the lack of conscientization among women. She ends with a
reminder of the achievements of the Hebrew women in mobilizing
Israel to the liberation of the Exodus event.

On the whole, Oduyoye's theological method follows the agenda
of EATWOT. She uses culture, primal religions, language, biblical
materials, women's experiences, and a concern for the predicament
of Africa as sources for doing theological ethics. Her goal is to build a
band of new African women, standing with confidence, under God's
empowering Spirit, to respond to the challenges of poverty and pluralism in Africa. Beyond mental reconstruction, she advocates an
organized quest for more economic and political space.Oduyoye's

posture has notable features that show the relationship between the various approaches, feeding one another and yet leaving distinctive African nuances. This may confuse some about her attitude towards the Bible, and some might question whether her theology is sufficiently Christocentric. Her rhetoric uses some of Schussler-Fiorenza's anti-androcentric declamations. She pays close attention to the concrete historical context as Schussler-Fiorenza advocates, that is, making experience the core hermeneutical principle and discounting the speech of God in passages that do not enhance the female cause.

On closer look, Oduyoye utilizes the resources of Schussler-Fiorenza's work at the descriptive and synthetic levels; but in appropriating the text for living, she posits the centrality of the Bible and deems some of the concerns of white theologians as irrelevant for the African context. Christian ethics do not operate in the air; they must be located within the worldview and culture of Africa. This is exactly what she does. To dismantle the antiwoman habits that have shackled the church and diminished its ability to mobilize its full resources to combat growing challenges, the roots of patriarchy in the society must be dealt with. This is what Walter Brueggemann calls moving back into the deepest memories of the community, activating those very symbols that have always been the basis for contradicting the regnant consciousness.[69] Has she succeeded in her manner of utilizing the proverbs? There is much doubt precisely because what is needed is not the re-reading of proverbs but, as Njoronge said, a consciousness-raising education or a program of enlightenment within the churches. Many churches must recover strong Bible study traditions, using new resources in Christian education and shifting from the old catechetics that emphasized indoctrination in the heat of virulent competition. This brings us to the fourth posture characterized by the *loyalist* voice. Attitude toward the Bible and how it could be used in Christian living is the core difference between the liberationists and the loyalists.

In *Engaging the Powers*, Walter Wink intoned that:

> Paul did not write Eph. 5:21-33; 1 Tim. 2:8-15; 5:3-16; or Titus 2:3-5, though they are ascribed to him. Someone in the early church did.[70]

The other three groups of feminists would treat these as satanic verses. The loyalist band emerges from the Roman Catholic sisters, Protestant Evangelicals, African indigenous churches, and Pentecostals. To various degrees, these share the Evangelicals's emphases on the centrality of the Bible, the cross, attestation of conversion and new birth, and the mandate to engage in social activism. They would not debate the authenticity of the biblical passages as high criticism would but would encourage Christians to accept the dictates and apply them to daily living. Like the others, they are against the male domination that hinders their practice of spiritual gifts in the church. They are also concerned that both males and females bear their God-given roles, which may differ in some aspects but are reciprocal. At stake is how to garner both personal freedom and the responsibilities of interdependent relationships. How much chance is there for partnership, given the historical and cultural realities?

As Mbugua's title, *Our Time Has Come* (1994) declared, Evangelical women believe that a resolution is possible by urging the men to obey the Bible. The belief is that the Scriptures contain enough to make the men less chauvinistic, more loving and family-responsible. The Bible is for them God's hope for women. For instance, the Ephesian passage demands that men love their wives as they love themselves, care for them as they care for their bodies. The Greek word, *ektrepho* requires men to nourish, bring up, care for, and protect their wives; *thalpo* demands that they cherish, foster, and keep their wives warm in their bosoms. Paul asked men to leave their parents and be joined to their wives. In defense of Paul, men have disregarded the texts of terror or the hindering statements on silence and restriction on preaching, as arising from the abuse of freedom in Christ by certain Corinthian women prophets. They note the sociocultural dimension: since the sacred and the secular spheres of Jewish society were intertwined, the inferiority and subordination of women was consequently present in both religious and civil areas of Jewish life. The resonance in African and Victorian morality should not be allowed in the new dispensation precisely because the Redemption restored women, after the Fall, to rule the earth jointly with men. Besides, many African women find nothing wrong with covering their hair which is an aspect of feminine fashion. Rather they note that Paul laid an enormous responsibility on menfolk, which, if fulfilled, would enhance the partnership necessary for a vibrant mission. Beyond the freedom that is in Christ, where there is neither male nor female, Paul's theology provided for the organization of the entire family (*oikonomos,*governance of the household*)*, and the requisite the ethic of mutual submission that would bring a sweet-smelling odor for God into that household. While reconstructionists regard Paul as a transitional figure with one foot in the old and the other in the new dispensation ushered by Christ, the loyalist position is that while some of Paul's pronouncements may have dire consequences for the woman cause, the church should take a more holistic view rather than hiding under Paul's mufti to practice discrimination. The Scriptures should be interpreted within their teleological framework to effect God's salvation history. The Scriptures lay emphasis on the power of the Word.

The loyalist debate is very vigorous among the Pentecostals, whose authority pattern declares that God is not a democrat. The pastor's power can be extensive. But the pneumatic emphasis in the Pentecostal theology provides a counterpoise. Can anyone prevent a female from exercising her spiritual gifts? Much to the contrary, argues Lois Wafula; the power of the woman's intercessory prayers is like the electric power plants carrying a powerful force that brings life and light into our homes. G. Mwiti buttresses this affirmation with a study of the Matthean passage,which declares that,you are the light of the world; it concludes that God's power can work just as forcefully in women.[71] Do we perceive here the complementarity in the Spirit between men and women that could provide an exit from the shackles of patriarchy? Wafula's is a different way of doing feminist theology: instead of trying to reread the proverbs, she taps the biblical resources for powerful images that would replace the dark images of women in traditional folktales.Women as light contradicts the dark imagery in primal myths and folktale. The question pulsates: how can these be reclaimed critically to empower the liberation of women?

Among white Pentecostals, it has been noted that women played elaborate roles until the 1940s when the close relationship with fundamentals brought a restrictive spirit into their fold. Since then, women do not rise above certain levels in the church hierarchy. Barfoot and Sheppard argue that the period of prophetic Pentecostalism, from the turn of the century till the 1920s was characterized by vibrant female mystical imagery and equality for women; thereafter, priestly Pentecostalism reigned supreme, institutionalizing the charisma and diminishing the role of women.[72] Margaret L.Bendroth,in *Fundamentalism and Gender, 1875 to Present,* has explored how the rise of fundamentalism brought the cult of domesticity and legalistic structures into Pentecostalism, which won them membership in the National Association of Evangelicals. Thus, the Assemblies of God, which ordains women, allows them to rise only to the rank of senior pastor, but bars the doors to the district and general council meetings.[73]

In Africa, the trend appears to be in the opposite direction; with the rapid explosion of the wind of God, there is an equal explosion

of ordained women. In many cases, the male leader needs his wife to
be ordained as copastor so as to control the finances and authority
within trusted bounds. In other cases, it is a response to enlargement of scale and the burst of innovation in the religious space. It
may take some while for the Weberian routinization of charisma
to emerge. However, the advocated family ethics are akin to those
of the Promise Keepers. In the midst of changing family patterns,
the high rate of divorce, and social instability, scholars have argued
that females find the certainties and securities of Pentecostal family
ethics reassuring and attractive; there is coherence and assurance of
the capacity to cope in the darkness that has hit Africa at noontide.
Ruth's example in the Bible comes in handy, as she is declared *a
woman of excellence*. At home and in the church, the woman works
as the bride of Christ, active in evangelism and ministry. Here, the
difference with the reformists appears: some women are afraid of the
powers of phallocracy in the Pentecostal position. What about men's
fears about the engulfing, entrapping powers of the female, often
expressed in terms of revulsion over body, blood, and milk; hence
the taboos on pregnant and menstruating women? Where do these
deep-seated deep fears come from? Teresa Okure would agree with
the loyalists that the Bible is the embodiment of the revealed will
of God, which plays a decisive role for Christians in their approach
to contemporary women issues.[74] However, she not only notes the
divine and human elements but observes that:

> Indeed, if the books of the bible can be said to agree on
> any issue with respect to women, it is that the woman
> suffers her greatest humiliation and subjection to the
> man in the institution of marriage.[75]

Both parties are concerned with the same problem albeit
approached from different postures: a reconstructed African church
needs to go beyond the achievements and inherited ideologies of the
missionary era;it needs to begin to listen to the women, hear their
cries; and deal justly within the precinct of the temple. This will
empower the church to foray into the society to combat the inequities of polygyny, female circumcision, early betrothal, forced mar-
riages, divorce rights, menstrual taboos, and widowhood customs.
The loyalists are emphasizing the loving relationship model that suffused Puritan literature; there is nothing to gainsay it, but how do
women engage the church to respond to the forces in the society that
scar the faces of women and children?As Oduyoye would say:

The daughters of Anowa, standing at the fork in the road, must determine which direction to take.[76]

4. THE EXIT: VICTIMIZED WOMEN AS HEALERS

Jennifer Whitaker wrote a book entitled *How Can Africa Survive?* She relates the larger issues of the legitimacy crises and the economic collapse in Africa to the fate of its female population and prophesied that conditions in Africa will never get better until the lot of women is improved.[77] There are several dimensions to the problem: the size of female population (and citizenry), the fact that women perform two-thirds of the productive work, which sustains the family and is dominant in reproduction; and the fact that the patriarchal ideology plays itself out in the ethics of power. Leadership has been identified as the key to the failure of the state in Africa, partially because the leader assumes to be the father of the nation, using national resources as his private wealth and brutally responding to opposition as sacrilegiously rebellious to divine authority. Thus, the leader clothes himself in symbols of sacred authority and chieftaincy regalia. The flywhisk, the leopard skin, the hat, the walking stick, the motorcade and siren, all symbolize the awe of patriarchal power which disdains accountability. Playing the village chief in political arena of the modern state has become a banal aspect of our political culture. The loyalists also point to the fact that the social wounds of the society such as AIDS, corruption, indiscipline, and violence are sourced from the dysfunctional structure of the modern family; this means that men and women need to work in partnership, standing in the glory of God and in shared humanity, to rebuild according to the demands of the gospel.

How can these things be? There seems to be a relationship between polities and gender practices among African churches. For instance, in the hierarchical polities such as among the Roman Catholics and the Anglicans, the emphases are on the institution and its traditions. The authority lines are well-defined and do not allow for much local initiative. Male priestcraft has bewitched these churches. Gender practices arise from ancient traditions and are resistant to the ordination of women. Among the congregationalist polities, there have been enormous shifts; for instance, the Presbyterians ordained women as ruling elders and, from the mid-1960s, started the ordination of female ministers who have full parity with male ministers.

Among the African indigenous churches, the utilization of African cultural forms, which appeared to be one of the elements of creativity, produced a biased attitude towards the role of women in the decision-making processes; except where they are the founders, they cannot head whole organizations. However, women have vast opportunities for creative roles based on spiritual power or charisma.[78] The intriguing irony is that the Church of the Lord that ordains women to certain limited leadership roles also bars them from such roles during menstruation, a taboo that has both traditional and biblical sources. As said earlier, among the Pentecostals, the distinctive character in Africa includes the large corps of ordained women in churches, women leaders, and founders of churches and women-led fellowships such as Women's Aglow. Even among the mainline churches, there has been a resurgence of lay power. Within this ambit, the power of women's organizations has become considerable. Numbers and financial influence tango. These organizations wield enormous power in the affairs of the church in spite of the powers of laymen. The priestly powers are increasingly confined to the monopoly of sacraments. In the recent mobilization of influential laity through knighthood orders, women participate. The vast array of social changes as well as the increased level of education have improved the roles of women in African churches. This suggests the first of three exits to the dilemma, namely, that women intensify the advocacy for improved legal, economic, and political power in the various nations. Already, the upsurge of working mothers, and the rise of professional women's organizations and non-governmental organizations devoted to women's causes have increased women's roles in civil society. Social activism is imperative because of the linkage between the victimization of women and the ethics of power in the wider society.

The second exit is suggested by the fact that women's access power in the church or religious space more easily through the exercise of their spirituality as seen among the groups that emphasize the pneumatic aspects. Initially, to talk about feminine spirituality appeared as one of those attempts to categorize women, when in fact the characteristic is culturally conditioned. Recent scholarship is connecting the feminist revolution with the desire to reunite sexuality with the experience of the sacred.[79] This is a larger issue that cannot be adequately dealt with here. Suffice it to say that women have always been healers; from ancient temple priestesses to the medieval herbalists to the alternative practitioners, nurses and midwives. The image of women as visionaries and spirit mediums is encrusted in the African worldview. The potency of feminine spirituality is equally acknowledged and used to explain the numerical strength of women in churches.

The founder of Full Gospel Businessmen's Fellowship, Demos Shakarian, started the fellowship because he noticed that men were reluctant to come to church. The strategy was to design an attractive project that would enable them to worship. That reluctance is increasing in many parts of Africa as new sodalities such as the Rotary Club, Lion's Club, Freemasonry and Rosicrucian Lodges have grown in popularity, offering promises of business contacts and male bonding and alternative religious quests. The challenge, therefore, for women is to push forward an agenda indicating how their innate spirituality could be used to revive the church. There is an equal need to mobilize sufficiently to counteract the forces that hinder their access to political and economic empowerment. Are the victims asked to save themselves? Yes and no. Quite often rights are not given, they are repossessed by those who have been robbed. The poor and oppressed have an innate power that must be aroused to counter the monopolized verdict of the oppressor.

Feminine spirituality is radicated in the Bible with images of God as a mother in Israel, the awesome power of God mediated in predominantly feminine imagery. God's salvation was first broached to and activated by Elizabeth, Mary, Anna, and Mary Magdalene. In each case, the heart of spirituality is yieldedness. They had the courage to say yes to the overshadowing power of the Holy Spirit and were able to see the invisible, have recourse to the sacred and became co-workers with God. Their apparent weakness turned into a powerful, prophetic recovery of both church and community. As one Church of England study group suggested:

> If women are now to bring into the ordained ministry their embodied realities, there will be a major shift in our symbolic structures – to metaphors and symbols drawn from the womb, from the breast, from birth and nourishment; from feelings and relationships; from the menstrual and other rhythms which are constant in their inconstancy.[80]

Marie Griffith (1993) used the case of Women's Aglow to illustrate how the banding of praying women can become an instrument of the struggle. The purpose of the fellowshipsays the brochure, is to

> provide,support, education, training, and ministry opportunities to help women worldwide discover their

true identity in Jesus Christ through the power of the
Holy Spirit.

Aglow's literature emphasizes their mission of bringing women
hope, healing, and reconciliation. They form a network of caring
women. During their meetings, every woman is invited to speak
about her life and to receive the prayers of others for healing. Each is
empowered to engage in social and economic pursuits with Christian
ethics and determination to be open to God's prospering grace. In
God's Daughters, Griffith explores the rich metaphor in the power
of submission. Surrender and submission to God become liberating
features both in concept and in practice as family ethics. Writing
about the *Righteous Discontent* in the women's movement in the
Black Baptist church, 1880-1920, Evelyn Higginbotham concluded
that:

> the feminist theologians had operated from a stance of
> radical obedience. And indeed it was this vantage of
> orthodoxy that compelled the brethren to listen. The
> theological nuances of these terms, the careers, and
> experiences of African- American women offer food for
> thought to African women.[81]

Thoroughly lacking in the literature of African women theologians is
the exploration of the power of prayer as a tool for hope or rousing
what Schussler- Fiorenza calls the angry power of the Spirit. Yet, as
Cheryl B. Johns argues, if women's advocacy taps into the pneumatic
resources in the Scriptures, they will discover that the Pentecost story
contains the story of the conscientization of women; that the mission
of the Pentecost involves both men and women as colabourers and
as joint heirs as members of God's new *ekklesia*. The Holy Spirit
empowered many spirit-filled women to perform priestly, charismatic
roles, to obey the call, to and move to mission without ordination
and institutional support and, in a revolutionary manner, to posture
themselves in the line of God's eschatological design. The Holy Spirit
is the power that will enable the Circle in Africa to achieve its goals.
This calls for abandoning the impressionistic and cursory attention
that they have shown toward the move of the Holy Spirit among the
women of contemporary Africa. Gordon Fee, in his *Gospel and Spirit
Issues in New Testament Hermeneutics,* attributes the prominence of
women as a result of the deeply populist roots of the New Testament
church.[82] It is, he says, the reviving of the elements of populism that
is providing women preachers of our contemporary period with new
ministry opportunities.

A third exit is a program of Christian education designed to enlighten and sensitize the people of God about the victimization of women. Most people act out of ignorance, without realizing that the full potentials of the community are underutilized. One should leave it to the women to design such a program. As Oduyoye has urged and done, Be a woman and Africa will be strong.[83]African women should move beyond hortatory theologizing and produce concrete materials for responding to the sins that have been so elaborately exposed. Victimized women and their sisters could become healers. However, they need the cooperation and willingness of the menfolk to realize that they should support women, renounce the abuse of power in the church, perceive partnership as the method provided by the Scriptures for mobilizing the people of God for mission. The church has no other reason for existence than mission. Isabel Phiri's discussion on the attitude of male Presbyterian leaders to the controversy about initiation of Chewa women in Malawi is a sad indication of the long road that the men will have to travel to be obedient to Christ.[84]

Notes

1. Sylvia Leith Ross, *African Women: A Study of the Ibo of Nigeria*. (London: Routledge, 1939), forword.

2. Jane L. Parpart ed, *Women and Development in Africa: Comparative Perspectives*. (New York: University of America Press, 1980);J. L. Parpart and K. A. Staudt eds., *Women and the State in Africa*. (Boulder, CO: Lynne Reinner Publishers, 1990).

3. M. Barrett, *Women Oppression Today: Problems in Marxist Feminist Analysis* (London: Verso Publications, 1980).

4. Nina Mba, *Nigerian Women Mobilized: Women's Political Activity in Southern Nigeria, 1900-1965* (Berkeley,CA: University of California, Institute of International Studies, 1982).

5. D. U. Iyam, *The Broken Hoe*. (The University of Chicago Press, 1995). see, Miriam Goheen,*Men Own the fields, Women own the crops:gender and power in the Cameroon Grassfields*.(Madison:The University of Wisconsin Press,1996);O.W.Ogbomo,*When men and Women Mattered:A history of gender relations among the Owan of Nigeria.*(Rochester:University of Rochester Press,1997)

6. Ify Amadiume, *Male Daughters and Female Husbands: Gender and Sex in an African Society.* (London: Zed Press, 1987); ibid., Reinventing Africa: Matriarchy, Religion and Culture (London: Zed Books Ltd., 1997);Christine Obbo, *African Women: Their Struggle for Economic*

Independence (London: Zed Press. 1988); C. Hoehler-Fatton, *Women of Spirit and Fire: History,Faith and Gender in Roho Religion in West Kenya. (*New York: Oxford University Press, 1996).

7. Teresia Hinga, ,Between Colonialism and Inculturation: Feminist Theologies in Africa',*Feminist Theology in Different Strokes.* ed., I E. Schussler-Fivrenza (London, SCM Press, 1996): 26-34

8. M. A. Oduyoue,(ed., *Will to Arise: Women, Tradition and the Church in Africa.* (Maryknoll, NY: Orbis Books, 1992); ibid.,*Talitha Qumi, Proceedings of the Convocation of African Women Theologians.* (Ibadan, Nigeria: Daystar Publishers, 1990), See, Musimbi Kanyoro's speech in Oduyoye, ed.,*Transforming Power.* (Accra: Sam-Woode Ltd., 1997), chap. 2.

9. Kofi Appiah-Kubi and Sergio Torres, eds., *African Theology En Route* (Maryknoll,,NY:Orbis Books, 1979).

10. Itumeng J. Mosala, "The Implications of the Text of Esther for African Women's Struggle for the Liberation in South Africa.", *Voices from the Margin.* ed., R. S. Sugirtharajah (Maryknoll, Orbis Books, 1995):168-178.

11. H. Kyung Chung, *Struggle to the Sun.* (Maryknoll,NY: Orbis Books, 1990).

12. M. A. Oduyoye and V. Fabella, eds., *With Passion and Compassion: Third World Women Doing Theology.* (Maryknoll,NY: Orbis Books, 1988), 60-65.

13. M. A. Oduyoye, ed., *Who Will Roll Away The Stone: Ecumenical Decade of the Churches In Solidarity With Women.* (Geneva, WCC, 1990).

14. N. J. Njoroge, "Resurrection People: Break the Chains of Injustice", *Reformed World*, 47, 1 (March 1997): 2-13.

15. Ursula King, ed., *Feminist Theology from the Third World: A Reader* (Maryknoll,NY: Orbis Books, 1994);E. Schussler-Forenza, ed., *Feminist Theology in Different Strokes* (London: SCM Press, 1996);S. B. Thistlewaite and M. P. Engel, eds.*Lift Every Voice: Constructing Christian Theology from the Underside* (San Francisco,CA: Harper, 1990);M. Mananzan et als eds, *Women Resisting Violence: Spirituality for Life* (Maryknoll,NY: Orbis, 1996);R. Gibellini ed., *Paths of African Theology.* (Maryknoll,NY:Orbis, 1995);Stuart and Thatcher, ed.,s *Sexuality and Gender.*

16. Eleanor Rae, *Women, the Earth, the Divine.* (Maryknoll,NY: Orbis, 1994), 4.

17. O. U. Kalu, "Gender Ideology in Igbo Religion", *Africa*, 42, 2 (1991),:184-202.

18. R. R. Ruether, *Women Healing Earth: Third World Women on Ecology, Feminism and Religion*. (Maryknoll,NY:Orbis, 1996):121-185.

19. W. Jakobsen, "Ethics in Feminist Theology", Doing *Ethics in Context: South African Perspectives* eds., C. V. Vicencio and W. DeGruchy (Maryknoll,NY:Orbis, 1994), vol. 2, chapt. 2.

20. M. A. Oduyoye, *Daughters of Anowa: African Women and Patriarchy* (Maryknoll, NY:Orbis, 1995).

21. G. Anderson and J. Clarke, *God Calls, Man Chooses: A Study of Women in Ministry*. (Burlington, Ontario: Trinity Press, 1990).

22. Chung, *Struggle to be the Sun*, 51.

23. E. Schussler-Fiorenza, *Bread Not Stone: The Challenge of Feminist Biblical Interpretation* (Boston: Beacon Press, 1984).

24. Linda Moody, *Women Encounter God: Theology Across the Boundaries of Difference*. (Maryknoll,NY: Orbis 1996), 81; Stephanie Y. Mitchem,*Introducing Womanist Theology.*(Maryknoll, NY: Orbis,2002).

25. Oduyoye, *Daughters of Anowa*, 88.

26. *Ibid.*, 170;Letty Russell, *Human Liberation in a Feminist Perspective Theology*. (Philadelphia,PA: Westminster Press, 1974).

27. Delores Williams, *Sisters in the Wilderness: The Challenge of Womanist God-talk*. (Maryknoll,NY: Orbis,1993), xiv.

28. Kwame Bediako, *Theology and Identity*. (Oxford: Regnum Press, 1992);Linda Moody, *Women Encounter God*, 148-150;Letty Russell, *Church in the Round : Feminist Interpretation of the Church* (Louiseville,KY: John Knox/Westminister Press, 1993).

29. M. A. Oduyoye, "Spirituality of Resistance and Reconstruction", *Women Resisting Violence.*ed., Mananzan, (Maryknoll,NY:Orbis, 1996),:161-171, esp.169.

30. D. Ramodibe, "Women and Men Building Together the Church in Africa", *With Passion and_Compassion*. eds., Oduyoye and Fabella, (Maryknoll,NY:Orbis, 1988),14.

31. Njoronge,'Resurrection People', *Reformed World*, 47 (1997), 9.

32. J. Mbugua, *Our Time Has Come : African Women Address Issues of Today*. (Channel Islands,UK.: Guernsey Press Co. Ltd., 1994).

33. Oduyoye, "Spirituality of Resistance",169.

34. Oduyoye, *Daughters of Anowa*, 34.

35. Adela Y. Collins, "An Inclusive Biblical Anthropology", *Theology Today*, 34, 4 (1978).

36. Oduyoye, "Spirituality of Resistance", 170.

37. Oduyoye and Fabella, *With Passion and Compassion*, 54-55.

38. H. G. Wells, "Trinitarian Feminism: Elizabeth Johnson's Wisdom Christology", *Theology Today*, 52, 3 (October 1995):330-343.

39. Brown and Parker, "For God So Loved the World?", *Christianity, Patriarchy and Abuse*: 1-30.

40. Ibid.

41. Ibid., 3.

42. Ruether, *Women Healing the Earth*, 161-171.

43. Elizabeth Johnson, *She Who Is: The Mystery of God in Feminist Discourse*. (New York: Crossroad Publishing Co., 1993),11-12.

44. Russell, *Human Liberation,* 20.

45. E. Schussler-Fiorenza, *In Memory of Her: A Feminist Theological Reconstrection of Christian Origins* (New York: Crossroad Publishing Co., 1983), 14-21, 27.

46. Ibid., 35.

47. Ibid., 32.

48. Ibid., 33.

49. Schussler-Fiorenza, *Bread not Stone*, 130.

50. R. B. Hays, *The Moral Vision of the New Testament.* (San Franscisco,CA:: Harper, 1996), 281-82.

51. Oduyoye and Fabella, *With Passion and Compassion*, 14.

52. Ibid,22. See, Elizabeth Agumba's Poem,"The Search for My Place in Society" in the theo-poetic section of Oduyoye (ed.) *Transforming Power: Women in the Household of God.* (Accra: Sam-Woode Ltd., 1997): 153-154: "Nobody can send me out of Church/ For I have a message for the disciples of Christ!"

53. Ibid., 47-59.

54. Gebara and M. C. Bingemer, *Mary Mother of God, Mother of the Poor* (Maryknoll,NY: Orbis Books, 1996).

55. Walter Wink, *Engaging the Powers* (Minneapolis, MN:Fortress Press, 1992), 134.

56. Cheryl Bridges Johns, "Pentecostal Spirituality and Conscientization of Women", *All Together in One Place*. eds. H. D. Hunter and P. D. Hocker (Sheffield: Academic Press, 1993): 153-165.

57. H. Kinukawa, Women and Jesus in Mark: A Japanese Perspective. (Maryknoll,NY: Orbis, 1994).

58. I.J. Mosala, "The Implications of the Text of Esther for African Women's Struggle for Liberation in South Africa", *Voices from the Margin* ed. Surgirtharajah (Maryknoll,NY: Orbis, 1995): 168-178; Oduyoye, *Daughters of Anowa*, 174-175.

59. P. Turner, "The Wisdom of the Fathers and the Gospel of Christ: some notes on the question of Christian Adaptation in Africa", *Journal of Religion In Africa*, 4 (1971): 46-58.

60. Amadiume, *Male Daughters*; Onunwa, "Feminity in Igbo Cosmology: Paradoxes and Ambiguities", Workshop on Igbo Worldview . Institute of African Studies, University of Nigeria, Nsukka, 1989;Ogbu U. Kalu, "Gender Ideology in Igbo Religion", *Africa*, 46 (1991).

61. Oduyoye, *Daughters of Anowa*, 34.

62. Ibid., 53.

63. Ibid., 97.

64. Ibid., 179.

65. Oduyoye and Fabella,eds.,With *Passion and Compassion*, 35, ff.

66. Oduyoye, "Spirituality and Resistance", 162.

67. Oduyoye, "The Empowering Spirit of Religion" eds., S. B. Thistlewaite and M. P. Engel *Lift Every Voice*, 249.

68. Ogbu U. Kalu, "Silent Victims: Violence Against Women in Tertiary Educational Institutions, Nigeria", UNIFEM-UNDP, Lagos, 1996. Musisi Kangoro echoes this in Oduyoye, ed.,*Transforming Power* (1997), 18-19

69. W. Brueggermann, *The Prophetic Imagination*. (Philadelphia,PA: Fortress Press, 1978), 66.

70. Wink, *Engaging the Powers*, 134.

71. See Mbugua, *Our Time Has Come*.

72. C. Barfoot and G. Sheppard, "Prophetic versus Priestly Religion: The Changing Role of Women Clergy in Classical Pentecostal Churches", *Review of Religions Research*, 22, 1 (September 1980): 2-17;D. G. Roebuck, "Pentecostal Women in Ministry: A Review of Selected Documents", *Perspectives in Religious Studies*,16, 1 (1989): 29-44.

73. Margaret L. Bendroth, *Fundamentalism and Gender, 1875 to Present* (1993).

74. Oduyoye and Fabella, *With Passion and Compassion, 52.*

75. Ibid., 54.

76. Oduyoye, *Daughters of Anowa*, 11.

77. M. Shank, "Unequal Partners", *West Africa*, 3720 (November 28, 1988): 2232.

78. Helen Callaway,"Women in Yoruba Tradition and in the Cherubim and Seraphim Society", *The History of Christianity in West Africa* ed. Ogbu U.Kalu (London, Longman, 1980), chap. 18.

79. Oduyoye in Mananzana,'Spirituality and Resistance'

80. *A Fearful Symmetry? The Complementarity of Men and Women in Ministry*. (London: SPCK, 1988), 18.

81. Marie Griffiths, "What Happens When Women Pray? Prayer and Paradox in Women's Aglow", Twenty-third Annual Meeting of the Society for Pentecostal Studies, Mexico City, 1993;ibid., *God's Daughters: Evangelical Women and the Power of Submission*. (Berkeley,CA: University of California Press, 1997), chap. 6;Evelyn Brooks Higginbotham, *Righteous Discontent: The Women's Movement in the Black Baptist Church, 1880-1920*. (Cambridge, MA:Harvard University Press, 1993), 149.

82. Johns, "Pentecostal Spirituality", 160-161; Gordon Fee, *Gospel and Spirit Issues in New Testament Hermeneutics*. (Peabody, MA: Hendericks, 1991).

83. L. M. Russell et al. eds., *Inheriting Our Mothers' Gardens* (Philadelphia,PA: Westminster Press, 1988), 39.

84. I. A. Phiri, "The Initiation fo Chewa Women of Malawi: A Presbyterian Woman's Perspective", *Religion in Malawi*, 5 (1995): 15-21;J. C. Chakanza, "The Unfinished Agenda: Puberty Rite and the Response of the Roman Catholic Church in Southern Malawi, 1901-1994", ibid., 3-7.

Conclusion
Unmasking the Powers

Candidus hid his face behind a mask, and Janus devised a double visage because both knew that the face defines who we are and how others see us. It reflects the image of God in us. When the relationship with the triune God is intense, His glory will be reflected in our faces; and there will be laughter. The opposite is equally true. When God's enemies rule, laughter will be banished and people's faces will be distorted with poverty and environmental degradation.

The story of the people of God in Africa in the last three decades is filled with irony; the spirit urges them in large numbers to the altar. Some commentators presume that they are driven by hunger and despair, especially as the quest leads to many different altars in an explosion of religious ferment. The spirit sometimes uses adversity, and one must feel the Wind of God. In spite of the increased cacophony of prayers, predatory powers conjugate the verb for corruption with dexterity and pour ashes on the people even as darkness stalks them at noontide. The leaders, like lions, eat up their people, exposing the poignant position of the church. Why is evil waxing strong in the midst of such massive religious ferment? Does the church see? Does it hear the cry? Does it possess the power to unmask the predatory powers?. The prophet Zechariah calls it shredding the horns which scattered Israel.

The Christian canon is full of resources for a spiritual warfare. After all, the good news is not that God reigns, but that Jesus' prophetic announcement of the hope for the coming of God's ultimate redemptive reign has begun. It is a sovereign rule by which God's people would be made socially, physically, and spiritually whole, and all forms of evil and the resistant wicked would be destroyed. Thus, the ministry of Jesus was characterized by binding, disarming, and plundering Satan. But the destruction of Satan is not yet. His exorcisms were an integral part of the work as he personally encountered the demoniac and responded to a parent's plea. Demons revealed their presence by words or conduct or through debilitating physical ailments. Sometimes they came singly and at other times in legions. At all times there was no contest as the master was in control. He urged his disciples to share in the ministry and gave them authority to cast out demons. As Adolf Harnack observed:

> Jesus had a strong and positive conviction of the aggressive and forward character of his message. I am come to send fire on earth, and he added, what if it be already kindled? The fire of the judgment of the forces of love was what he wanted to summon up, so as to create a new humanity.[1]

Thus, there is a power and an enduring force within Christianity to counter the predatory state and the scourge of poverty and reenvision a more environmental-sensitive development. The love of God demands it, and the history of the church is designed to interpret how the task has been done.

Commentators observe that the problem with Africa is leadership. A historical analysis with a strong theological bias would demur. Fingers would point to ethics of power or the moral dimension or value system that undergirds the exercise of power. A number of World Bank reports focus on both the economic problems as well as the environment for recovery. They lay emphasis on bad governance as the root cause of developmental failure, arguing that the moral context in which corruption vitiates efficiency causes economic collapse. This means that the problem is systemic. A good leader may have his dreams thwarted by the system, just as a moral man may be overpowered by an immoral social structure. Bishop David Gitari, therefore, calls African governments back to a moral culture that respects the sanctity of life.[2] Some surmise that these deeper social structural constraints are engendered by historical, social, and political factors. Richard Sandbrook argues that the softness of African states is the result of colonial rule and the attendant social transformation; or more specifically, the failure of externally-imposed authority structures to gain legitimacy by establishing effective linkages with indigenous social groups. Such forces are fostered by contradictory policies associated with the administrative exigencies and the economic requirements of colonial rule, limited class formation, a fluid pattern of overlapping ethnic identities, and an un-integrated peasantry. They have served to undermine the state's coherence and legitimacy and to accentuate the dilemma of governance in post-colonial Africa. This disjunction between the state and society has facilitated the rise of personal rule. For Sandbrook, personal rule thus represents a logical adaptation of colonial-inspired political institutions to a concomitantly peculiar historical and social conditions of contemporary Africa. Personal rule debauches the political culture.[3]

The immorality of personal rule ensures that the state, in spite of its metaphysical pretensions, cannot adequately deal with moral issues, which leaves the field wide open for the churches, the followers of Jesus. As Harnack also intones:

> The image of Christ remains the sole basis of all moral
> culture, and in the measure in which it succeeds in
> making its light penetrate is the moral culture of the
> nations increased or diminished.[4]

Our historical excursion indicates that many congregations in African churches have not become fully aware of their mission to baptize all aspects of their culture including the political. Little is done at the local church level to posture the church as a suffering church, suffering with the poor, enabling them to fight back and to unmask the powers of domination. Increasingly, projects are mounted because the Western partner desires and funds it. This tendency has grown with the new model or paradigm of mission. As Stanley Skreslet argued, there has been a paradigm shift in mission because the criticism against the old is that it produced the collusion with both colonialism and new predatory one-party states. A new model of networking with partner churches is inherently more flexible, essentially egalitarian, and holistically oriented. It postures the partner churches as civil society:

> concerned with community values and the ways citizens
> can contribute to the building up of stronger local,
> regional, national and global forms of society.[5]

It is supposed to be oppositional or antisystemic towards an unjust economic system and engaged in fighting for participatory democracy. Skreslet realized, however, that this new model is not working adequately because of the lack of capacity for such a model. African churches tend to perceive development matters along the line of the old charitable institutions. Thus, there is need for enlightenment programs or for a Christian education re-fashioned in a manner that could sensitize congregations to perceive the political roots of their plight and the need to build the capacity for response-data, institutions, and manpower.

This is the task designated as unmasking the powers. It is taken from the second of Walter Wink's trilogy, which set out to do five things: (i) give readers a broad, extensive understanding of the language of power in the New Testament as well as in the extra-canonical literatures of the period; (ii) attempt to provide a consistent interpretation of the meaning of the biblical language of power for human existence in order to bridge the gap between the biblical period and the postmodern twenty-first century; (iii) demythologize the power clothed in an unintelligible robe to the postmoderns; (iv) help to discern and transform the powers now and here in terms of racism, sexism, political oppression, ecological degradation, militarism, patriarchy, homelessness, hunger, economic greed, exploitation and so forth; and (v) contribute to completing a newly emerging worldview in order to overcoming materialism. The thesis undergirding Wink's trilogy is that the New Testament's principalities and powers are a generic category referring to the determining forces of physical, psychic, and social existence. Power is perceived in a bifocal manner, as possessing an outer visible form (constitutions, judges, police, leaders, office complexes) and an inner, invisible spirit that provides it with legitimacy, compliance, credibility, and clout. The Western worldview may find it difficult to comprehend a gallery of demons and suchlike but Wink believes that social analysis would benefit by

> unmasking these antiquated, repudiated and neglected powers (and thereby) open new awareness of the richly textured plenitude of life. The goal of such unmasking is to enable people to see how they have been determined, and to free them to choose.

It is a means of attacking the materialism that dominates us, our social structures, and our world. Wink concludes that:

> the demonic can be identified as the psychic or spiritual power emanated by societies or institutions or individuals or sub-aspects of individuals whose energies are bent on overpowering others.

The term, angels of nations, reflects the collective soul or actual spirituality of a nation; sometimes a nation acts as a butting goat, hurting others and, thereby, falling under the anvil of divine judgment.[6]

We can borrow from Wink's study to emphasize the moral dimension to the stagnation in Africa. The church must engage in a meaningful discussion about the inner spirituality and ethics manifested in the outward institutions of the state and unmask the limits of state power. The church has the distinctive capacity and obligation to assist African societies conceptualize political power and authority. Useful in this task is a strand in African church historiography that draws attention to the African roots of Christian spirituality and to ecological ethics. It has been difficult for church historians and the many sociologists who interpret African Christianity to connect between ecology and the conditions and mission of the churches. Yet the African primal worldview not only provides the problematics but also the idiom and a salient ethic to ensure that development is organically integrated. As Wilmot Blyden intoned:

> the African has developed and organized a system useful
> to him for all needs of life, a system as his environment
> have suggested-to be improved not changed by larger
> knowledge.[7]

Wink draws attention to this in his discussion of the angels of nature, an emerging, transformed worldview, replacing the life-threatening materialistic worldview. Justice is the ethos of God's creation; therefore, environmental justice is directly linked with social and economic justice. The angels of nature can broaden and deepen our sense of worship. The necessity for wonder, praise, and awe of God's creation cannot be stressed too much. The angels of nature are the code names for the numinous interiority of created things.

Perhaps, it should be explained that environmental theology, which exploded from the 1980s after two decades of the doldrums, has different nuances: creation spirituality or ecospirituality emphasizes the theodicy factor in environmental issues and the holistic continuity between humans and the natural world; to pluck a flower is to touch a star. As Jay McDaniel says:

> It springs from a deep-seated hope, not utopia, but for
> a more just, sustainable, and spiritually satisfying world.
> It is shaped by a distinctive way of thinking and feeling:
> one that emphasizes the interconnectedness of all things,
> the intrinsic value of all life, the continuity of human
> with non-human life, and the compassion of God of
> life...it images the divine mystery as the mind or heart
> of the universe.[8]

Eco-justice focuses on the inequality and marginalization of humans in society, and this has been the staple diet of ecumenical social policy. The World Council of Churches labels the ideal as justice, peace and the integrity of creation. These ideal relations incorporate several core modern values such as equality, human rights, progress, individual and collective self- determination, tolerance, and the celebration of diversity. Eco-traditionalists argue that received religions already contain the ethical resources for addressing the problems of the environment; that traditional religious symbols and the canon contain the religious answer to ecological crisis. They avoid the pantheism and sacramental approach to nature and call for the redemption of all creation through Christ. The mandate to steward nature is their compelling goal. These variations do not hide a global perception of the environmental crisis; all would acknowledge that:

> religion cannot do anything direct about environmental problems. It can offer ethical principles of sustainability and living in harmony with the constraints of the extra-human world. Its professionals and adherents can posit the efficacy of religious rituals, belief and ethics in the hoped-for solution to the problems.[9]

Worship and prayer as a means of human response to untoward physical circumstances was a predominant model in ancient Israel and the preoccupation of the psalms. It is coming back into African Christianity through the Intercessors for Africa. As the political field widens for religious actors, a new political theology of engagement is emerging from the periphery, namely, among the Charismatics and women. This suggests the need to mobilize the full resources of the church; the depths of its spirituality and gender. The church must reenvision and utilize its spiritual energy, including the charismatic gifts that were released at Pentecost as empowerment for the arduous task of witness in terrains overshadowed by principalities and powers. It is becoming increasingly untenable to ignore or underutilize the contributions of the largest sector-women and youth. To purvey justice in the outside world, it must first act righteously within its walls. The history of women in African Christianity indicates that the process of mobilizing women theologians is underway and has yielded much reflective resources. The women have refused to sing the same song as white feminists; nor have they nor accepted the rejectionist position typical of the Western trend. They utilize the academic resources of the reconstructionists without discounting the speech of God. The Bible remains a central resource for theologizing. Like all third world theologians, they seek other native sources. They are for the most part liberationist-reformists. Many are loyalists with a difference; they ask the men to obey the biblical mandates and seek to liberate the church by applying biblical principles. Traditionalism must break down, through the power of the word, so that new life forces can be encountered and mobilized.

The outside world is a pluralistic context. Ironically, successful religious opposition to predators in Africa has been achieved only in situations where multifaith groups have acted in concert. The results can be quite strange. For instance, in Malawi, the Roman Catholics fired the first verbal salvo; the Presbyterians threw in their numerical strength, and the Muslims joined the PAC. At the end of the day, the PAC supported a Muslim candidate for the presidency, and he won! The obvious lesson is that holy Christian huddles may deter the ouster of dictators. Nigerian ecumenical leaders need to learn this lesson. Indeed, a political consciousness would inform the open-field risk of dialogue. It would demand the harvesting of salient political values in other religions so as to build a force that could scatter the horns and unmask the powers which pour ashes on our faces. Having risked all, we can stand stronger in affirming that Jesus is Lord in the new land, where the state does not banish speeches.

The basic contention here is that the history of Christianity in Africa should be written from the perspective of the church's core task to mission. The measuring rod is the degree of faithfulness exhibited in nurturing the spiritual growth of the people and in responding to the socioeconomic and political needs of the people. The church in Africa has come of age.It has acquired an identity that could be characterized as African Christianity. A mature church can engage no longer in missionary-bashing but rather in self-criticism. The history of Christianity in Africa is not what the missionaries did or did not do, but what Africans did with the gospel entrusted to their care. The church must be understood by the quality of its being or presence in communities, its doing as it responds to the problems of that community, and in its saying or teaching.

We have tried to interpret, in time perspective, how the different faces, types, and phases of Christianity in Africa responded to the urgent life and death realities of the continent. The presence of Christianity in Africa is measured by its saltiness. It is not enough to affirm that the Christian presence has grown, and that there has been a shift in Christianity's center of gravity to the southern hemisphere; the

nature and solidity of that presence must be critically examined lest
idolatry set in. It is not a matter of numbers. The encroaching power
of the state, the scourge of poverty, the implosion of international
and fundamentalist Islam, environmental degradation and abuse of
human rights constitute the challenges that define the measure of the
witnessing power of the church's prayerful existence. Moreover, effort
has been made to portray Christianity as a band of African peoples
with faces. Institutions are important, but the church is essentially
the people of God. How we define the church influences the type
of church history we write. In this study, the church has been the
African people; the history has been their story as they struggle to
rerspond to the gospel mandate in a challenging environment and
life conditions.

Finally, it is impossible to do any serious academics in the African
context, at the edge of the twenty-first century, without concern for
the ashes on our faces. Those who should tell the story and inspire
their brethren are ill-equipped to do so because the infrastructure of
the educational institutions has broken down. The immoral political
culture has created the untoward downward spiral that has pauperized the populace. As religious actors respond to the challenges, they
operate with inadequate data and sometimes adopt strategies that risk
the balance in a pluralistic society. The contention here is that these
challenges must be addressed as the key aspects of African church
historiography. This is the knowledge of the past, not as consumer
goods, but investment and commitment for the future.

Notes

1. Adolf Harnack, *What is Christianity?* (New York,NY: Harper and Bros.,
    1957), 122.

2. David Gitari, "Sanctity of Human Life: Priority for Africa", *Transfor-
    mation*, 14, 3 (1997): 19-23.

3. Richard Sandbrook, *The Politics of Africa's Economic Stagnation* (Cam-
    bridge:Cambridge University Press, 1985).

4. Harnack, *What is Christianity?*, 123.

5. S. H. Skreslet, "Net-working, Civil Society and the NGO: A New
    Model for Ecumenical Mission" *Missiology*, 25, 3 (1997): 307-319.

6. Walter Wink, *Unmasking the Powers* (Minneapolis,MN:Fortress
    Press,1996), 7, 9, 68, 169.

7. Bediako, *Christianity in Africa*, 10.

8. Jay McDaniel, *Earth, Sky, God and Mortals: Developing an Ecological Spirituality*. (Mystic, CT: Twenty-Third Publications, 1990),182.

9. Peter Beyer, *Religion and Globalization*. (London: SAGE Publications, 1994), 222.

Index